RETURN TO
GLORY

RETURN TO
GLORY

INSIDE TYRONE WILLINGHAM'S
AMAZING FIRST SEASON AT
NOTRE DAME

ALAN GRANT

LITTLE, BROWN AND COMPANY
Boston New York London

First Edition

ISBN 0-316-60765-7

10 9 8 7 6 5 4 3 2 1

Q-FF

Designed by Oksana Kushnir

Printed in the United States of America

To all those who refuse to let others define them

*"When those disciples were sitting in the boat
and the sea was calm, they didn't need Jesus, did they?
But when the storm hit,* that's *when they needed leadership."*
— Tyrone Willingham

CONTENTS

Prologue   *3*
1. Rock Bottom   5
2. Waking Up Echoes   20
3. Training Camp   32
4. "Something's Happening Here!"   45
5. Maryland   59
6. Purdue and the Media   77
7. Michigan   97
8. Michigan State   110
9. Stanford   129
10. Pittsburgh   146
11. Air Force   159
12. Florida State   171
13. Boston College   185
14. Navy   207
15. Rutgers   218
16. USC   230
17. Season of Change?   242
18. Validation   252
19. The Gator Bowl   259
20. Return to Glory   272
Acknowledgments   *281*
Index   *283*

RETURN TO
GLORY

MICHIGAN

September 14, 2002, Notre Dame Stadium

NOTRE DAME WAS LOSING. That's why Tyrone Willingham showed up when he did.

With four seconds left in the third quarter, Notre Dame trailed Michigan 17–16. It was the first time they had trailed the whole season, so it only made sense that something would happen right then.

Just two minutes earlier, receiver Arnaz Battle, easily the best athlete on Notre Dame's team, had fumbled a kickoff, leading to a Michigan touchdown. Battle, though a senior, was in his first season as a kick returner, and his running style was hard, almost defiant. After taking the kick at the 15-yard line, Battle had lunged forward, knees high and head erect. He was the type of runner who never gave much thought to the first defender; instead, he looked *through* him as he planned to evade the next potential tackler. But after contact, while fighting for an extra five yards, he had momentarily forgotten about the ball in his right arm. As he was being dragged down by the waist, the ball had been stripped, and the Wolverines had recovered. Six plays later, Michigan running back Chris Perry had bulled in from the two, and Notre Dame was losing.

Now the Irish had to receive another kickoff. As the kickoff return team huddled on the sideline, Battle stood on the outside edge of the group. To his left was Buzz Preston, the special teams and running backs coach. Preston had seven years experience coaching special teams, but he'd spent the last eight away from them, and now Preston and his units were struggling. The week before, Purdue had returned a punt 76 yards for a touchdown, and, making matters worse, earlier that day Michigan had blocked a field goal attempt. Now Battle, Preston, and the rest of the unit huddled at the 40-yard line. Around them, the other Irish players solemnly stood on the sideline, each one holding up four fingers, the traditional sign for the last quarter.

Several hundred feet above the huddle, the student section ushered in the fourth quarter in Notre Dame fashion. Dressed in green T-shirts, they paid tribute to the head coach in signature style, forming W's with thumbs pressed together and index fingers pointed toward heaven. Across the field, the band played Tchaikovsky's *1812* Overture. In unison, the students waved their hands up and down in a continuous, fluid motion as the song came to its dramatic conclusion, horns spiraling, drums thundering, and cymbals crashing.

As the song ended, Tyrone Willingham joined the huddle. His team was losing, but he knew all the elements were in place for them to start winning again. He knew that what they needed was a unifying force — a focused conduit of energy that could fuse the team's talent, the fans' desire, and the university's grand tradition into a cohesive unit. They needed him.

Willingham calmly walked up and stood between Preston and Battle. He didn't say anything; he offered only his presence. Flanked by these two individuals who, like Notre Dame itself, had walked into the unfortunate spotlight of temporary failure, Willingham would not let them walk it alone. After Preston called middle return, they broke the huddle, and Willingham broke it with them. He forcefully slapped the rolled-up program he held in his left hand, standing straight-backed with arms folded as the spirit of expectation danced around him.

ROCK BOTTOM

November 24, 2001, Stanford Stadium

THE NOTRE DAME HEAD COACH had fought through failures before, but when he saw his team collapse this time, he knew there was no coming back from it.

With over seven minutes left in the game, Bob Davie's team was leading Stanford 13–3. It was third-and-ten, and the Cardinal had the ball on its own 19-yard line. Stanford had no chance. Well, they weren't *supposed* to have a chance. But after Stanford quarterback Randy Fasani threw a strike to receiver Nick Sebes for a gain of 46 yards, something strange happened.

The Stanford team, in this case the "other" team, acted as though *they* were supposed to win. Even though they were the "academic" team that was supposed to just make things respectable against teams like Notre Dame, Stanford acted as though they were the dominant program in college football. They carried themselves as if they set the standards for excellence. That was probably because their head coach, Tyrone Willingham, thought anything was possible.

Even after Sebes's long gain, things looked grim for the Cardinal, but with the clock ticking down, neither Willingham nor his team seemed worried. They marched down the field, and Stanford fullback Casey Moore scored a nine-yard touchdown to make the score 13–10. A few minutes later, after the Irish failed to move the ball, Stanford got it right back, and Cardinal running back Kenneth Tolon scored from the one to make it 17–13.

That's the way it would end. That's why Bob Davie, Notre Dame's head coach, said what he did after the game. "In the second half of Stanford," Davie told the media, "we hit rock bottom."

That rainy night may have been when their coach and their fans realized just how fast they were sinking, but in fact, Notre Dame had been plummeting for a while. They had been in trouble back on September 29, after a 24–3 loss to Texas A&M left them at 0–3 for the year. It was the first time in history that any Notre Dame team had started the season with three straight losses. Though they continued to practice and prepare each week, their chances for a berth in a Bowl Championship Series (BCS) game had evaporated before the end of September, making it all but impossible to do anything but go through the motions.

It wasn't just the team, though. The spirit of Notre Dame had also declined, slipping from its rightful place in the pantheon of college athletics. The most conspicuous evidence was displayed during a game against Nebraska a year earlier, on September 9, 2000. The disheartening 27–24 loss in overtime wasn't the real tragedy; after all, the loss — to the number one team in the nation — was one of only three defeats the Irish suffered that year. The biggest blow was the overwhelming presence of Cornhuskers fans in Notre Dame Stadium.

Nebraska had been allotted just 4,000 tickets for the game. But when the Cornhuskers team emerged from the tunnel, 30,000 screaming fans greeted them — each and every one dressed in bright red. That afternoon, as Nebraska quarterback Eric Crouch sprinted down the sideline in overtime for the game-winning score, that rowdy cartel of Huskers fans erupted in unison. Oh, they may have just been visiting Knute Rockne's house, but for the moment, those fans took over the stadium and treated it as though it were *their* house.

It was a sign of the times. Notre Dame fans were still coming to campus on Saturday afternoons; they just had other things to do once they got there. They had to take in a Mass, check out the Golden Dome atop the Main Building, pray in the Grotto, browse the bookstore, and tailgate all weekend long. But the actual football game, once the crown jewel of an autumn Saturday, had become merely another item on the list. So when Nebraska fans rolled into town, money in hand, looking to score several thousand tickets to support their team, Notre Dame fans said, "What the hell?" and gave them up.

Things had certainly changed since Bob Davie helmed the Notre Dame program in 1997. Davie was a coach who wanted to move the program forward. He once said that the administration, in terms of their standards of recruiting and expectations, was "living in the past." Davie would finish his Notre Dame tenure with a decent, though unspectacular 35–25–0 record, and in January 2001, he did take the Irish to the Fiesta Bowl, their first ever Bowl Championship Series game since the series was instituted in 1998. But at Notre Dame, a coach has to do more than just win football games. He has to embrace the university, with all its history and traditions. But Bob Davie didn't completely "get" the Notre Dame culture. And his failure to grasp it, as much as his record, led to his undoing.

Prior to becoming the Irish defensive coordinator in 1994, Davie had been the defensive coordinator for the Texas A&M Aggies. When Davie was named Notre Dame's head coach in 1996, some Irish fans thought he'd never really left his old school behind. And Freudian slips of the tongue, like replacing the word *Irish* with the word *Aggies* at Notre Dame pep rallies, didn't exactly endear him to Irish fans. But the truth was, Davie was just the kind of coach the administration wanted at the time.

The Notre Dame football universe is no stranger to peaks and valleys. It's a program that operates on a regular cycle, as the university tries to balance wins, losses, and image. When the football team is winning, all is good around the Dome. But when it gets a little too big, when Notre Dame football eclipses Notre Dame the university, the administration feels the need to remind themselves and their fans that their primary mission is scholastic. That's when admission standards for athletes receive more attention. And as the university solidifies its academic image, the high-profile football coach, still the school's most visible representative, suddenly becomes persona non grata. The shift usually involves hiring a new, less dominant coach — at least until the university and its alums start itching for more wins on the field again.

You might recall the Gerry Faust era, from 1981 to 1985.

Perhaps no other coach, save Knute Rockne himself, loved Notre Dame more than Faust. He knew what Notre Dame was about and tried to uphold the tradition of the student-athlete. He was Catholic, had coached at Cincinnati's Moeller High School, a Catholic powerhouse, and he had always dreamed of coaching at Notre Dame. He recruited and signed a lot of great guys. Problem was, he didn't sign a lot of great football players. As a result, he never won more than seven games in a single season. His woeful tenure came to an end on November 30, 1985, inside Orange Bowl Stadium. There, the Miami Hurricanes put it on the Irish 58–7.

Enter Lou Holtz in 1986. The diminutive fire-and-brimstone leader was handed the reins and told to restore the program to its rightful place. Holtz instantly obliged. He'd come to Notre Dame because it was his dream job. The crown jewel in Holtz's first recruiting class was a marvelously talented quarterback from Woodruff, South Carolina, named Tony Rice. Rice was one of the few Notre Dame players ever admitted under the NCAA rules of Proposition 48, which stated that in order to participate during his (or her) freshman year, an athlete must (1) be a high school graduate; (2) have a high school grade point average of 2.0 in an 11-course core curriculum; and (3) have scored 700 (out of a possible 1600) on the SAT or 17 (out of a possible 36) on the ACT. If he (or she) failed to meet those standards, the athlete would not be allowed to play or practice with a college team his (or her) freshman year. And that was the punishment — just three years of athletic eligibility.

That was the case with Tony Rice. Because he had scored just 690 on his SAT, Rice wasn't eligible to play for the Irish during his freshman year. In the past, Notre Dame may not have relaxed its standards to admit a Proposition 48 student. But allowing Rice entrance paid handsome dividends. Two years later, on January 1, 1989, Rice led his teammates off the field of the Fiesta Bowl with Notre Dame's eleventh consensus national championship in tow.

During Lou Holtz's 11-year reign, the Irish came within two games of winning two more titles after 1988. Holtz had come in and done exactly what he had been asked to do: restore the power of the football program. But for the folks up top, whose priorities were slowly shifting back to academic pursuits, that was just about enough. For Holtz, the beginning of the end came in 1995. Coming off a 6–5–1 season, Holtz tried, unsuccessfully, to convince the admissions department to embrace a fleet "precocious" kid named Randy Moss. At the time, Moss was the West Virginia high school player of the year in both football and basketball, and he had committed to come to Notre Dame. But after Moss had been in several fights at school and was arrested for kicking a student who he mistakenly believed had written racial slurs on a desk, Notre Dame withdrew its commitment to him.

Had it been 1985 rather than 1995, things may have been different. But that trophy from 1988 still maintained a pretty fresh glow, so the admissions department decided it could do without Randy Moss. Soon it became fairly apparent that Notre Dame could do without Lou Holtz as well. But it was more than just his "ambitious" recruiting that led to his departure. A dynamic and colorful public speaker, Holtz was paid thousands of dollars by corporations for his appearances. As the Notre Dame team gained more success, the demand for Holtz grew, and before long, his face was everywhere. The administration never wants its coach to upstage the university; friction was unavoidable.

Holtz resigned after the 1996 season. But since he had such an intense passion for his job, many Irish fans are convinced that he was forced out of Notre Dame. He won't say anything against the school now, but Holtz once complained to a *South Bend Tribune* writer that "not only do they want you to win every game, but by big scores." There was talk that Holtz was "burned out" and that coaching had passed him by. But after a two-year stint as a college football commentator for CBS, Holtz returned to the sideline at the University of South Carolina in 1999. There, Holtz transformed the Gamecocks into winners, while Bob Davie was leading Notre Dame down the path of mediocrity.

Notre Dame isn't the only university concerned with its image. There's a certain status that accompanies any scholastic university with successful sports teams. Take Duke University for instance. Some folks in Durham, North Carolina, swear that there's a vested interest in keeping the performance of the school's football team well below that of its storied basketball team. There's a reason for that. To field a good hoops team, you need just two or three excellent players. Schools like Duke, and Stanford for that matter, can dominate on the hardwood without visibly compromising their academic integrity. But football demands more than two or three bodies. It demands at least 50 guys who can compete with anyone in the country. And with 117 schools on the Division I-A level, all vying for those same players, it's just a fact that you can't routinely sign enough guys to fill your team without sacrificing some of your academic standards.

In other words, if you field a consistently dominant football team, your school's "meathead factor" is raised exponentially. Therein lay the rub for Notre Dame. They wanted it all. They desperately wanted to compare themselves to Duke and Stanford in the classroom, but they also wanted to be like Nebraska and Miami on the football field. Bob Davie had repeatedly said that what Notre Dame was asking him to do — compete for the national championship with players who were held to a higher academic standard than their opponents — was impossible. This was the same struggle that had plagued Notre Dame football for decades. It made the position of Notre Dame head coach one of the most demanding in college football.

Offensive guard Dusty Zeigler, a second-team All-America at Notre Dame in 1995, summed it up nicely. "They've got to decide what they want to be — an academic school or an athletic school. They've made it very hard to recruit because of their high standards. Maybe they should take a look at another program to teach them how to do it. Stanford has very high academic standards, and they seem to be able to get quality athletes."

It was an interesting point — and it wasn't lost on the Stanford coach. Tyrone Willingham had spent a lot of time thinking about academic standards. In the late 80s, Willingham had noticed the guy who was coaching the Duke football team. Willingham knew that the Blue Devils had never produced a winning football program until Steve Spurrier — an ultracompetitive cat much like Willingham — had arrived on the scene. On Spurrier's watch, Duke went 20–13–1, even winning an ACC championship.

After Spurrier left Duke in favor of a big-time program at the University of Florida, Willingham continued to keep an eye on him. While at Florida, Spurrier won seven SEC titles, and in 1996 he won it all when Florida beat Florida State for the national championship. Spurrier's path — from unprecedented success at an academic institution, to even more success at a big-time football program — captured Willingham's imagination. He didn't know exactly how Spurrier had succeeded at Duke, but he knew a part of it centered on making players *believe* they could win.

In 1999, perhaps taking a page from Spurrier's playbook, Willingham led Stanford to its first Rose Bowl in 28 years, a feat not even NFL coaches Bill Walsh and Denny Green had accomplished while there. And his 2001 team, along with a 9–3 record, would go on to compile an 83 percent graduation rate. Academic achievement coupled with football success underscored one of Willingham's basic philosophies. Wherever competition manifested itself, on the field, in the classroom, or in any social realm where success or failure could be tangibly measured, Willingham had one purpose. "The goal," he said, "is to win."

High academic standards were not an insuperable barrier to athletic success, but the academic culture at Stanford affected Willingham in other ways. Despite his success on the field, the university had never rallied around his team. Football simply would never be a prominent part of Stanford's identity.

On the November evening of Stanford's unexpected win over Notre Dame, Willingham was reminded of how Stanford's attitude toward its football program had limited him. Before his team took control of the game in the third quarter, he noticed an unsettling presence in Stanford Stadium. A paltry 51,000 people had shown up in a stadium that housed 80,000, and the loudest cheers weren't even for Stanford, who at the time was ranked No. 13 and on the verge of winning *nine* games that season. Sure, there were scattered cheers each time Stanford scored, but each time Notre Dame scored, a loud and clear "Go Irish" came from one section of the stands. Even when Notre Dame wasn't itself in terms of spirit or dominance, they still commanded more of a presence than Stanford did.

Maybe Stanford's apathy that night was a sign that Willingham's tenure at that particular academic institution was just about over. Maybe it was time for him to start thinking about doing the same thing Steve Spurrier had done, making the leap to a big-time football program. And maybe his timing was just right, since after that game, Notre Dame, the academic school with the big-time football program, would search for ways to maintain its academic image *and* win football games. How fitting that Tyrone Willingham, the coach who beat Notre Dame that night, just happened to be a man who knew how to strike that balance.

After the game, Notre Dame had fallen to 4–6, and Davie wasn't the only one who was frustrated. Inside the locker room, Notre Dame linebacker Courtney Watson quietly dressed. A junior, Watson hadn't chosen to play for Notre Dame just to win football games, but he hadn't expected to lose so much either. That night, Watson and his teammates knew that Bob Davie's job was in serious jeopardy, but it was out of their hands. They just prepared for what they could control, which was their last game of the season against Purdue.

Over the next several weeks, Watson and his teammates would hear rumors about several coaches who might be headed to Notre Dame — including Tyrone Willingham. Watson had met the man before. He was a senior at Riverview High School in Sarasota, Florida, when Willingham came to offer him a scholarship to Stanford. Well, Willingham had *wanted* to offer him a scholarship. At the time, Watson was a highly sought after running back who, in addition to rushing for more than 2,000 yards, had scored 1000 on his SAT. Willingham wanted him, but he also knew that Watson might be more attractive to the Stanford admissions department if he had gotten another 100 points on that test.

Watson thought about that. Sure, he could take the test again, but what would be the point? The football powers like Miami and Florida State wanted him, and so did Duke, another academic school. One night, as Watson lay in bed, it suddenly occurred to him that Notre Dame was the ideal place for him. He could do it all there. He could win football games without compromising his academic beliefs or his personal goals. Watson had no idea that little more than a month after the loss to Stanford, his new coach would arrive, bringing with him that very same conviction.

At Notre Dame, "image is everything." At one time, it may have been thought that Bob Davie reflected the dynamic, disciplined, clean-cut image that once defined the university. But by the end of the 2001 season, it was clear that Davie hadn't lived up to his billing.

After firing Bob Davie on Sunday, December 2, 2001, Notre Dame athletic director Kevin White began his search for the new Irish head coach in the Bay Area. White, who was in his second year at Notre Dame, "contacted" Willingham on Tuesday afternoon. Now it should be noted that "contact" in this case means the two had a brief conversation on the phone. But Willingham wasn't offered the job that day.

White and Willingham had met before. Back in 1978 at Central Michigan University, Willingham was a young secondary coach while White assisted the cross-country team. They weren't close then, but they became more acquainted with each other during the years Kevin White was the athletic director at Arizona State and Willingham chaired the Pacific-10 coaching committee. With that personal link in their past, it made sense that Notre Dame's initial interest in Willingham was actually Kevin White's interest in Willingham.

After the brief conversation, White told local and national pundits how "passionate" Willingham had seemed about the job. When Stanford athletic director Ted Leland got wind of the conversation, he called Willingham and asked him the deal. Willingham confirmed that he had spoken to White, but he told Leland "they weren't very interested." That's because the real purpose of White's West Coast tour was to meet with Oakland Raiders coach Jon Gruden and San Francisco 49ers coach Steve Mariucci.

Gruden was the Holy Grail of coaches. At 38, Gruden was not only the youngest head coach in the NFL but also an energetic, blond, and strikingly handsome man who had played high school football in South Bend while his father was a Notre Dame assistant and had once professed that coaching Notre Dame was his dream job. But at the time, Gruden was the most popular coach in the pro ranks, and he had another year remaining on his contract with the Raiders. He was a long shot to ever coach the Irish. He turned them down.

On Wednesday, White took a trip to Santa Clara, California, to the 49ers' training facility. Notre Dame was interested in Mariucci for the same reasons it was interested in Gruden. He was young, energetic, and good-looking. But in Mariucci's case there was more. There was exactly one degree of separation from San Francisco to South Bend. The 49ers facility is named the Marie DeBartolo Complex. That would be the late mother of former 49ers owner Eddie DeBartolo, the same Eddie DeBartolo whose name adorns a building adjacent to Notre Dame Stadium. DeBartolo is among the biggest and most powerful of the Notre Dame alums. But Mariucci was an even longer shot to coach the Irish than Gruden was. Mariucci had taken his team to the playoffs that year, and he had just signed a long-term contract. After admitting he was "intrigued" by the Notre Dame job, Mariucci also told White no.

On Thursday afternoon, White was on a plane to Atlanta, Georgia, with his sights set squarely on Georgia Tech coach George O'Leary. O'Leary wasn't a handsome youngster like Gruden and Mariucci, but he did fit the Notre Dame image.

Kevin White even said as much. "George kind of appeared to us all like something out of central casting," he explained. "Second-generation Irish Catholic. Good football coach. Good track record of success. And a great institutional fit. On top of all that, George expressed a great passion for the job. It was his lifetime ambition to be at Notre Dame."

That last part had actually been documented. When O'Leary became the Georgia Tech coach in 1994, his deal contained a "Notre Dame" clause, which allowed him to break his contract to take the Notre Dame job without a buyout. When he signed a new deal in 2001, that clause was removed, but now he looked like such a good match for Notre Dame that White and his gang wouldn't balk at paying $1.5 million to Georgia Tech.

White called Willingham after making his decision to hire O'Leary. Willingham hadn't campaigned for the job, but once he had a shot at it, he wasn't about to let it slip away. Willingham, while intensely private and humble, is still at heart a competitor.

He knew the most demanding position in college football could only be filled by the most demanding man in college football. "You're hiring the wrong guy," Willingham told White. "You *need* to hire me." But it was too late to change anyone's mind. White offered the job to O'Leary, and he accepted.

O'Leary had coached Georgia Tech the previous eight years, but he resigned on December 5, right before Georgia Tech's Seattle Bowl appearance, to take the Notre Dame job. When his hiring was announced on December 9, his first order of business was to gather his team in the meeting room at Notre Dame Stadium. Like any new coach, he had to establish the rules for his new regime. Before him sat a team that had finished the season a very un–Notre Damelike 5–6. O'Leary, with his ruddy face, perpetually tousled white hair, and pale blue eyes, looked his team in the eyes and told them, "Always tell me the truth. Don't you ever lie to me."

On December 14, O'Leary, in one of the most damaging public relations debacles in college football history, was forced to resign from Notre Dame after it was discovered that *he* had lied. His résumé stated that he had received three letters in football at the University of New Hampshire and that he had attained a master's degree in education from New York University. None of it was true. After 34 years of coaching, O'Leary's reputation had been destroyed in one fell swoop. More important, Notre Dame's already staggering reputation had suffered another crippling blow.

The timing couldn't have been worse for the Irish-Catholic university. Not only had its football team, long the bearer of Catholic pride and might, lost its luster in the college football community, but now its moral credibility was in question. In South Bend, football is just about everything, so in order to reburnish its image, Notre Dame needed to kick some ass on the field. But before the Irish could reach a peak high enough to wake up the echoes, they had to descend into the dark, funky abyss of rock bottom. O'Leary's resignation and the search to replace him turned out to be just that.

Remember that scene from the movie *Trading Places*? The

one in which the orange juice stock is plummeting and Randolph (Ralph Bellamy) and Mortimer (Don Ameche), the two antiquated millionaires, are trying to sell their positions, but no one is buying? The same scenario now applied to Notre Dame and the position of football coach. A job that at one time had such unquestioned value was no longer worth a damn.

Word spread that Notre Dame was interested in Jacksonville Jaguars coach Tom Coughlin, who had coached the Boston College Eagles to an upset win over the top-ranked Irish in 1993. Coughlin himself seemed amused by the rumor. He asked publicly: "Why, because I'm an Irish Catholic who beat Notre Dame?" Another rumor was that Notre Dame returned to Mariucci and Gruden. "Are you *suuure* you don't want the job?" Once again, both said no. When Willingham's name was tossed into the rumor mill once again, Ted Leland called Notre Dame. He told them Stanford was withdrawing permission for them to speak to Willingham unless they were offering him the job. "And they backed away after that," said Leland.

Willingham was the ideal man for Notre Dame, but for some reason the administration just wasn't seeing it. Notre Dame is a university that fields sixteen varsity sports and hadn't had one black head coach in its 114 years of intercollegiate athletics. Since lining up against Michigan in its first football game in 1887, crowning seven Heisman Trophy winners, winning eleven consensus national championships, and being immortalized in the films *Knute Rockne, All American* and *Rudy,* one thing had remained constant in South Bend: no black head coaches.

If the Notre Dame administration had a face, it was university president Reverend Edward A. Malloy, C.S.C. He had succeeded the legendary Theodore Hesburgh in 1986, and was in his sixteenth year as the university president. Father "Monk" Malloy was a very tall man, about 6′5″, with silver hair, square wire-rimmed glasses, and large ears. A 1963 graduate of Notre Dame, a scholarship athlete on the Irish basketball team, residence hall rector, teacher, and administrator, Malloy was, in many ways, a Notre Dame "lifer."

It only made sense that Malloy seek a coach who understood the "Notre Dame way" of doing things. He was looking for someone who understood the significance of Knute Rockne and the Four Horsemen. The fact that every person who had ever helmed a Notre Dame team was white may have been coincidence, but white men were familiar to Malloy. And perhaps that's what took Malloy to Seattle, where University of Washington coach Rick Neuheisel was preparing his team to play Texas in the Holiday Bowl.

In Rick Neuheisel, Malloy had identified a proven coach who was good-looking and educated, one who had a law degree from USC. But Neuheisel was also a coach who, while at Colorado from 1995 to 1998, had gained a bit of a reputation for his "liberal" interpretation of NCAA rules. It was never anything really heinous, but just enough to keep things interesting and to maintain his reputation as college football's most precocious young coach.

In fact, Neuheisel had a rep similar to Lou Holtz's while Holtz was coaching at Minnesota. One year, Holtz allegedly gave money to a couple of his players for their personal needs — a transgression of NCAA rules. Neuheisel, in the summer of 2002, would tell the NCAA committee that he and his staff had "accidental encounters" with some of their recruits on high school campuses. Neuheisel didn't think it was much of an advantage, but committee chairman Tom Yeager thought otherwise. Since seven of the 26 kids the coach bumped into eventually signed with Colorado, Yeager considered it unfair. "In most instances," Yeager said, "these seven athletes were among the top recruits in their respective classes. In the end, the institution benefited."

Neuheisel rightly and craftily defended himself. "I was reading the NCAA rules as an attorney," he said, "meaning that it doesn't say, 'You can't do that.'" After Neuheisel left for Washington, Colorado was slapped with 53 violations, 51 having occurred while Neuheisel was there. Most significant to Notre Dame was that Neuheisel's punishment would follow him to his next job. Had he taken the Notre Dame job, Neuheisel would have been barred from making any off-season recruiting visits for the Irish through May 31, 2003. (But in the spring of 2003 things got even worse for Neuheisel after it was discovered he had bet on the NCAA men's basketball tournament the past two years. Gambling on college sports, in any form, is forbidden by the NCAA, and the University of Washington fired Neuheisel.)

But perhaps Malloy wasn't aware of Neuheisel's antics as he sold his school to the coach that night. Or perhaps Malloy was thinking about the immediate future, not necessarily the long term. It didn't matter, though, because in the wee hours of the morning, Neuheisel decided Washington was the place for him. He told Malloy thanks but no thanks.

The next morning, Neuheisel boarded a plane to catch up with his team in San Diego, and Notre Dame went to its final option. On December 22, Kevin White called Willingham and asked him if he was still interested in the job. Willingham said yes. After he had the job, Willingham told a friend, "I never had to campaign for this job. A lot of coaches do that. When they wanted me, they called me." But Willingham had not forgotten his first conversation with White. After he'd accepted White's offer, Willingham coolly told him, "You should have hired me the first time."

On Thursday afternoon, December 27, 2001, in a half-empty stadium on a typically dreary Seattle day, Willingham's Stanford squad couldn't engineer another miracle comeback as Georgia Tech defeated Stanford 24–14 in the inaugural Seattle Bowl. Afterward, Willingham looked devastated. It wasn't just the loss. His seven-year tenure at Stanford, one of the longest in school history, had officially come to an end.

Willingham's staff would have some choices to make. That Friday night, Buzz Preston, who coached the Stanford running backs, sat on his sofa watching Texas beat Washington 47–43 in the Holiday Bowl. While in Seattle, preparing for their game, Preston and the rest of Willingham's staff had heard the Notre Dame jet was in town, so they naturally assumed it was there for Neuheisel. Willingham, guarding against leaks, hadn't even informed his staff of his decision.

As he watched the clock run out on the Holiday Bowl, Preston casually remarked to his wife, Audrey, "Rick Neuheisel is going to Notre Dame." With that, Preston went out to get some ice-cream sandwiches, preparing to just chill out for the next two days. But when he returned, there was a message that Willingham had called. Preston immediately feared the worst.

"Uh-oh," he said, "I must have done something wrong. Did I lose a recruit or something?"

Instead, Willingham told him he had officially accepted the job at Notre Dame. "Well, do *I* still have a job?" asked Preston.

Willingham chuckled. "Of course you do." It would be a major change for Preston's high school–age daughter, but the family was moving to Indiana.

Bill Diedrick, the Stanford offensive coordinator, had grown accustomed to the Tyrone Willingham rumor mill. "Working with Ty was always interesting because it seemed like every year someone would make a run at him," he said. After Notre Dame hired O'Leary, Diedrick just moved on. "Hey, we escaped another one, and we'll be here another year," he thought.

After the Seattle Bowl, Diedrick and his wife flew home to the Bay Area, and the next day they took off for San Diego. But the next night, on New Year's Eve, while Diedrick watched the Washington State–Purdue game on television, it was announced there'd be a Tyrone Willingham update at halftime. A few minutes later, he watched the Willingham family walk across the Notre Dame campus. *Wow, I'd better go check my messages,* thought Diedrick.

Before leaving for San Diego, he had turned off his cell phone, and when he clicked it on, there were fifty-two messages for him. The first two were from Willingham. "Bill, call me back; I need to visit with you."

The next one was slightly more urgent. "Bill, this is Ty again. It's *really* important that I speak to you."

When Diedrick called Willingham back, the coach asked his offensive coordinator to join him.

"Notre Dame? That one was a no-brainer," said Diedrick. Two days later, Diedrick, Preston, and four other coaches from Willingham's staff at Stanford (Mike Denbrock, Trent Miles, John McDonell, and Kent Baer) joined him as he headed for South Bend.

2

WAKING UP ECHOES

Lionel Tyrone Willingham was born in Kinston, North Carolina, a small town near a military base about sixty miles east of Raleigh, and grew up in nearby Jacksonville. Like most black families in the South, the Willinghams knew they were surrounded by hate. That's why they countered it with love. That's why they went to church. And most black kids who grew up in the South knew that Sundays were for church — not a prescribed, time-limited service on Sunday morning or afternoon, either. For religious Southern black folks, church meant sitting on a hard polished wooden pew pretty much *all day* long.

Sunday afternoons created a conflict of interest for an adolescent Tyrone Willingham. He would go to Jacksonville Methodist with his parents; younger brother, Jerome; and his two younger sisters, Joyce and Gail, but at a certain time of day, he would give in to the lust in his heart.

In 1966, at 13 years old, he already had a passion for football, and the coaching part of his personality had already manifested itself in one of his hobbies. "Remember those electric football games? I used to turn off the electricity, usually because it didn't work that well anyway, and just line the players up in all kinds of formations." But on Sunday afternoons in the fall, Willingham was preoccupied with watching *real* football.

"Services in a Methodist church could go past noon," said

Willingham. "You have to understand, Notre Dame highlights started around noon. So part of my responsibility to myself was to slip out of church and watch those highlights." He's quick to point out that he wasn't necessarily a Notre Dame fan, but he was a college football fan.

"Growing up in North Carolina at the time, it was difficult to be a fan of *any* team. There weren't a lot of African-Americans allowed to play in Division One schools. And there weren't a lot of venues for people in Jacksonville. On Sunday, you had NFL games and you had Notre Dame highlights."

It's fitting that Jacksonville, a town of 16,000, sat in the shadow of the Camp Lejeune Marine Corps Base, because every inhabitant of the Willingham house on Kerr Street embodied discipline, especially Tyrone. That practiced, rigid trot Willingham makes to the practice field each day reeks of a military influence. But look closer, and it reeks of something else too. That focused gait is a manifestation of the sometimes written but always loudly spoken rule of the segregated South: If "niggers" had to be seen, they sure as hell shouldn't be heard. Wherever he went, he moved with a honed sense of purpose. And if he had to pass through a white neighborhood, he did so in silence. But as he matured, his silence wasn't steeped in fear as much as it was fueled by pride.

Never mind the 1954 *Brown v. Board of Education* Supreme Court ruling, in the mid-60s, in segregated Jacksonville, the black kids went to Georgetown High School and the whites went to Jacksonville High. But in the spring of 1966, on graduation day, Georgetown High was destroyed by a fire. At the time, the federal government was waging war on segregated education, and Georgetown was slated for integration the following fall. The origins of that fire were never determined, but Willingham, like many in the black community, said that he is still convinced the demise of Georgetown High School was the result of a fire-bomb.

By the time Willingham was a teenager, schools may have been integrated, but race relations remained tense. Willingham's daily trek to Jacksonville High School was two miles of humble silence. Blacks, or "colored" people as they were called then, knew better than to call attention to themselves. "I never actually witnessed or experienced anything really bad," says Willingham now, "but I knew there was hate around me."

If there wasn't visible hate in his own community, the nearby town of Smithfield, North Carolina, certainly had no shame in its game. When Willingham was 12, his Little League baseball team took a bus to Smithfield for a tournament. Once they entered Smithfield's city limits, Willingham, the team's lone black player, poked his head out of the window to get a closer look at a large billboard in the distance. Written underneath a charcoal sketch of a hooded rider on a rearing stallion were the words: "Welcome to the home of the United Klan."

That image burned into his head, Willingham approached high school the same way he had junior high. Even after he became the school's first black quarterback, and the Jacksonville Cardinals Most Valuable Player, neither the measured carriage of his walk to school nor the foundation of his philosophy ever changed. Any type of statement that could be construed as self-aggrandizement, he considered taboo. He still does. Willingham gets visibly uncomfortable when asked to speak about himself. While talking about his high school days, he interrupted himself with a laugh and a disbelieving nod of his head. "This should not be the focus." He doesn't ever want it to be about him. It's nothing personal, he just hates for anything to be about himself.

His selflessness and sense of community are proof that the man sprang from the loins of Nathaniel Willingham. His father thought manic energy was better utilized erecting programs than bolstering his own self-image. A self-taught contractor, Nathaniel built Jacksonville's Masonic temple and converted the bottom half of the Willingham's two-story home into a recreation center for neighborhood kids.

If Tyrone Willingham inherited the gene for practical thought from his father, then the strand of DNA that helped him become an educational pioneer came courtesy of his mother, Lillian. She spent most of her life as an elementary school teacher, pouring herself into Jacksonville community projects. Her most astonishing achievement may have been the master's degree she earned from Columbia University. There weren't too many black women who left the South in the 50s and returned with sheepskin from an Ivy League school. Today, in honor of her accomplishments, Lillian Willingham Parkway will take you directly to the manicured lawns of Lillian Willingham Park, located in downtown Jacksonville.

Willingham's parents left him with a practical view of raising children. "Some of these parents today are out clubbing and drinking," says Willingham now. "See, I was blessed to have had older parents. They had already done all that and didn't have to worry about it. These days, you have parents who, when they have kids, are still into that. You know that commercial with Kid Rock? It's the one where he picks up his friend and tells his [friend's] wife, 'I'll bring him home early.' He doesn't come back until early the next morning. That promotes that kind of behavior." Willingham leaned back in his chair, rocking back and forth, and allowing himself to smile. "Nothing against anyone else's parents, but I'm glad I had mine."

Maybe Willingham's balance, his unyielding emotional equilibrium, came from taking the bitter with the sweet. In January 1984, shortly after he and his wife, Kim, welcomed their first child into the world, he lost his mother. As he celebrated the birth of Cassidy Willingham, he mourned the death of Lillian Willingham, who had suffered a stroke. "After she died, we were worried about our father for a while there," said Willingham. "But we knew how strong he was."

In January 1995, Willingham was named head coach at Stanford. Several weeks later, Willingham needed his father's strength. While Tyrone Willingham celebrated the fulfillment of his professional dream, his father, Nathaniel Willingham, passed away. Willingham asked questions then, but he doesn't anymore. "You ask God, 'Why me?' But you come out of that mode because you realize we're not smart enough to have the vision God does. So you don't need to question anymore. You just thank God for all the positives you had with them, and you have a better understanding of how to travel in this life."

By the time they passed away, Willingham's parents had instilled in all four of their children the one prerequisite skill vital to many black youths' success in the segregated South. "My parents taught us to dream," he said. In fact, it was a healthy dose of dreaming that led Willingham onto the field at Jacksonville High School.

Willingham was 5'7" and 139 pounds. His shoulders didn't appear broad enough to support his pads, let alone his dreams, but they were large enough to support a man-size chip. A small feisty quarterback, he became the all-time leading passer at Jacksonville High School. By the time he graduated, he owned MVP trophies in football, basketball, and baseball. And in 2000, he was inducted into Jacksonville's Athletic Hall of Fame. He doesn't like to reflect much on the past, preferring to move forward with the unrelenting passion of one who makes history rather than one who dwells on it. But that's not to say he doesn't remember things.

Willingham particularly remembers his high school football coach, Ken Miller. He doesn't recall some pregame speech or crunch-time tactic, but the way Miller treated people, shaping Willingham's personal and professional focus. "It wasn't his words, it was his actions," said Willingham. "He was one of those who saw the good in you, regardless of what color you were." Throughout his 20-year career, Willingham has applied that philosophy to each of his players.

And, of course, Willingham remembers his parents. "Oh, I think about my parents every day," he says. "But I'm not one to say, 'Oh, I wonder if they're looking down and watching me.' They were always active, and knowing them, they're probably still busy doing things. They aren't worried about me. They know they raised me right and did a good job."

If Willingham's parents *were* watching, they must have seen that he had his work cut out for him at Notre Dame.

Willingham had just earned a spot in the most visible office in the land, but before he could sit down behind his desk and make sense of it all, he had to hit the road. With just one month left before national letter-of-intent day on February 5, 2002, he scrambled to make up for lost time and lost recruits. He went to Indianapolis to speak to James Banks, Notre Dame's top priority at quarterback, but found that Banks had canceled his trip to campus and was leaning toward Tennessee. In the time Notre Dame spent searching for Bob Davie's successor, they had lost five blue-chip recruits. Tight end Dominique Byrd had chosen USC, quarterback Gavin Dickey had committed to Florida, defensive lineman Julian Jenkins had chosen Stanford, and tight end Eric Winston was deciding between Miami (Fla.) or Texas A&M. Linebacker Jeremy Van Alstyne, from Greenwood, Indiana, who had originally committed to Notre Dame, had changed his mind and committed to Michigan.

Among Willingham's top priorities was receiver — because of the West Coast offense. If he was going to successfully implement his new offense, one that had seen much success at Stanford, he desperately needed some speed and more than a few able bodies at that particular position. So it was especially disconcerting when Josh Hannum, a receiver from Wallingford, Pennsylvania, called offensive coordinator Bill Diedrick and told him he had chosen Penn State over Notre Dame. Hannum supposedly ran a legitimate 4.3 forty meters, and that time would have made him the fastest wideout on the Notre Dame team. But just one week later, disappointment turned to fortune when Willingham received a call from Maurice Stovall.

Stovall, from Archbishop Carroll High School in Radnor, Pennsylvania, was 6'5", weighed 200 pounds, and possessed maturity beyond his years. He was rated by recruiting guru Tom Lemming as one of the top two receivers in the country — and he was only 16. Willingham told Stovall he needed a big receiver, and Stovall liked what he heard.

"He seemed like a pretty good coach," said Stovall after meeting Willingham. He chose Notre Dame over Michigan, Temple, and Virginia. "After discussing things with my family, I decided Notre Dame was the best choice, especially as far as earning a degree," said Stovall.

Things got even better for Willingham and his staff when they received a call from another receiver, Rhema McKnight. At 6'1" and 190 pounds, McKnight was smaller than Stovall, but of the two he was actually the more explosive and more polished player. Since he was from Los Angeles, the staff knew they had to do a great sales job to get him to dreary South Bend. And Trent Miles, the receivers coach, did just that.

"You're gonna play," Miles told him. "In this offense we need a lot of guys, and you're gonna be one of 'em."

McKnight heard enough and committed. Just those two young men made Willingham's first recruiting class a successful one. Willingham had told every potential recruit that there was only one team that would be televised every Saturday afternoon, and that was Notre Dame. And Willingham was telling Irish fans that when they tuned in, they would see an exciting group of players.

In the show-and-tell that is football coaching, Tyrone Willingham was always more about the showing than the telling. But in the beginning, he had to tell his new team some things — 247 things to be exact. Willingham gathered the team in the meeting room at the stadium. It was the same room where Bob Davie had once smashed a desk to show his disgust when one of his players had the audacity to talk during a meeting. It was the same room where, just a couple of weeks earlier, George O'Leary had told them to always tell the truth. After walking into the room, Willingham made his first point with an apology. He apologized for being fifteen seconds late. He then turned on an overhead projector and highlighted 247 different points, each leading to one specific directive: Win.

Only two weeks after that meeting, Willingham used winter conditioning to show his new team what was expected of them in the months ahead. To do that, he had to wake them up. Early. On Saturday mornings, the Notre Dame football team walked to the indoor field at the Loftus Sports Center for 6:30 A.M. workouts. The two-hour sessions were grueling. They consisted of old-school calisthenics such as jumping rope, doing push-ups and sit-ups, and holding the legs six inches in the air, doing the old together-apart routine for several minutes at a time. The workouts often culminated with players lying on the ground and throwing up from sheer exhaustion. During one of those sessions, Gerome Sapp, a senior strong safety, looked over at Courtney Watson and whimpered, "Who is this guy, and why is he doing this to us?" Other players weren't as discreet and openly moaned out loud. During one of those times, Willingham just looked at them and, maintaining eye contact, blew his whistle three sharp times. He then told them simply, "Stop whining."

While Willingham was getting things started on the football end, the university took action on the scholastic side. Junior running back Julius Jones, whose 718 yards led the team in rushing in 2001, had been placed on academic probation for the second time in his collegiate career. He was expelled from school and would have to spend the next two semesters at a junior college. Willingham met with Jones before his departure and told him that after he had completed the requisite coursework, he could reapply the following year.

For Willingham, the main point wasn't that Jones was expelled. Based on his academic performance, he deserved to be. But Willingham wanted Jones to get another chance to prove himself. He didn't want Jones to be discarded because of his lack of production in the classroom if there was a chance for improvement. Willingham's philosophy was simple. Throughout the course of the year, Willingham would repeat it ad nauseam. He wanted to win. But for him, winning didn't mean compromising a school's scholastic integrity. Even more important, it didn't mean compromising a kid's professional future.

"The key is, whomever you bring to college, you have to educate," said Willingham. "Years ago, people said it was better that the kid just went to college, even if he didn't graduate. They felt that was progress. But that's not enough. That's a loser's mentality. You have to educate. That's the goal. Then the kid can really do something with it afterward."

In Jones's absence, Willingham was left with sophomore Ryan Grant, who had only 29 carries in 2001, as the most experienced running back on the team. Grant's backups, fellow sophomores Marcus Wilson and Rashon Powers-Neal, didn't have a carry between them. But Willingham wasn't especially concerned. He knew X's and O's were a major issue but that's what his assistant coaches were for. For the moment, he was dealing with the big picture.

Part of that picture involved leadership. To get everyone involved in the leadership process, Willingham changed the policy on electing captains. He decided they would be better served by electing captains each week than by selecting a few for the entire year. It was just the second time in the history of Notre Dame football that captains were chosen on a game-by-game basis. The only other time Notre Dame picked captains in that fashion was under Frank Leahy in 1946. Players from any class could be captains, but Willingham was looking primarily at the seniors for leadership. "It depends on where the seniors are though," he said. "Some lead, some are indifferent, and some follow."

Willingham was all about moving forward, but before he could do that, he had to take a step back. The vital ingredient to the lasting success of Notre Dame football was the maintenance of its tradition. Although Willingham hadn't been Notre Dame's first choice, he knew enough of the school's heritage to teach his team. In recent years, tradition had become a cliché among the current Notre Dame players, as very few gave any thought to the past. Jordan Black, a fifth-year senior offensive tackle, confessed that prior to his recruiting visit in 1998, he had no idea what the Golden Dome was. And when a reporter from Channel 2 News quizzed the current Notre Dame players on Irish football trivia, the results were abysmal. The questions were (1) How many Heisman Trophy winners has Notre Dame had? (2) Name at least two of those winners. (3) When was the last time Notre Dame won a bowl game? (4) What bowl was it? (5) Sing the words to the school's fight song.

Vontez Duff, a junior cornerback from Texas, may have turned in the worst performance. He got only one question *partially* right — he could name only one Heisman Trophy winner. And the reason he knew that Tim Brown had won the 1987 Heisman was Brown, like Duff, was from Texas. The reporter offered Duff a hint on another Heisman winner by saying that "one of them is here every week for games and is nicknamed the Golden Boy." Duff paused before blurting out, "Rick Mirer!"

"No," the reporter said. "It's Paul Hornung."

But that was the sign of the times around campus. It seemed

that when Lou Holtz made his exit in 1996, so too did the grand tradition of Notre Dame football. In his zeal to make the Notre Dame program modern, Bob Davie threw out tradition and was never big on former players hanging around his team. As a result, many of them said they didn't feel welcome.

Once Willingham arrived, however, all that changed. He thought the best way to build the future was to use the foundation from the past. And he knew he needed former players to breathe life into that tradition. Over the course of the season, Willingham would repeat one particular phrase a few hundred times: "I want all the players who have worn this uniform to be proud." To entice former players to visit the campus, he introduced certain activities, including an alumni flag football game and a dinner each spring. All past players were invited to attend.

But Willingham was very particular about whom he asked to address his team. "There are some people who want to speak to the team simply because they want to tell people they spoke to the team," said Willingham. "I'm not looking for them. I'm looking for the pure in spirit. They're easy to detect because they're the ones who don't usually want to speak. They're the ones who don't know how much they have to offer."

Former offensive lineman Chris Clevenger was one of those guys. Clevenger was back at Notre Dame working on his M.B.A. when he stopped by practice for the first time since he quit playing after the 1997 season. Willingham asked him if he would like to address the Irish offensive line. Clevenger declined to speak, but the gesture carried much weight for him. "It means a lot," said Clevenger. "It means a lot when the head coach takes an interest in the former players, what the former players think."

Although he failed to get Clevenger to speak to the team, Willingham, hell-bent on recovering lost school spirit, set his sights on one of Notre Dame's more dynamic personalities.

Willingham got word that Raghib "Rocket" Ismail was returning to South Bend that spring to speak at a luncheon at the College Football Hall of Fame. "I have no idea how he found me," said Ismail. He was driving from San Diego to Los Angeles when Willingham called him on his cell phone. Willingham introduced himself to the Dallas Cowboys receiver as the new coach and then proceeded to ask him about himself, his life, and his memories of Notre Dame.

"The first thing that came to mind was [that] he was listening to me," said Ismail. "He was *digesting* what I was saying. It was like his mind was always going and always computing. This was on the phone, so it was over the airwaves that I got this impression."

After that conversation, Willingham could have said, "Okay, Rocket, feel free to come on down and watch practice one day," but he didn't. He asked him to address the squad; an honor not lost on Ismail. "It's very smart for him to be particular about his speakers," said Ismail. "The most powerful position in any society is the position that enables the person who holds it to mold the perceptions of the masses. So as a coach, or as a leader, or someone with great authority, you have to recognize that. You can't just let someone with a shiny suit come in and start feeding things to people who don't know any better."

When Ismail walked into the Loftus Center field house before practice, the team left an impression that for him was far from scintillating. Standing before him was a group of guys who in no way, shape, or form resembled the dominant teams for which he had played in the late 80s and early 90s. "I was thinking this cat was in for a rude awakening," said Ismail. "From a purely physical standpoint, how the team looked, I thought Coach Willingham was at least three recruiting classes away from cracking the top twenty again."

As Ismail stood there, he thought about what to tell the players. He was trying to come up with something to say that was relevant beyond that particular phase in their lives, something that went beyond just spring practice. That's when he remembered Lou Holtz.

"Coach Holtz had a way of saying things we could identify with," said Ismail. "When things got hot, we could recall a particular saying. And one thing he said was 'Don't ever flinch.'"

Later, Ismail would explain why he used that example with the young Irish team. "Young people can relate to that because they want respect," he said. "Respect comes from other people perceiving that you're powerful. If someone comes up and tries to punk you, you're not gonna flinch. I knew the seeds would be planted for them later in the school year, and later in life."

Ismail spoke wisely. Willingham's first team was a group who would be punked, who had been punked on a regular basis, and who desperately needed to regain the edge and not-so-subtle insolence that marked Notre Dame teams of old. They all quietly listened that day, but none more closely than junior receiver Omar Jenkins. A Dallas native and a graduate of Jesuit High School, Jenkins was also a huge Cowboys fan.

The 2002 season would mark Jenkins's first as a starter. Although he had just seven receptions in his college career, he was the team's best overall route runner. As Jenkins listened to Rocket that day, he had no idea that several months later, the very same electric presence would show up again. And it would be at a time when Jenkins and the rest of his offensive teammates needed some inspiration.

3

TRAINING CAMP

PRIOR TO TAKING the field, all teams gather in the dark, shady confines of a stadium passageway. There, each one is alone with his thoughts, and for a few moments, everything is perfect. The game plan is flawless, the uniforms are clean, and the coach has yet to make a poor decision. So it was fitting that a month before the season began, one of the most salient moments of the Tyrone Willingham era took place inside the concourse of Notre Dame Stadium. That was the day Willingham, in no uncertain terms, let Notre Dame fans know that his expectations were as great as theirs were.

On Friday, August 9, 2002, one day before training camp started, in an annual ritual called Fan Appreciation Day, the players sat at seven long tables, in their blue home jerseys, markers in hand, signing autographs for fans. Willingham sat at the first table, alone. The line of fans, consisting mostly of parents and small children, cheerfully snaked its way toward him. As he smiled, shaking hands and patiently posing for pictures, it was clear that a statement he'd made just 20 minutes earlier wasn't part of some impassive shtick.

Earlier that day, seated on a platform in the Joyce Athletic and Convocation Center arena, 10 feet above a throng of 30 journalists, Willingham had answered a reporter's question about his "leisure activities." "My life can be summed up by something I call 'F.F.G.G.,'" he said. "Football, family, God, and golf."

Now, since the crowd of 200 people waiting in line to see him were mostly families, three quarters of Willingham's earthly axis was represented. Willingham, dressed in a dark-blue polo shirt, khakis, and old-school shell-toe Adidas shoes, soaked up the fans' energy as much as they feasted on his celebrity. He smiled warmly, gently placing his arms around kids as he posed for pictures.

"How are you gonna do against Maryland, Coach?" asked a white-haired gentleman in a coral-blue golf shirt and white fishing hat, referring to the first game on the Notre Dame schedule.

"We'll just do our best," said an ever-polite Willingham.

Another man, holding a Notre Dame calendar, asked Willingham when his birthday was. "It's in December," Willingham answered.

"December twenty-fifth?" the man asked.

Tickled by the question's obvious implication, Willingham laughed. "I wish."

At precisely 2:00 P.M., a pear-shaped mother of two, dressed in white shorts and a blue Notre Dame T-shirt, led her two sons toward Willingham. The boys, one in a gold number 12 jersey and the other in a blue number 7 jersey, wore huge grins as Willingham posed with them. After the picture, as Willingham signed their jerseys, he said to the one wearing number 7, "That's a good number right there." It was a subtle reference to his starting quarterback, Carlyle Holiday, seated several tables away. He knew the athletically gifted Holiday would be under a lot of scrutiny this season. Willingham's comment was his subtle way of getting fans to stand behind the signal caller. When he finished signing, Willingham said softly to the boy, "Maybe *you* can come play quarterback for me one day."

But 15 seconds later, Willingham sent a not-so-subtle message to his team and all who were watching. As the two boys walked away, the coach abruptly stood up, put a whistle in his mouth, leaned forward, and blew. The atmosphere of good, wholesome family cheer was momentarily displaced by the business at hand.

After two piercing seconds, he stopped blowing that whistle, and for two more seconds he stood, maintaining a slight forward lean, making eye contact with as many players as he could. His stare spoke volumes to all who fell into its line: *We're here to win football games, and it's time to get to work.*

And according to his finely tuned schedule, at 2:00 P.M., it was time to stop celebrating the Notre Dame football program and to start rebuilding it. Willingham and his team were signing autographs and being congratulated, but they had yet to play a game. With a flick of his hand, he motioned for the players to exit, and without hesitation, they silently filed from the stadium and back to the locker room to put away their home jerseys. It wouldn't be time to *really* wear them until they played Purdue on September 7, in what would be their first home game under the Willingham regime. Willingham sat down at his table, resumed his smile, and signed a gold football that had been placed in front of him.

The next morning, at precisely 8:45 A.M., camp began with intense sunlight and frenzied passion. The team had a long, arduous road ahead of them. Over the next two weeks, their days would consist of breakfast, practice, lunch, followed by another practice, dinner, and an evening of meetings reviewing everything they'd done that day. That morning, the excitement extended to prepractice stretching. Strength coach Mickey Marotti, whose stout body and square features fit his profession, barked out each stretch, interspersing directions with the same weird coaching clichés you'll hear at the start of every organized football practice in America: "Workday, men. It's a workday!"

Over the next 10 days, Willingham would push his team harder than ever. But he didn't set out to break their spirit. Minus the freshman class, Willingham had inherited 97 youngsters with no direction who had practiced and played inconsistently and gone to class only when it wasn't an inconvenience. He wanted to provide confidence, spirit, and a sense of pride, all of which had been lost in the last five years.

The two perfectly manicured practice fields lay in between the golf course and the Hammes bookstore. As the players sat on the dewy grass, heels together, grasping their cleats and stretching their groins, they did look confident, but also expectant and eager, like children on the first day of school. As Willingham navigated his way through the players, he looked neat, calm, and focused. Wearing khaki shorts and a green nylon vest, he said nothing, just stalked up and down each row, taking it all in. His body language — the quick steps, erect head, squared shoulders — making him a conduit of intensity. Every ounce of energy and passion he provided was being soaked up by the kids seated at his feet. The players, each of whom wore a shiny gold helmet, peered up at their new teacher as he passed by. Though it was silent, save for Marotti's exhortations, the sense of expectation was palpable.

From one of two yellow towers overlooking the practice field, an air horn sounded. As soon as every player had scrambled to his feet and was sprinting toward his station, Willingham voiced the thoughts of every Notre Dame fan in the country who was upset that the team had fallen to the depths of mediocrity and expected to see them return to familiar heights — not next year, not in five years, but *that* season. "You should already be there!" he said.

The defensive players, on one field, broke into three units and opened practice with a pursuit drill. One of the defensive backs would simulate a running back, and after he was handed the ball, he would sprint down the sideline with the defenders pursuing him. When they caught him, each player would run in place, furiously chopping his feet until the whistle blew to end the drill. Each unit repeated this three times.

On the other field, quarterback Carlyle Holiday brought the first offense to the line of scrimmage. He barked the signals: "Black Eighteen! Black Eighteen!" and handed the ball to Ryan Grant, who sprinted into the end zone. Freshman Chris Olsen and sophomore Pat Dillingham, the backup quarterbacks, put their groups through the same drill.

At one of his early press conferences, Willingham had told his audience something they all wanted to hear. The option, which is predicated on a running quarterback, would no longer be the main focus of the Notre Dame attack. Notre Dame fans didn't mind the old-fashioned offense when they were winning, but once they started losing, many felt it should have been replaced by something "modern." As a disciple of the West Coast offense, Willingham was planning to have the offense throw the ball more than any recent Notre Dame team had. Over the previous four years, while Notre Dame's teams had been stagnant in the option, his Stanford teams had averaged more than 30 points and 400 yards per game.

The origins of the West Coast offense can be traced back to Paul Brown, former head coach of the Cleveland Browns and owner and founder of the Cincinnati Bengals. But most citizens of the football culture credit former 49ers coach Bill Walsh with shaping the modern version of the quick passing attack. Behind it, the 49ers, throughout the 80s and 90s, were easily the most prolific and entertaining offense in the league. Jerry Rice and, to a lesser degree, John Taylor were the most visible receivers in the game. Each made a habit of turning a 10-yard slant into a long touchdown run. And if the West Coast offense could be condensed into one simple objective, it was precisely that — to use 10- to 15-yard passes to get receivers in one-on-one positions with defenders so that they would have room to break tackles. This was a welcome change for Notre Dame fans, who had become accustomed to, then tired of, the power option game. Occasionally in the West Coast offense, the ball was thrown deep downfield in posts, corners, and fades, but most of the receivers' routes, each defined by its own code word, were the standard 10 to 15 yards.

It fell on receivers coach Trent Miles to teach the code to players like Arnaz Battle and Omar Jenkins. Though both were veterans, they had to learn a completely new offense. By the afternoon practice, Miles was leading them through route recognition drills. "Thunder," he yelled. The receivers, in groups of three, sprinted five yards upfield and abruptly stopped. This was called a "hitch" route. There was no quarterback and no ball. It was strictly a mental drill. Miles wanted each receiver to commit to memory the terminology that accompanies and defines the West Coast offense. And he wanted each route to be quick and precise. "Okay. Omaha," yelled Miles. Each receiver ran a quick five-yard route toward the sideline. "Keep your elbows up!" Miles yelled at Omar Jenkins.

At 39, Miles was the second youngest member of the staff behind only Mike Denbrock, who coached the tackles and tight ends. Miles, who stood about 5'6", was bald, friendly, and one of the more animated members of the staff. His energy was boundless, and his attention to detail never seemed to wane. It was his second year as an assistant on Willingham's staff. After spending the 2000 season as a quality control coach for the Green Bay Packers, he had joined Willingham at Stanford in 2001. Miles was a native of Terre Haute, Indiana, and had played receiver for Indiana State from 1982 to 1986. Being born and bred a Hoosier, the transition from Palo Alto to Notre Dame hadn't been too difficult for him.

"Okay. Lion," yelled Miles. The command was met by a quick five-yard slant toward the middle of the field. Where the routes got their names is unknown, but legend has it that Bill Walsh just made up names that sounded cool.

Willingham emphasized the scheme's balance of run and pass. He pointed out how in 1985, in this particular scheme, 49ers running back Roger Craig rushed for 1,050 yards and had 1,016 yards receiving. But Notre Dame starting running back Ryan Grant was inexperienced as a receiver. He joked about making his mark strictly as a runner. "I think I've caught one pass in my career," he said.

For Grant, this season would be an unexpected chance to shine. A sophomore who had been third on the depth chart in 2001, Grant wasn't supposed to be a part of the offense for at least another year. But with Julius Jones on probation, he would have to perform.

The other backs from the 2001 season believed Grant was the quintessential overachiever. "Even if Ryan isn't necessarily ready to be the main guy, he'll step up," remarked Tony Fisher, who was now enjoying a good rookie year with the Green Bay Packers.

Grant lacked the explosive step of Julius Jones, but he was a fluent, long-striding runner who had unusual patience for a youngster. On zone plays, in which the offensive linemen blocked a zone rather than a specific defensive player, Grant was known to slow down and wait for an opening before making his move. He was also a perfectionist. He wasn't going to be satisfied with anything less than excellence. Willingham put it bluntly: "He's a young man who likes to beat himself up."

But part of Grant's ambition came in response to Willingham's presence. He liked Willingham's focus and attention to detail. Grant was also one of the few players on the team to state the cultural significance of having the first black head coach in Notre Dame's history. "Man, this is something I can tell my grandkids one day," he said.

The one thing Grant lacked was the ability to finish a run, to punish a defender on contact. He didn't have the confidence to break a tackler's will. But that would come in time, with the help of the ideal mentor, running backs coach Buzz Preston.

Like Grant, Preston was also a perfectionist. In many ways, he was one of the team's "attitude coaches," someone who always lifted morale. Preston, 45 years old, with a round, cheerful face, maintained a relentlessly upbeat mood and always sought to inject that mood on the practice tempo. He was known to pepper his onfield chatter with words like *dagnabbit!* or *dadgummit!* His motto: "I always look at the bright side, even when things are going down the toilet!"

That perspective had been forged following his one-year stint as offensive coordinator at UNLV in 1998. The Rebels had little success, and Preston was fired after one year. "Man, back then, I thought I had *arrived.* I thought I was the man. But I found out I wasn't ready for that." As a reminder of that experience, Preston keeps a red UNLV baseball cap near his desk. "It keeps me humble," he said.

Preston met Willingham while he was a running backs coach at Washington State from 1995 to 1997. The two would chat after each time their teams played each other. "We weren't friends or anything back then," said Preston of Willingham. "But he liked the way my backs performed on the field." After Willingham heard Preston was available, he added him to his staff in 1999.

Before Grant and the other backs could be fully utilized as receivers, Carlyle Holiday had to become a polished passer, a real challenge for a quarterback who had been trained in the option scheme. In fact, a few weeks after the press conference in which Willingham had announced his plan to abandon the option, he amended his earlier declaration. He said he would incorporate *some* option into the offense, explaining that "every team should have more than one dimension in its offensive philosophy." One had to wonder if he was saying that the option was still part of his plans just to make opposing defenses *worry* about stopping it. Whether or not he was actually planning to use it was anyone's guess. But if the option was part of his plans, Carlyle Holiday was the reason why.

Quick, strong, and explosive, Holiday was the quintessential option quarterback. And he was easily the most gifted athlete Willingham had ever had at that position. While he developed into a passer, Holiday would not be discouraged from using his strengths as a runner. It was a philosophy wonderfully articulated by New York Jets coach Herman Edwards. "The players dictate your system," he said. "You don't walk into the meeting room and tell the guys this is what we're doing, now adapt to it. You have to tailor something to the strengths of your best guys because the players *are* your system."

Notre Dame's proposed two-pronged offensive philosophy — the old-fashioned option attack blended with the en vogue passing game of the West Coast offense — was clearly a scheme that could utilize the gifts of Holiday.

During his senior year at San Antonio's Roosevelt High School, Holiday's skills were coveted by colleges from all over the country. At 6'3" and 214 pounds, he had a fearless slashing running style. "Texas A&M, Nebraska, and Syracuse were all recruiting me," said Holiday. All of these teams were big on running the ball, and although he was a natural running quarterback, Holiday yearned to do more.

"Since I was a little kid, I always dreamed of throwing the ball for so many yards," he said. "As an option quarterback, taking all those hits, it takes away from your throwing ability. This is the offense I always wanted to be in."

But at the start of camp, Holiday obviously had some catching up to do. The short pass, or "long handoff," of the West Coast offense was a particularly difficult throw to execute, and though Holiday had always wanted to throw the ball, now he found that his blessing as an option quarterback — speed — was also his curse.

Offensive coordinator Bill Diedrick took the quarterbacks through footwork drills. The passing game was predicated on the quarterback taking three- and five-step drops into the pocket and making quick throws. Holiday was already fast as a hiccup, but when he hurried to set his feet, he sometimes hurried his throws too, especially backside passes, when he threw across his body. Diedrick's goal was to have Holiday improve with each game. But he knew the difficulty factor was extremely high. He likened Holiday's crash course in the passing offense to learning a foreign language. "It's like jumping into a third-year Latin class without having taken the other two years," said Diedrick.

Diedrick was small in stature and direct in manner. He was 55 years old and had brown hair, kind eyes, and a soft smile. In some ways, he had the demeanor of a hard-nosed yet trustworthy accountant who always shot straight with his client. And the cat knew some offense. During his four years as the offensive coordinator at Stanford, his teams had averaged 30 points and more than 400 total yards per game. The previous season, they had averaged 37 points a game, the ninth highest average in the nation. Diedrick also knew quarterbacks. In 1989 and 1990, while serving as offensive coordinator at Washington State, Diedrick had coached Drew Bledsoe, who became the number one NFL draft pick in 1993.

In Carlyle Holiday, Diedrick knew he had a player who was extremely talented but also fairly reserved and a bit of a loner. "He's a very quiet young man," said Diedrick. "He needs to develop more of an assertive role and be a leader. That comes natural for some kids, and for others it doesn't. But there is a tremendous amount of pressure put on a young man to play that position at this university. People can sometimes become consumed with that. I try to deflect all that and take it myself."

But Diedrick knew he would have only so much time to spend with Holiday and that he couldn't shield him from all the criticism. "These guys are at school all day," he said. "They're around the students, who are as hyped-up or even more hyped-up than most of the alumni."

It was the same pressure all the players would face, and Willingham was pushing them hard to prepare them for it. By the afternoon of the first day of practice, when the temperature hit 90 degrees, the team already looked lethargic. It was obvious this was a team in transition and one that needed to be repeatedly kicked in the ass.

Practice was broken into several periods, about fifteen minutes each. After the first individual period, the quarterbacks, tight ends, and offensive line finished a drill and broke for the next station. But they were moving too slowly, and Diedrick furiously blew his whistle and had them come back and break again.

"You guys don't seem to understand yet," he said. "When we break, we are running! We are *not walking!*"

With a renewed urgency, the entire group returned to the same spot and broke again. This time, Holiday led a sprint to the next drill.

Later that afternoon, during the team session, when it was offense against defense, the offensive line was clearly sluggish. The players were still in shorts and helmets, so it wasn't a full-speed drill. It was an up-tempo period commonly called "thud." Linemen were required to burst off the ball; backs and receivers to run to the end zone; and defenders to run to the ball carrier, get into tackling position, and drive a shoulder into him. Midway through the period, reserve center Zachary Giles failed to fire out of his stance after snapping the ball. Standing with the rest of the offense behind the drill, offensive line coach John McDonell lost it.

Prior to joining Willingham at Stanford, McDonell had spent seven seasons as the offensive coordinator for Washington State. In 1997, he had engineered an offense that took the Cougars to their first Rose Bowl in 67 years. He was a large, friendly man with a pleasant round face and easy smile, but that wasn't the case right then. Before the whistle blew the play dead, he removed his hat, threw it to the ground, and kicked it. "We can't have that shit, Zachary!" he yelled. "It starts right now! Fire off the ball!" It may have been done for effect, but his point was certainly well taken. Sheepishly, Giles slunk behind the rest of the offense and did his penance for lack of effort — 20 push-ups.

In the middle of the two practice fields was a large wooden sawhorse. Atop it was a large placard with a number on it, marking the practice session periods. At about 4:45 P.M., the sign read PERIOD 6. When the air horn blew, it was time for the seventh period, another team session, a full-on offense-versus-defense half-speed scrimmage. The players started toward the middle of the field, but this time it was Willingham who hated what he saw. They moved like a herd of dumb sheep going to the next station simply because the horn had signaled them to do so, not because *they* were in a hurry to get there. Willingham blew his whistle, summoning them back to where they began, and then reiterated Diedrick's message about running to stations. He blew the whistle again, leaning forward to ensure a long, drawn-out screeching command, demanding that each player sprint to the middle of the field. It was something he'd learned from Denny Green.

While at Stanford, Green would routinely send the team back to the previous station if he thought they were dragging. Once, 30 minutes into practice, Green disgustedly blew his whistle and announced that the whole thing would start from the beginning. "Just so you know, no one's going to feel sorry for you out here!" he screamed.

Willingham applied a similar approach, though more subtly. He never screamed, relying instead on his lecture voice and death stare. But he made it clear that self-pity would not be allowed on his watch. "*Now men . . .* when the horn blows, you should already be at your next station." Willingham loathed raising his voice.

"Kids don't want people yelling at them," he later said. "When you address them, you gotta have a plan, otherwise you're just wasting time."

After practice, Willingham spoke to a visitor about the week's schedule. He sat on the brick wall that separated the field from the courtyard outside O'Neill Hall, the players' dorm for summer camp. He was pleased with the way things had been going thus far. "Weather permitting, hopefully we'll have three straight days of double day practices," he said cheerfully. Then he shook his head and laughed at what he'd just said. Willingham was as old school as they came, and the smirk on his face indicated that he was about to slip into one of those yarns that old folks tend to slip into whenever the opportunity presents itself. It was the type of story that begins with *"When I was your age, I had to walk to school in ten feet of snow . . ."*

He cleared his throat. "When I was at Michigan State, we had two straight weeks of double days," he said. "We walked like zombies from the dorm to the locker room." For effect, he imitated the glazed look and stumbling walk of a zombie. "See, players today don't know how good they have it."

Willingham said the philosophy about summer camp had changed since then, becoming less physically demanding and more mentally focused, after coaches who had been in the pros returned to the college game. "See, it wasn't just the emphasis on the passing game, but the *mental* approach to the game," he said. "It was about conserving energy and teaching rather than wearing players down physically."

During the summer sessions, practices were open to the public, allowing Irish fans an up-close and personal view of the team and its new coach. That was like Christmas Day for the so-called subway alumni — the people who never attended Notre Dame but who claim the Irish football team as their own. (The term *subway alumni* refers to the subways that New York City Irish Catholics used to get to the Polo Grounds when Notre Dame played Army during the Rockne era.) Notre Dame subway alums can be found all over the country, but the ones in South Bend are some of the most fanatic. Willingham understood the passion of the local Notre Dame fans. He knew what the university represented to people around South Bend. "If you go to a school and graduate from a school, you can brag about *that*," he said. "But if you don't go to a school, what you brag about is that school's athletic success. And that definitely applies to a lot of Irish Catholics who live in this community."

Willingham noted that "the best thing about living in a fishbowl was being able to swim with the fish," but one day, the adulation from a visiting subway alum made things tricky for the fiercely private Willingham. For fifteen minutes, Willingham was trapped by a persistent, subtly flirtatious angler who, if she caught him, clearly had no intention of throwing his little black ass back into the pond. She was a plump, round-cheeked, and attractive dark-haired woman in her early forties who spoke in a slow, breathy voice.

"We drove here from Las Vegas *just* to watch practice," she said. Willingham, startled by her flirtatious vibe, repeated the words, "Las Vegas."

"You should see our home," she said. "It's a Notre Dame shrine. When we enter the house, we bow." Willingham politely listened, gazing up at the sun glaring off the windows of O'Neill Hall.

"So what will the students do when you enter the stadium?" she asked. It was a question in reference to a tradition in which the students salute the coach in the fourth quarter of games and at pep rallies. The woman offered her own suggestion. "Maybe it will be a W," she said while holding up both hands with the middle and ring fingers crossed — perhaps not knowing that, in hip-hop terms, she was flashing the universal sign for "West Side."

Willingham politely laughed. "I'll leave that up to the students," he said. "They're much more creative than I."

She finally asked him to autograph a piece of paper. As he signed, she crept close enough to kiss his neck if she so desired. Like a punt returner who feels the first tackler before he actually sees him, Willingham made a quick move to his right, but she made one final pitch to him.

"Oh, I speak three languages," she blurted. "French, Spanish, German, and, of course, English."

Gazing briefly at the sky, Willingham nodded.

"So if you need an assistant . . ."

Chuckling, Willingham replied, "I think we've got that covered." With that, he finally, mercifully, got away and headed to the locker room.

4

"SOMETHING'S HAPPENING HERE!"

O N THE THIRD DAY of camp, Willingham got involved. It was the early part of practice, during a warm-up drill in which the receivers practiced releasing from the line of scrimmage and the quarterbacks lobbed the ball downfield. One receiver would simulate a defensive back in bump-and-run position, and the other receiver would make a move to get by the defender and sprint upfield. Willingham, playing defensive back, lined up in front of freshman Maurice Stovall, in bump-and-run position. At 6'5", Stovall dwarfed the 5'7" Willingham. Willingham provided a stiff forearm to Stovall's chest, momentarily knocking him off balance as the freshman released upfield.

After Stovall made the catch, it was Willingham's turn to play receiver. He took his stance, left foot forward, back straight. Omar Jenkins lightly punched his shoulder, and Willingham slipped past him, but after two steps he fell to the ground, bounced up, made the catch, and sprinted 10 yards upfield. Knowing he hadn't lost any cool points for having stumbled, Willingham calmly took his place at the end of the other line. On his next rep, Willingham released upfield, but Holiday's pass was behind him and it hit Willingham's hands and fell to the turf. Willingham picked up the ball and ran to the next line. He handed the ball to backup quarterback Pat Dillingham, dropped down, and did 10 push-ups, the same penance any receiver did for a dropped ball.

The scene being played out wasn't Willingham showing off for his young team or for the spectators who lined the field. It was something he had always done with his teams. But it also served a purpose, actually two purposes. For one, it allowed him to apply his strong sense of historical perspective to Notre Dame tradition. Knute Rockne, in addition to his "win one for the Gipper" speech, was known for mixing it up with the kids on occasion. In fact, Rockne's doctor would blame such activity for the bad case of phlebitis Rockne got in his early forties. Very subtly, and very carefully, Willingham was making history at Notre Dame by simply taking a few pages from Irish lore and signing his name to them. And he was doing something else.

The minute Willingham inserted himself into the drill, the pace quickened and everyone, not just the receivers, had new life. Everything he did was for a purpose, and that day Willingham's goal was to get his guys past that initial self-loathing period that inevitably falls on the third or fourth double day. And he wanted to show that one of his many mantras, "We're all in this thing together," wasn't just a bunch of empty coaching rhetoric. That's the way he reached people. He didn't tell them what he wanted. He found out what *they* wanted, discovered where they wanted to go, and found ways, both subtle and not so subtle, to get them there. This was the players' program, and he desperately, intensely, and sincerely wanted to make himself a part of it. He also knew that turning these guys into an actual team would be a long, often painful process, and he had to show them that they didn't have to do it by themselves.

About a month after he'd taken the job, Willingham was told that there were some guys he'd be better off without. "A few people told me that I had some guys who hadn't done anything, who would never do anything for me, and that I should get rid of them," he said.

One of those guys was Arnaz Battle. On the fifth day of practice, at the afternoon session, Battle, a fifth-year senior, lined up with his left foot forward. His gloved hands were balled into fists, and he held his chest-high. At the snap, he exploded off the ball and abruptly angled five yards toward the middle of the field. Without breaking stride, he snatched the ball, which was headed toward his face mask, and continued toward the middle before bursting upfield and sprinting to the end zone. It was called the "hitch screen," one of the staples in Willingham's version of the West Coast offense. The play was football's equivalent of clearing out the lane in basketball and allowing your best player to go one-on-one, having his way with a defender as he takes it to the hole. Any coach worth a damn knows that there are times when you throw out tendencies and stat sheets and just let your big dog eat. After watching Battle during spring practice, Diedrick and Willingham agreed that while still very raw as a receiver, he was their big dog.

Battle was the one player who would benefit most from the new coaching staff and probably leave with the most regrets at having played only one year under them. At 22, he was physically and athletically one of the most mature members of the team. When speaking to him, Trent Miles often referred to him as "old man," and he treated him with a certain reverence that coaches reserve for special players. And Battle was special. Approachable and friendly, yet possessing a cut-your-throat competitive fire, he was, in many ways, *the* emblematic player on Willingham's first Notre Dame team.

In addition to his maturity and athletic gifts, Battle owned one intangible that transcended his other easily defined characteristics — depth. His eyes revealed a depth of emotion, a layer of sorrow, and a comprehension of loss that your average 22-year-old shouldn't have. He had seen something when he was nine years old, something no one needs to see, least of all a boy whose view of the world is still expectant and pure.

In November 1989, Battle was invited to display his marvelous adolescent skills in a Pee Wee football game called the Independence Bowl. Afterward, his family, which consisted of his 3-year-old brother, Brandon, and his mother, Sandra, went to Battle's grandmother's house in Shreveport, Louisiana. While the grown folks convened in the living room, Brandon quietly slipped outside. After several minutes, one of the adults noticed that Brandon was missing, and when they recalled that Brandon had been talking about his grandmother's pool all day, collective terror seized them.

When they found him, Brandon was floating facedown in the water. Sandra dived in and retrieved him. And as she laid his body on the pavement and pumped his chest, trying to revive him, Arnaz did the only thing a big brother could do. He reflexively laid a hand on his brother's forehead and prayed.

But Brandon was already dead.

Battle moved on, of course. He had no choice. He didn't try to forget that night, and he didn't try to forget Brandon's face, ever — but he didn't want to remember *that* face, the lifeless one. That wasn't his brother's face at all. He wanted to remember the lively one, the one with the bright eyes, the one that begged to play football with him in the backyard, the little face with the big appetite, the one that ate his big brother's food when his back was turned. So Battle carried pictures of Brandon in his wallet, but that just didn't cut it. In trying to remember Brandon, he kept forgetting his wallet or, worse, losing it. Besides, their bond had been too strong to be captured by simple film. He needed something more enduring.

When he turned 18, Battle did what a lot of 18-year-old boys do: He got a tattoo. He went to the tattoo parlor, sat in the chair, bared his left shoulder, presented a picture of Brandon, and asked the man to draw his brother's face. The man complied, and when he was done, it wasn't just Brandon's face that adorned the muscular deltoid, it was Battle's own. The little brother had the big brother's countenance. He had his dark, serious eyes, his full lips, and his round chin. With the tattoo done, Battle could move on. Now he could finally stop worrying about forgetting. Now he could always take Brandon with him. And he took him a lot of places.

Brandon was with him at C. E. Byrd High School, when he got to play on the varsity team as a freshman, when he took a kickoff eighty yards for a score, through his junior year when he threw for over 800 yards and ran for 1,000 yards. He was with him when he was named a *Parade* All-America. He accompanied him on the recruiting trips to Nebraska, Auburn, and Texas A&M, and finally to Notre Dame.

It was when Battle got to South Bend that he needed Brandon the most. Who better to remind him that good things can often turn into painful things? Of course, Battle never thought that for him the leap from good thing to painful thing would be so commonplace. He never thought lost opportunity, lost time, and lost years would frame his college career.

When Battle chose Notre Dame, he chose great expectations. He chose the pressure to live up to his legendary high school exploits, and he chose jersey number 3, Joe Montana's number. Why wouldn't he? He was, after all, a quarterback and a playmaker. He had a strong arm, though he wasn't a fluent passer yet. He couldn't be tackled, not by just one person, and he had a knack for taking over a game whenever it was needed. He tried to do that in the last game of his freshman year, against USC at the L.A. Coliseum.

On November 28, 1998, starting quarterback Jarious Jackson got hurt, and with 11:53 left in the first half, Battle calmly trotted into the huddle. How perfect for the playmaker. It was the school's biggest rivalry, a chance to lead his team to a BCS bowl berth and thrust himself forever into Irish lore — as a true freshman no less.

On second-and-12, the ball was on the USC 16-yard line. Battle dropped back, quickly surveyed the scene, saw nothing, and burst upfield. He ran through four tackles before getting hit again at the two-yard line. But as he went down, an instant before his knee hit the ground, the ball popped out and was scooped up by Trojan linebacker Ken Haslip, who returned it to the 30-yard line. The Irish ended up losing 10–0, and instead of going to a BCS bowl, they went to the Gator Bowl.

After sitting out the 1999 season behind Jarious Jackson, the next time Battle ran onto the field for the Irish, it was for real. When 2000 rolled around, Jarious Jackson had gone to the Denver Broncos, and Arnaz Battle, by virtue of being the starting quarterback, was *the man*. Though he was sacked on his first attempt from scrimmage, Battle led his team to a 24–10 victory against the Texas A&M Aggies. And the next week, well, the next week would tell the story of Arnaz Battle.

Notre Dame was playing Nebraska, and on the first play of the game, Battle ran a little bootleg. But as he threw, he was hit. He put his left hand down to break his fall, and when he did, he broke his wrist. But he didn't know this at the time, so he kept playing, and he played hard. He had more than 100 yards rushing. The next morning, after the 27–24 loss in overtime, his wrist was sore and swollen. It turned out he needed surgery to repair the navicular bone, and because of that his 2000 season was done.

That was the strangest year of all for Battle. That was the year you could say Arnaz Battle broke even. He lost that season, but he gained another in the form of a medical redshirt. That wasn't all. In Battle's absence, a freshman named Carlyle Holiday began to show his skills. As a runner, he and Battle were about even, but Holiday had a bigger arm. Davie told Battle that Holiday would be his quarterback, and he moved Battle to receiver. Truth was, Battle didn't mind playing receiver. In fact, he told his high school coach as much his junior year. The coach appreciated that, but he told Battle the reality of the situation — there wasn't anyone else who could get him the ball.

But that wouldn't be a problem now, playing for Notre Dame. Maybe now Battle could do some of the things he had planned to do when he got there. But midway through the second quarter of his second game as a receiver, Battle lost again. They were playing Michigan State, and Battle, who was making his first start at his new position, was also playing the gunner on the punt team. He was sprinting downfield when the returner made a move to his left, and Battle, planting to move to his right, heard a pop. He'd never broken his leg before, but he knew that whenever you heard something pop, it was always bad, really bad.

He had broken his right fibula and would lose four more games of his career.

When he returned to the field, he caught two balls against Boston College. Those two receptions, plus two he caught against Nebraska and one he caught against Michigan State before getting injured — five receptions in all — were the only shred of proof that Arnaz Battle had spent time as a flanker at Notre Dame.

But Tyrone Willingham didn't have time for stats or for the opinions of outsiders. It wasn't that he wanted to change people's perception of Arnaz Battle. That wasn't his job. He just had a feeling that if given a chance and put into the right position, Arnaz Battle could change some minds all by himself.

Before one afternoon practice near the end of camp, a few members of the 2001 World Series–champion Arizona Diamondbacks showed up at the field. Willingham was given a white Diamondbacks jersey with "Willingham '02" on the back. "This is a hell of a place," he told a visitor. "You have the world champions coming here. They have a game in Chicago, but they want to come *here* first. They want to run on the field like little kids. That should tell you how special this place is."

Willingham was clearly excited to be at Notre Dame. It was a place that valued football, a place where football meant something. He said it all the time, but it was especially clear at that particular moment: "Stanford was a great place, but on the football landscape, it's just not Notre Dame."

That same afternoon, a half-hour after practice ended, Willingham stood with his son, Nathaniel. The 12-year-old had a smooth round face that matched his mother's and serious, focused eyes that matched his dad's. Willingham looked down at Nathaniel and said, "I saw you running sprints today. You feel good now, don't you? No one should have to tell you to do that. You should do that on your own. That's exactly what I tell the team."

He put his hand around Nathaniel's neck and pulled him in close, his grip a mixture of love and exhortation. That afternoon, more than any other, told the story of why Willingham came to Notre Dame. The passion, the expectation, and the challenge of pulling a team together in a place where people really cared about football had him almost giddy with enthusiasm.

At 6:15 P.M., directly behind Willingham, the sun reflected off the windows of O'Neill Hall. With his large jersey hanging off of him, his sunglasses resting atop his head, and his arm around Nathaniel, he looked nothing like the most visible coach in college football. He looked like any dad who had just spent the day playing catch with his kids. And in some ways that's exactly what he was to his team — a dad. When he played catch or ran routes with the receivers, when he got *involved,* it wasn't a feeble gesture of pretending to relate to them. It was his way of showing that he was in this thing with them. Hell, they *needed* their coach to be in this thing with them.

The offense, most of all, was in need of good coaching now. Just before the team started camp, Bill Diedrick had come across some notes he had scribbled on a schedule at the beginning of 2002. In the margins he had concluded that they could be at least 9–3 for the season. After their opener against Maryland, they would face Big Ten rivals Purdue, Michigan, and Michigan State. And later in the season, they would also have to contend with perennial college football powers Florida State and USC. In all, five of their opponents were ranked in the Top 25 in the Associated Press preseason poll.

At the conclusion of spring practice in April, Diedrick knew the offense wasn't anywhere near where he wanted it to be. "If the coaches had taken a poll of how many games we would win, and the answer was six games, we would have all been pleased and excited about that."

Diedrick knew that installing a new system while they played one of the most demanding schedules in college football could lead to some difficult times. And that was the benefit of having all five of the offensive coaches from Stanford. Each one knew what to expect while trying to teach the new offense. "We all knew how frustrating an experience it might be," said Diedrick. "But together we could work through it and not get that frustration across to our kids."

On Friday afternoon, exactly nine days from their August 31 opener against Maryland, the offense looked like crap. After a light rain, it was painfully muggy and overcast, with gnats hovering above the practice field in tiny little funnel clouds. In the last session of the day, during the team period, the offense hit the wall. On one play, tackle Jordan Black jumped offside. On the next, Carlyle Holiday fumbled the snap, and Rhema McKnight dropped an easy hitch pass. During the series, the one play they did manage to run was a dive, in which Grant was stopped five yards deep in the backfield by nose tackle Cedric Hilliard. The defense was excited. Cries of "That's it, D! I see you, defense!" came from the sideline, where those not involved were watching. Later in the season, the defense would rely on this same offense to score and would encourage them from the sideline, but at that moment those thoughts were a million miles away. Right then, the defense was content to beat the shit out of any offense in front of them, including their own.

At the end of practice, Willingham delivered a message. He had the entire team line up and do a series of up-downs. It was the oldest drill in the manual of football corporal punishment. They lined up by position behind the goal line. Willingham blew the whistle, and the first group ran in place. When he blew it again, they dropped to the ground, then quickly sprang to their feet. When he blew it again, the next group stepped forward and so on. It was an exhausting drill and took nearly 15 minutes to complete. When it was over, the team congregated in the far end zone, the offensive and defensive linemen doubled over, gasping for breath.

Willingham applied his typical glass-half-full spin on the practice. Everyone who had seen the practice knew the offense was miles away from getting anywhere near respectability, but that didn't deter their consistently optimistic leader. "When one group does really well," Willingham said, "it usually means the other group doesn't do as well."

The very next day, on the last double day, the day before the players broke camp and moved into their own dorms, the whole team had a great practice. Afterward, Willingham put them through another series of "gassers." He blew his whistle, and in groups, they sprinted across the width of the field, back and forth, back and forth. A firm believer in conditioning, Willingham cited Vince Lombardi's philosophy on the fatigue factor. "Fatigue is one of those things that can make people cowards." The backs and receivers were allotted 30 seconds, linebackers 35, and linemen 40. After three series of gassers, Willingham mercifully blew his whistle, and the players gathered at midfield, clapping in unison. They were beat and weary, and they still had a long road ahead of them. But even while working them to exhaustion, Willingham had already inspired in them a renewed sense of optimism and pride. As they clapped, senior offensive lineman Sean Mahan began to yell, "Something's happening here! Something's happening here!"

Willingham's presence at Notre Dame extended beyond the two football fields that lay between the golf course and the bookstore. When Notre Dame hired its first black head football coach, it represented change. There was already a new energy around campus, a buzz that something was different. And it couldn't have come at a better time. Not so far beneath the surface there had always been unrest among the minority population at Notre Dame. There were more than 8,000 undergraduates at Notre Dame, but only 3% of them were black. And just about anyone who wasn't white and male had some reservations about the school.

In 1987, the Alumni Association conducted a study to find out who wasn't participating in alumni events. The study revealed that minorities, women, athletes, and graduate students were least likely to participate. In response, officers established the Minority Alumni Network, which aimed to help minorities feel they were a part of the Notre Dame community. In 1990, the university appointed former Notre Dame football player D'Juan Francisco director of the Minority Alumni Network. Francisco had graduated from Cincinnati's famed Moeller High and was a member of the 1988 national championship team.

Francisco said that because of some basic cultural differences, like music and religion, many minorities felt alienated. "People assumed they were here for athletics," said Francisco. "Many people didn't realize that some of the minorities got into Notre Dame because they were great students."

Yet one biracial female student said that one day she and a few of her friends counted the number of black men on campus who weren't athletes. "We could only come up with ten," she said.

The Minority Alumni Network consists of three ethnically defined subgroups: black, Hispanic, and Asian and Pacific islanders. They recruit prospective minority students, mentor current minority students, and meet with prospective students. Since its inception, the network has seen increased participation by all groups on the alumni level. "You can say that they [the parents] were called spiteful names [while at Notre Dame]," said Francisco. "But in spite of all that, the alumni continue to encourage their children to look at the university." When their parents were there, the issue of race wasn't discussed. But now that the minority network acknowledged that there was a clear discrepancy in minority representation, there was reason for hope.

That promise of change, however, did not extend beyond the campus boundaries. South Bend had never had good race relations, and an incident that summer showed that things weren't getting any better. On August 10, about an hour after the Irish had finished their first day of practice, two African-American 18-year-olds, Sidney Hockaday and Mario McGrew, rode their bikes through a little strip mall located directly behind the Turtle Creek apartment complex near the campus. As they pedaled past a popular sports bar called Between the Buns, three white men came staggering into the parking lot. One of them screamed racial epithets at the teens and another said, "We should hang your asses!"

Hockaday stopped pedaling and asked what the problem was. Just then, one of the men pushed McGrew off his bike, and Hockaday took off his belt and started swinging the buckle at his attackers. But when the men got close enough to tackle the kids, one of the men took Hockaday's belt and put it around his neck. "I told you I was gonna hang you!" he screamed. The scuffle lasted 10 minutes, during which time a worker at Papa John's came out, saw the violence, emptied the trash, and went back in.

"Nobody called the police," said Hockaday. "And there were a lot of people there." When it was over, the boys went into the sports bar and called police. Hockaday came away with only bruises, but McGrew suffered a broken wrist that required surgery later that night. It was South Bend's first hate crime since 1997, and it all went down less than one mile from the football department in Joyce Center — Tyrone Willingham's office.

This was Indiana, though. It was the same Indiana once considered the cradle of the Ku Klux Klan. It was the same Indiana that took 34 years to charge Kenneth Richmond with brutally stabbing a black woman named Carol Marie Jenkins in 1968. And it was the same state where, in 1998, the black members of the Bloomington North High School basketball team were called "nigger" and "coon" by some members of an all-white Martinsville High team. Today, there's still a faint, if not menacing, Klan presence, even around South Bend. In the fall of 2001, on a farm in Osceola, just miles from the Notre Dame campus, Richard Loy was welcomed to the community. Loy's father, Raillon, is the imperial wizard of Indiana. In December 2000, citizens of Osceola ushered in the holiday season with a Christmas party that included a good old-fashioned cross burning.

Fortunately, hooded Knight Riders and the first hate crime since 1997 weren't the sole barometer of what was taking place in South Bend in the summer of 2002. This was the same Indiana that boasted four black coaches in major professional and collegiate sports. In addition to Willingham at Notre Dame, there was Indiana University basketball coach Mike Davis, Isiah Thomas of the Indiana Pacers, and Tony Dungy of the Indianapolis Colts. Sports are important in these parts, so it only made sense that such a quartet could inspire those who watched them. That's exactly what happened in South Bend that summer.

On one August evening, a few hours after the team had finished the afternoon practice, something was happening to the South Bend community. About six miles from campus was a small bar and grill called Simeris. During the summer, the courtyard featured an outdoor stage where local bands performed cover songs of recent Top 40 hits by singers like Alanis Morissette, Blues Traveler, and Hootie and the Blowfish.

Three weeks before the start of football season, Darryl Buchanan, or Darryl B, a short, muscular black man with braids, took the stage. The last song of his set was a song he'd written about Notre Dame. As he began to dance, he dropped a little history on the crowd. "Okay," he said, "football season is about to start, and y'all know we have a new coach!" He paused as the crowd screamed its approval. They were happy to have a new coach because it symbolized a new beginning. But it was fairly obvious that for Darryl B, it meant a great deal more than that.

"I wrote this song for y'all."

As he strutted around the big wooden stage, it was obvious that this particular black man was happy to see another black man, short in stature but tall in pride, command such a high-profile position. The music started, and he began to dance. It was your standard drum and bass beat, with some keyboards to make it funky. Coupled with the beat was a voice-over doing the play-by-play from the 1993 Notre Dame–Florida State game. It was the game in which second-ranked Notre Dame upset number one–ranked Florida State. Perhaps he had chosen that game because both schools were led by black quarterbacks — Kevin McDougal for Notre Dame and Charlie Ward for Florida State — or perhaps it was just coincidence. "Ward drops back to pass and is sacked by the Irish!"

Up until that point, he had belted out songs with an old-school Motown flavor. But this, his latest creation, was a rap, which was, in lyrical content and presentation, very, *very* old school. The song's refrain went: "What's the name? Notre Dame!" The crowd, completely white, was filled with unabashed Notre Dame fans. Each time Darryl B asked, "What's the name?" they responded in unison: "Notre Dame!"

Midway through the song, he poked out his chest, allowing the bass in his voice to take over as he delivered the lyric of which he was most proud. He tightly gripped the mike, threw his head back, and yelled, "It's two thousand two, and *Will-ing-ham's the man!*"

It was the kind of voice that until Willingham's arrival had been largely quiet, and a face that, for the most part, had remained invisible. But when a university chooses a man who happens to look like you as its most high-profile representative, a man whose parents look like your parents, you become "the man" as much as he does. For a brief moment that night, Darryl B really was the man. And while he sang, it was clear that Willingham's impact had extended beyond the football stadium.

There was a spirit of inclusion that night. There had always been a few black folks at Notre Dame. There were some black students, a lot of black athletes, some black faculty members, and even some local black folks who worked in the dining halls on campus. But this was different. This was the Notre Dame football coach — the most dynamic representative of the university. In Tyrone Willingham, the South Bend black community had more than just a black face; it had a strong black voice, one that commanded some actual respect and authority.

And Darryl B wasn't about to let anyone forget it.

5

MARYLAND

ON MONDAY NIGHT, August 26, 2002, Willingham was in his office when a friend dropped by. Willingham was five days away from perhaps the biggest game of his life. His friend asked him if he was excited, and as if on cue, Willingham purposefully unfurrowed his brow. "It's like playing golf," he said. "You go out there and see those *hackers* on the course getting all excited when they birdie or par a hole. Then, on the next few holes, they're too excited to concentrate on what they're supposed to be doing. See, I'm *not* one of those hackers."

His attention to detail, to the scope of what he wanted the football program to be, was one thing that kept him focused. Later that night, as he passed by the secretary's office, he saw that week's offensive scouting report strewn about the floor. The copy machine had broken, and Julie, the assistant to the offensive coaches, was on her hands and knees trying to make sense of it all. Willingham, giving up on his dream of going home early, dropped his briefcase and asked what she needed him to do. She told him not to worry about it and to go home, but he repeated his mantra: "We're all in this together." By 1:00 A.M., the scouting report was done, and by the following week, the office had a new copy machine.

* * *

The next afternoon, the second day of game week, Willingham strode onto the practice field, looking as though he might break into a sprint. Tuesday's practice coincided with the second day of classes for the fall semester — and after two weeks of camp and double-day sessions, the team didn't appear to share Willingham's excitement. They were sluggish and in obvious need of some "inspiration." Linebacker coach Bob Simmons did the honors in a tackling drill.

The head coach at Oklahoma State from 1995 to 2000, Simmons had spent 2001 as a volunteer consultant for the Big 12 conference. His primary duties included coordinating game-day officials. It was good work, and he got to travel frequently and see a lot of games. But he really missed coaching. For Bob Simmons, the Maryland game was more than just the season opener; it marked his return to the sideline.

Earlier in his career, Simmons had been an assistant coach at the University of Colorado under Bill McCartney for seven years. When McCartney retired after the 1994 season, he was certain that Simmons would be named the next head coach. After all, McCartney had pretty much groomed Simmons for the position. Instead, Colorado athletic director Bill Marolt gave the job to another Buffaloes assistant, Rick Neuheisel. Simmons was disappointed but undeterred. He asked around about other openings, and when the Oklahoma State job came up, he faxed in his résumé and told Bill McCartney about it. McCartney looked him in the eye and said, "You know you have no chance at that job."

Simmons didn't have a shot at the job unless he had someone — preferably someone white — to back him up. So McCartney provided that backup. He made some phone calls, recommending Simmons and supporting his character. Soon after, McCartney got a call from Oklahoma State athletic director Terry Phillips. McCartney had gotten Simmons in the door. After he interviewed with Phillips and university officials, Simmons returned to Boulder and waited. Then, on the evening of December 14, 1994, Simmons got a call from Phillips, who offered him the job. Six days later, Simmons became the first black head coach in Big 12 history.

Oklahoma State finished 4–8 his first year, shutting out

archrival Oklahoma on its home field in Norman for the first time in 19 years along the way. Simmons followed that season with a 5–6 finish in 1996; then came the improbable 1997 season. While his team was rolling to an 8–4 record, Simmons began to experience fatigue and stiffness in his back and joints. On top of that, his skin had taken on a dull grayish color. He made an appointment with a urologist, who told him that his kidneys had deteriorated and that he would eventually need a transplant.

"At the time, I wasn't really thinking about it, and I wasn't taking it seriously," said Simmons. "I was at peace about everything in my life."

In December, Oklahoma State received an invitation to the Alamo Bowl. But before he left for San Antonio, Simmons had another appointment with his urologist. This time, the doctor put Simmons's name on the transplant list. Simmons and his wife, Linda, discussed all the possibilities. They didn't tell a soul about his condition, not his team, not his kids, not the other coaches. They didn't even tell his parents.

The wait for a cadaver kidney averaged two years in the state of Oklahoma, so Simmons was facing the threat of kidney dialysis. His best shot at full recovery was through a living donor. Linda volunteered. She was the only one he would consider; he had already dismissed the possibility of his kids, his two sisters, or his parents acting as donors.

Eventually, Bob and Linda Simmons got the okay to go under the knife — together. As they lay next to each other, Linda leaned over and told her husband that a miracle was at hand. The surgery was performed on March 10, and by March 22, Simmons was standing before his team, trying to tell them his story without breaking down. He wasn't successful.

Unfortunately, Simmons and his team couldn't match the success of the 1997 season, and after successive 5–6 campaigns, Simmons was fired. But during the 2001 season, Simmons made a trip to Stanford. He had met Willingham several years before and immediately respected him as a man and a coach. "I was very intrigued by the consistency with which he developed Stanford's program," Simmons said. "They did put academics first, but he kept winning.

"I always respected Tyrone and admired him from a distance," Simmons continued. "I spent three or four days with him, talking and playing golf. We talked about his experience out there. Actually, I tried to implement some of the things he had done at Stanford at Oklahoma State. He did things with the alums, like implementing them into the program. I always respected how he kept consistently winning and how he always stayed with what he believed in."

In January 2002, when he heard Willingham had been hired by Notre Dame, Simmons called to congratulate him. "I also told him I wanted to get back in. I told him that if anything happened, I would be very interested in being part of his staff." Fortunately for Simmons, linebacker coach Phil Zacharias left for the NFL in March, and a spot opened up. Willingham called to offer Simmons the position, and Simmons accepted.

Now, just four days before the opener against Maryland, Bob Simmons was fired up, to say the least. And he was determined to pass along his spirit to his troops. It was the first time since practice started that the defensive players had engaged in a full-fledged tackling drill. In order to save the players from injury and fatigue, the staff had had them practice only thud until this point — and it showed.

The defensive backs were the ball carriers, and the backers did the tackling. Mike Goolsby was first in the tackling line, and freshman Mike Richardson was the ball carrier. After Richardson made a move and cut inside, Goolsby nearly broke his own ankles as he dived and grabbed nothing but air. Simmons began to boil. "Wake up!" he growled. "This is game week. Your attitude should change now. I know mine has! Do it again!"

Goolsby took his place at the front of the line. A junior from Joliet Catholic Academy near Chicago, Goolsby's outstanding spring practice and summer camp allowed him to beat out senior Carlos Pierre-Antoine for the starting inside backer spot. But just to be sure he was ready, Simmons still pushed him.

Richardson ran toward Goolsby again. This time, Goolsby squatted, lowered his shoulder, and exploded into Richardson, driving him back five yards. After he separated from Richardson, Goolsby shoved him in the chest. Because Richardson was just a freshman, he didn't retaliate. "That's more like it!" said a satisfied Simmons.

Next in line was Derek Curry. A junior, Curry was set to replace Rocky Boiman, who was now playing for the Tennessee Titans, at the outside linebacker spot. Corner Shane Walton ran toward Curry, faked to the sideline, then dipped back inside, allowing Curry only to slap his shoulder pad as he ran by. "You better wake up," yelled Simmons. "You guys are gonna get me pissed off the very first day of game week! We're supposed to be getting ready for Maryland!"

The same two repeated the drill, and Walton, being a senior, was savvy enough to know that the best thing to do when a coach is getting pissed off is to create the perfect scenario for his drill. Sometimes that means taking one for the team. Walton ran right at Curry, who slammed into him, snapping Walton's head back like a crash-test dummy.

"That's it!" Simmons yelled.

After 10 minutes, the tackling got a little better, but only marginally. When the drill ended, the defensive backs ran over to their coach, Trent Walters, while Simmons huddled his guys for a chat. "I'll tell you one thing," he said, "you guys better be ready to practice better than that. We don't practice that way. From now on, you'd better be prepared to *work* every damn day."

A few days before the Maryland game a colorful presence made his way to the practice field. Joe Theismann, who played quarterback for the Irish from 1968 to 1970, showed up to address the team. Dressed in black, with windswept hair and an impeccable tan, he looked like a cross between Johnny Cash and a more athletic version of 80s singer Huey Lewis. The players took a knee as Theismann told them what it meant to be a part of the Notre Dame legacy. He told them that when they took the field before a national audience, they should be aware that Notre Dame had always been and always will be the focus of college football. "They make movies about us," he said, "like *Knute Rockne* and *Rudy*."

The best part of Theismann's speech was the end. He looked at the players and told them, "I'm fifty-four years old, and I can still throw the ball as well as anyone out there. That's the kind of arrogance I want each of you to have when you take the field on Saturday night."

While Theismann spoke, Willingham also took a knee, listening with a little grin. It was a comically odd picture because the guy addressing the team, from a self-promotional point of view, was Willingham's polar opposite. As an ESPN football analyst, Theismann often peppered a telecast with self-referential anecdotes. Willingham, however, sprinted away from the spotlight as fast as his legs would carry him, and he desperately wanted his team to adopt that approach as well.

He liked Theismann's message, but Theismann's reference to Notre Dame always being the focus of college football obviously had Willingham a little concerned. The last thing he wanted was for Maryland, his very first opponent, to have any added incentive to prepare for his team. To squash that possibility, as soon as Theismann was done speaking, Willingham walked over to the group of media people gathered on the sideline and told them in a stern voice, "I think you understand my policy when I ask that none of this be publicized."

But the game itself had to be publicized. Aside from the fact that it was the coming-out party for the marriage of Tyrone Willingham and Notre Dame, this game meant something more. Soon after Willingham had taken the job, much had been made of the fact that there were only four black head coaches in college football — Tony Samuel at New Mexico State, Bobby Williams at Michigan State, Fitz Hill at San Jose State, and, of course, Willingham. It couldn't have been more fitting that Willingham, easily the most visible coach at the most visible school, would begin his Notre Dame career in the most traditional and generically titled of all the preseason games — the Kickoff Classic, which was first played in 1983 and is the original preseason game.

In the week leading up to the Kickoff Classic, there were two other games that also carried some social significance, if only in the labels attached to them. On August 24, in Kansas City's Arrowhead Stadium, Florida State beat Iowa State 38–31 in the Eddie Robinson Classic. Eddie Robinson was the best-known black coach in college football history. Over a 56-year career at

Grambling State, Robinson won 408 games, eclipsing the legendary Bear Bryant for most wins in college football.

In another preseason game, the John Thompson Foundation Challenge Football Classic, Wisconsin beat Fresno State, 23–21, on August 23. That game was named after the former Georgetown basketball coach who led the Hoyas to three Final Fours and to a national title in 1984. Like Willingham, Thompson had a strong interest in education. Thompson had demonstrated his feelings in 1989 when he staged his own silent protest of Proposition 42, a controversial NCAA rule passed that year. Proposition 42 stated that while a student failing to meet all the freshman eligibility requirements of Proposition 48 could still be admitted to school, he would no longer be eligible for a scholarship. The student would have to pay his own way, an option that John Thompson and many others felt would not be viable for a majority of the athletes who had trouble with the academic requirements. Tony Rice, the star of Notre Dame's 1988 national championship team, would not have been able to attend the school had this rule been in place when he was recruited.

So, right before tip-off at a game against Boston College on January 14, 1989, the 6′10″ Thompson walked from the court. With this gesture, the stage was set for the NCAA, and for all college sports fans, to not only take black coaches seriously but also take an even more stringent look at academic standards in collegiate sports. Thompson saw Proposition 42 as legislation that denied opportunities to needy students (many of them minorities) in the interest of saving schools millions of dollars in scholarship money. It was also a form of punishment for kids with low test scores. Thompson was among those who argued that standardized test scores were a measure of a student's socioeconomic circumstances, not his intelligence. In other words, standardized test scores couldn't measure a student's ability for academic growth. It was the same reasoning that said a kid's time in the 40-yard dash couldn't really determine what kind of a football player he could be.

Thompson's silent protest, which took place 13 years before Tyrone Willingham ever took the field for Notre Dame, let people know that there were certain coaches whose interest in their players extended beyond athletic ability. And when that was the case, the players who benefited were forever loyal. Seventeen years after Lou Holtz gave him the chance to attend Notre Dame, Tony Rice still sang the praises of his old coach. "He believed in me," said Rice. "And he kept me going. He said if I didn't graduate, he would never coach again." In 1990, Rice graduated from Notre Dame with a degree in psychology.

Of course, protest in the form of walking out wasn't an option for Willingham. Though he agreed with Thompson's argument that socioeconomic disparity affects education and believed that the NCAA's standards weren't always fair, his response to anything in his professional life, whether it was discrimination, injustice, or misconception, was fairly simple — just keep winning.

On Saturday night, August 31, 2002, a little after 8:00 P.M., Willingham was consumed by that very thought. After leaving the locker room at Giants Stadium, where the Kickoff Classic has been held every year since 1983, Willingham led his team down a long dark path to the stadium tunnel. The last 20 feet of the tunnel went underneath the stadium, ending with a pale light that bathed a small patch of the end zone. The team, while crammed into the tunnel, had one final moment to meditate on great expectations.

While starting cornerbacks Shane Walton and Vontez Duff got fired up, talking shit, Willingham was silent. As he stood there in front of his team, he was enveloped by the words he'd told his guys all week: *Be aware but not focused.*

He wanted them to be aware of but not focused on the distractions around them. Willingham was *aware* that because this was Notre Dame, everyone would be watching. But he was *focused* on the business at hand — beating Maryland. Maryland was ranked 21st in the AP preseason poll. They were the defending ACC champions and their coach, Ralph Friedgen, who led them to a 10–2 record in 2001, had been voted National Coach of the Year in his first season.

Willingham didn't know who Maryland's starting quarterback would be that night, but he knew who led their defense. He knew all about 6'2", 250-pound middle linebacker E. J. Henderson, who had earned ACC Player of the Year honors in 2001.

Henderson was already the favorite to win the Butkus Award, given annually to the nation's best linebacker. In fact, many in college football felt Henderson was the best overall defensive player in the country.

But for the time being, Willingham had to think about his own team. He knew that, for the moment, Notre Dame was unranked and unknown. As he stood in the tunnel that night, Willingham had the same thought he always had at such a time. Standing with his arms folded, he thought to himself: *When are they going to let us on the field?*

Until that moment, there had been only anticipation and speculation. No one knew how good this team was or how good a coach Tyrone Willingham could be. Notre Dame hiring a black head coach had been the feel-good story of the off-season. He was a symbol of change for a university that was in desperate need of change. So far, Tyrone Willingham had been, at least in theory, *perfect*. But every coach and player knows perfection is always left in the tunnel.

When a stadium official stepped aside and motioned toward the field, Willingham turned to his team and said, "Let's go to work!" They stormed from the tunnel and were greeted by 72,903 spectators. About half the crowd was Irish fans. Some were there to see Notre Dame's shiny new coach; some had come to see the much-hyped new offense. But most of the Notre Dame faithful had come to see if the lifeless unit from the year before had rediscovered its spirit.

It wouldn't take long for the players to prove it had. The West Coast offense is one predicated on speed. At the start of games, teams who run it often resemble boxers who enter the ring already loose, sweaty, and funky, not wasting precious time measuring an opponent and feeling him out. In that kind of offense, the goal is to come out ready to throw hands and land immediate blows.

Notre Dame won the toss and deferred their choice to the second half. Willingham liked to have the ball to start the second half, a time when a team can either come from behind or pull away from its opponent. So the Notre Dame fans would have to wait to see the new offense. But it was fitting that the defense took the field first that night, because Shane Walton had something to prove.

On Maryland's third offensive play of the game, Walton squared up to the line of scrimmage and jammed the receiver in the chest. Then he backed off him several yards and drifted toward the flat, all the while reading Maryland quarterback Scott McBrien's eyes. Not seeing Walton, the quarterback tried to lob the ball to the sideline, where the receiver had run an out route. But Walton rose, snatched the rock, darted toward the middle of the field, and got five yards.

Walton had been selected captain for the Maryland game. It was a good, sound, logical choice based on how he had performed during the previous weeks. But months later, that decision would make Willingham look even more worthy of the nickname bestowed on him by his players — Prophet Ty.

Walton had entered the season a pro prospect, but he wasn't the kind of prospect who got love from scouts because of his weight-room physique. All of 5'11" and barely 185 pounds, he didn't have an impressive body. But he did have enough skills to enter the year with a preseason "classification." On the list of potential NFL cornerbacks, Walton was listed at a very decent but ordinary No. 12. But there was more to him because he had *that story* behind him.

By the time they teed it up that night, the story had been told a thousand times by at least a thousand people. Walton was a soccer player and had been since he was three years old. That's when his mother took his little hyperactive ass to the soccer field so he could do something with all of his energy. With his socks pulled up under his shorts, he could run around and kick the ball and chatter until he got tired. But he didn't get tired. He never got tired. That's why his mom had brought him to the soccer field in the first place.

At one point during that first practice, the coach took him out and put another kid in. He told Walton to take a rest, but the kid didn't want to rest. He was there to run around and kick the ball. So he came to the sideline, where his mom was kneeling, and he put his arm around his mom's neck and wept. "What did I do wrong?" he asked her.

His mom's name was Shari Cassingham. She and Shane's pop, Lin Walton, were divorced. With light-brown hair and light-brown eyes, Shari had a calm confidence. She was that cool mom, the one who doesn't look like the other moms and doesn't dress like the other moms. She'll tell you she wasn't like other moms because she's not old-fashioned, but the truth is, she wasn't like other moms because she couldn't be matronly if she tried.

Shari and her son had the same nose. It was a prominent nose, perfectly shaped and proud, except hers had freckles on it. They looked very much like mother and son, even though Shane had the smooth light skin of a biracial kid. He also got the black features, or the *one* telling black feature — the nappy hair. But he had Shari's raised cheekbones, square chin, and naturally raised eyebrows, which gave both of them a look of perpetual curiosity.

That's the look Shane had when Shari tried to explain that the coach didn't take him off the field because he'd done something wrong. The coach just wanted to give someone else a chance. His mom knew even then that her son possessed a wicked intensity. He couldn't stand losing. When they played cards, she let him win, and later she wondered if that was such a wise thing to do.

Shari and Shane lived in La Jolla, a suburb of San Diego, about 30 miles north of the Mexican border. A logistics analyst for a military company, Shari knew that soccer was a perfect fit for Shane, so she put him in the La Jolla Nomads, the local soccer club. When it was time for high school, Shari enrolled him in the Bishop's School, a small Episcopal prep school with a 93-year-old foundation of spiritual and academic excellence. Since soccer and football are two separate seasons in California, Walton was allowed to do his thing as both a scrappy forward and a big-play cornerback. He was also an exceptional punt returner, quick but not fast, amassing more than 1,000 yards of punt-return yardage his senior year alone.

But it was through soccer that most would recognize that he

was special. In the summer of 1998, Walton, then a member of the Nomads' under-19 team, went to Indianapolis to play the Tulsa Pride in the under-19 national club championship game. With 34 minutes left, the Nomads trailed the Pride 4–1. The Nomads scored two quick goals to bring them within one. Then Walton took over.

That afternoon he served notice that he possessed a special gift, a knack that all legitimate big ballers have — the ability to raise his game at money time. He quickly scored the tying goal, sending the game to overtime. Then, nine minutes later, Walton stole a pass from a defender, dribbled to the top of the penalty area, and drilled the winning shot.

Mike Berticelli, then the soccer coach at Notre Dame, had noticed Walton before. He asked him if he wanted to attend Notre Dame on a scholarship. Even though he was a legitimate soccer star, Walton still wanted in on the big-time football cachet. But since Fresno State was the only school showing him any love on the football front, he said, "Bet," and accepted Berticelli's offer.

Sensing that Berticelli was a forthright and honorable man, the kind of man who was more than just a coach, Walton asked him for something. He told him that he would come to Notre Dame only if Berticelli would help him get a tryout on the football team. Berticelli agreed, and Walton came to South Bend.

His freshman season was great, if not unexpected. Walton scored 10 goals and was named second-team All–Big East. But as had been his plan, it was one and done with the soccer team; he set his sights on the Irish football team the following season. Some of the other football players in his class may have heard of him, but not many. How many football players pay attention to soccer? And because they didn't know him, they couldn't immediately respect him. Arnaz Battle, on seeing Walton, said to himself, *Who is this little bowlegged dude coming out here from the soccer team?*

But Walton paid no attention to what others thought. He had a plan. During the first season, he would just learn the defense and adjust to the speed of the collegiate level. He would learn how to get his hands on a receiver and get a feel for the combination coverages he never ran in high school. He did all that the first year and in the process had his soccer scholarship converted to a football scholarship. Through it all, he continued to speak to and seek the counsel of Mike Berticelli. Walton was, after all, a couple of thousand miles from home and away from his mother for the first time. And even though he no longer played soccer, Walton knew Berticelli was his guy, someone who saw him as more than just an athlete.

But what Walton didn't know, what no one knew, was that Berticelli had a heart condition, cardiomyopathy, that enlarges and weakens the heart. On the morning of January 25, 2000, Berticelli had a heart attack and died in his home. It makes sense that a man who was known for having a big heart eventually died because his heart was too big, right? But no, it didn't make sense. Not to anyone, least of all to Shane Walton.

Berticelli had been like a generous pop, bringing Walton to Notre Dame and giving him a chance to play another sport, for another coach. It didn't make any sense for him to die. But Walton did try to make sense of it by making a personal statement: "Everything I do I dedicate to him." The next year, Walton was a starter. And two years later, he entered his final season as an experienced collegiate cornerback and a team leader.

Tyrone Willingham had heard this story. He'd heard how Walton had walked on, made the team, and made himself. But Willingham was a guy who needed to *see* something to believe it. He saw Walton come out to practice two days early, while just the freshmen were practicing, and help out the younger guys. That was enough for him to name Walton a captain for the first game.

After Berticelli's death, Walton had been left without a strong role model — until Willingham arrived. Willingham's concern for developing student-athletes fit perfectly with Walton's own plans.

"I always wanted to go to a good academic school," said Walton. "In fact, it was either Stanford or Notre Dame. At my high school, everyone went to an Ivy League school, like Harvard or Yale. It was always important for me to be seen as both a student and an athlete."

In Berticelli's absence, and in Walton's last year at Notre

Dame, his last opportunity to blossom, Walton was lucky enough to end up playing for another coach who saw his guys as more than just bodies to fill out a team.

After Walton's pick in the opening minutes of the game, it was time for the offense to make its long-awaited debut. On the first play, Carlyle Holiday took a one-step drop and fired a quick hitch to Omar Jenkins for seven yards. Willingham, arms folded, watched from 30 yards downfield. That was his normal spot; from there, he had a panoramic view of the offense and defense. The play ended, and he leaned forward and clapped furiously in Jenkins's direction. But after Ryan Grant had back-to-back carries that netted only two yards, Notre Dame faced a fourth-and-one. Without hesitation, Willingham sent Nicholas Setta to kick a 56-yard field goal.

That Setta's kick sailed wide seemed irrelevant at the time. Starting with the opening play, the manner in which the team came in and out of the huddle on that first series had set an unmistakable tone. A mixture of confidence and pride, two ingredients sorely missing in 2001, had shaped those three plays, and the Notre Dame faithful stood and applauded. Willingham had brought them here to beat Maryland, but he knew this game, like every practice and meeting session, was also part of a process. As he transformed them into a winning team, he also rebuilt their sagging confidence. As the unit came to the sideline, Willingham extended his hand to each player and said, "Good job, good job."

If that first series of plays served as a public service announcement for the "New Notre Dame," the second series was like a trailer for an action-adventure film. On the fourth play, Holiday hit Arnaz Battle on the hitch screen. Battle exploded toward the middle of the field, and when he reached the opposite hash mark, he bolted upfield, hitting another gear and outrunning the Maryland corner. He was headed to the end zone, or so he thought, and never anticipated getting touched. So when the safety clipped his left heel just enough to knock him off stride, Battle lurched forward, falling hard to the ground.

The 29-yard play got a standing ovation from the Notre Dame fans. But it wasn't just Battle's effort. Only five minutes into the game, the current team bore absolutely no resemblance to last year's squad, and for Irish fans, it was a truly pleasing sight.

But the fans didn't want improvement; they wanted points. Toward the end of the first quarter, with Notre Dame leading 3–0, the Irish embarked on a 12-play drive. They made it all the way to the 13-yard line before the offense was shut down inside the 20.

The area inside the 20 is called the "red zone" because it's hot; it's the place where the offense has the best chance to score a touchdown. But it's also the place where a defense can easily blanket the field. In the red zone, receivers can't run deep routes, and an offense that lacks a power running game is laid bare, then laid to rest. That's exactly what happened to the Irish that night as their weakness inside the red zone was exposed.

First Ryan Grant was dropped for a loss of one; then Holiday was sacked, losing 11 in the process. And on third-and-22, after Holiday's pass to Carlos Campbell fell incomplete, it was suddenly fourth-and-11 from the 14-yard line. They settled for a 32-yard field goal to make it 6–0. On the next two drives, the Irish made it to the one-yard line. But after a penalty for delay of game, and after Holiday was sacked for a six-yard loss, it was fourth-and-goal.

When Willingham sent Nicholas Setta out to kick another field goal, the perfect glow of Tyrone Willingham's first season officially wore off. The Notre Dame fans booed. Later, Willingham pretended he didn't hear it. "They booed?" he said with a smirk. But he had reasons for kicking a field goal.

"We scrambled to get there," he said. "We were going backward, not forward. I don't have a specific plan for fourth down. If we don't make it, there's a huge momentum boost for [the other team]. But if we kick it and miss, who cares? Now if it's blocked and they pick it up . . . well."

But Nicholas Setta's kick would neither miss nor be blocked; his 18-yard field goal gave them a 9–0 lead. In fact, Setta's five field goals that night set a record for most in a Kickoff Classic game. More important, he provided all the offensive scoring as Holiday and his teammates still struggled to establish themselves.

But the defense had already established itself. And Shane Walton was proving to be the unit's heart and soul. In earning a reputation as a leader, Walton had also earned a nickname — Big Head — because of his ceaseless on-field conversations with opposing players.

Before the game, one Maryland receiver said, "Playing Notre Dame is like playing a scout team." But the Maryland offense was doing nothing that night, so each time Walton made a play, he escorted the receiver back to his huddle, asking him who the *real* scout team was.

Because Walton had such an infectious personality, the other defensive backs wanted to be like him, especially Vontez Duff. Duff was so eager to be like Walton that teammates had bestowed on him the name Little Head.

That night, with Walton in the process of establishing himself as a defensive force, Duff wanted in on the action. Duff was listed as 6', but was closer to 5'10". He hadn't mastered the technical aspects of football, and he didn't have Walton's instincts or anticipation. But his coach, Trent Walters, knew that Duff was the best raw athlete in the secondary, and to make him work, Walters made fun of his technique, especially his goofy backpedal.

Like Walton, Duff also returned punts, but unlike Walton, he had long speed, the kind of speed that breaks a game wide open. Returning punts was the one area in which he had Walton beat. With 10:28 left in the third quarter, Notre Dame led Maryland 9–0, and with Big Head basking in the spotlight, Little Head caught a punt and took it 76 yards to the house, a Kickoff Classic record, giving Notre Dame a 16–0 lead. Two more field goals by Nicholas Setta made it 22–0.

But Walton wasn't quite done with his show. In the last 13 minutes of the game, he picked two more passes to give him three for the night and a record for most interceptions in a Kickoff Classic. With four seconds left, Walton ran over to Willingham and hugged him.

The ultraconservative Willingham proudly embracing the

trash-talking Walton completed the perfect portrait for the evening. This was a new Notre Dame football program. Any of the 72,903 fans would have been hard-pressed to deny that this particular image symbolized an awakening of the Notre Dame spirit. But it was a new spirit, one that looked and felt different from the old one. The helmets were still gold and the nameless jerseys still made the players anonymous, but the sight of the black coach hugging the kid with the braided hair made the old tradition look, well, *modern*.

Several minutes after the game, the Notre Dame team was presented the Kickoff Classic trophy. Though the offense hadn't scored a touchdown and still looked very much like a work in progress, it was a truly great victory for Willingham and his team. No one had known if he could coach them, or if this group of guys would even play for him. But those questions were answered by a 22–0 shutout.

Yet as a photographer asked the team to gather around their coach and asked the coach to hold the trophy over his head, the look on Willingham's face was almost pained. Carlyle Holiday had completed 17 of 27 passes for a career-high 226 yards, and the defense had allowed Maryland just eight first downs and 16 yards rushing. But this was only one victory, and Willingham was determined to prove to anyone who was watching right then, and to anyone who would see that picture later, that he was not satisfied with just *one damn victory*. He refused to smile or even slightly part his lips, and when the photographer took that picture, Willingham was almost frowning.

On the Monday night after the game, a friend dropped by the head coach's office. It was still warm, about 80 degrees, and rather than sit in the office, Willingham opted to talk outside the Joyce Center, on a bench just across the street from the life-size statue of former Notre Dame coach Frank Leahy. He had just attended his first victory dinner, a tradition that accompanied each Irish win. He sat down on the bench and apologized for being late. He had planned to see his friend an hour before, but he'd been told of the victory dinner just before it started — perhaps because no one in the athletic department wanted to give him the added pressure of win-to-eat. It was rare for the hyperprepared Willing-ham to ever be caught off guard.

As Willingham began to spoon vanilla ice cream from a foam bowl, three women volleyball players, each wearing baggy shorts and holding ice bags, came from the gym. One, acknowledging the fact that the offense had changed for the better, said, "Great game. It was really fun to watch." Willingham, looking up from his dessert, sincerely surprised, said, "Thank you."

He was expressionless until his friend asked him about his favorite play of the game. For every coach in every game there are a few plays that stand out, that only he notices. "Actually, there's always one particular play I look for in every game," said Willingham. "It's the play that puts them away, that play that says 'Okay, we got 'em now.' I thought we had it on Duff's punt return. But after their long return [51 yards] on the following kickoff, that moment was over. So I don't know if I have a favorite moment for that game."

It would be that ideal, that decisive moment in a game when his team broke its opponent's will and ripped out its heart, that would become the Holy Grail of Willingham's first season at Notre Dame. But on that early evening, seated on the bench, eating ice cream, he didn't seem especially worried by it. He knew his team would eventually get the hang of it.

Finished with his ice cream, he checked his watch and sprang off the bench. USC was playing a televised game against Auburn, and he wanted to catch at least a few minutes of it. He glanced back over his shoulder. "You know we play them at the end of the year."

6

PURDUE AND THE MEDIA

IF YOU'RE ROLLING DOWN Edison Road, on your way to Notre Dame Stadium, standing before you is the true grandeur of the university. To the right of the stadium is Hesburgh Library. Of course, the most colorful feature of the library is a 134-foot mosaic of Jesus, standing triumphant with His arms raised overhead — Touchdown Jesus. And to the left of the library is the university's Main Building, better known by its Golden Dome. On any late afternoon in the fall, extended sunbeams make the Dome glisten, warm the stadium, and light up Touchdown Jesus, giving Him that certain bling-bling that is synonymous with Notre Dame football. But none of these is the most sacred totem on campus. The holiest of holies lies in the bowels of the Joyce Center — the head football coach's office. Oh, you've been inside that office at least once. We all have.

You know the scene. Admit it. You know the scene, and you love the scene. It's that scene from *Rudy*. It's the one that makes you cry. It's the one that makes *everybody* cry. It's the scene in which the whole starting lineup, one after another, marches silently into Coach Dan Devine's office, jerseys in hand, demanding that Daniel "Rudy" Ruettiger get the chance to suit up for the final game of the season. It's a softer, yet more sober 90s reinvention of the "win one for the Gipper" scene from *Knute Rockne, All American.* This time the tone is less dramatic and a great deal more, well, pathetic. There's no gridiron icon lying on his death-bed. It's just a nice gesture by a bunch of guys who have both the integrity and the balls to say, "Come on, Coach, let the scrub get some run."

Remember the guy who led the Rudy movement? As he stands before Devine, his nostrils flare, his top lip curls over his teeth, and his chiseled face is the mask of a snarling Doberman. Until that moment, we know him only as number 21, but as he lays his jersey on Devine's desk, saying, "I want Rudy to dress in my place," we see the name "Steele" emblazoned on the back of his shirt.

When Devine says to him, "You're a captain, a team leader, now act like it," Steele answers tersely, "I am." But it's the unspo-ken dialogue that makes this exchange so significant. As Steele says the words, he and Devine lock eyes, and before Steele exits, he holds his stare for several uncomfortable seconds. At that instant, it's clear that Steele is telling the coach that even though Devine's name is stenciled on the office door, he isn't controlling this situation.

You know why this scene worked? Why we're moved to tears? It's because we suspend all disbelief. That's why we believe a man can walk into the most hallowed football office and, in the name of a greater good, upset the delicate balance of all the men who have ever sat behind that desk — and leave everyone happy. This works in the teary-eyed sentimentalism of *Rudy*. And it works in *theory*. But in reality, things don't go so smoothly when the under-dog who takes over the coach's office is a dignified, proud, unyielding man named *Tyrone*, who says, right off the bat, "I tend to be brief with the media."

Willingham's approach to privacy and his subsequent rela-tionship with the media were actually reminiscent of Dan Devine's. Like Willingham, Devine was an intensely private, guarded man. After practice, Devine wasn't hanging around jok-ing with reporters. A family man, he wanted to coach his team and go home. Devine was prickly and was never fully embraced as one of Notre Dame's beloved figures. Though he'd won a national championship in 1977, the name Dan Devine rarely conjured warm, fuzzy images among Notre Dame fans. By the time Willingham made his first appearance in Notre Dame Stadium, some folks probably felt the same about him.

Long before the Purdue game on September 7, Willingham had taken decisive action to close the ranks, shutting out anyone or anything that could manifest itself as a "distraction" — the consensus taboo for all football coaches. At the conclusion of spring practice, he had requested that the annual Blue-Gold Game, pitting one half of the Irish team against the other, be blacked out by local television stations. While at Stanford, Willingham had used that game to scout the Irish, and his record against them was 3–2. Willingham also had his weekly press conferences reduced from one hour to a half-hour. Because of these acts of public privacy, he had already gained a reputation among the local media. "I read somewhere I was a control freak," he said. He lifted his eyebrows and shrugged. "Now, what that says to me is *that* person is a control freak, and they're mad because they want control of what goes on in here and they can't have it."

In the past, the Notre Dame players and their coach had been open to local media — understandably so, since they were the crown jewels of the South Bend community. But Willingham also saw openness as an opportunity for failure. Though his players varied in age and maturity, they were still kids, and because of the stage on which they performed, they were open to intense scrutiny and ridicule. After 22 years in college football, Willingham knew that whenever a kid said something that could be used against him, it probably would be. And, as he was fond of saying, "Some things are better off kept within the football family."

But the Willingham Privacy Act didn't go over so well with the local media. First he announced that neither he nor his players would be available on Sunday or Monday afternoons. In the past, those two days had been open for the media. In addition, Sports Information Director John Heisler and members of his staff were told that the media would no longer be permitted to call players at their dorms. That made the relationship between coach and media a bit chilly.

Among the local media, it was understood that any man who took the head coaching job at Notre Dame was someone willing to deal with tremendous pressure. He had to handle more than just the expectation that he would win every game; he had to deal with a little "hazing" as well. It wasn't necessarily personal, but in the first few weeks of the season, there did seem to be an unspoken code that required a few members of the media to get under the coach's skin whenever possible.

Tim Prister was the editor for *Blue & Gold Illustrated,* a publication that represents the direct link between the team and its extremely loyal and curious fans. It was Prister's job to get every bit of information he could for his readers. So when Willingham came to town and, at his very first press conference, declared, "I tend to be brief with the media," there was bound to be a tremor in the local press force. There was never any real animosity between Willingham and Prister, or any other member of the local media. But from the beginning there was certainly some "tension."

On the Thursday afternoon before the Purdue game, Willingham, in two separate instances, made his stance even clearer. While the team was warming up, a cameraman from Channel 2 lugged his tripod perilously close to the field. Willingham, standing a few feet away, said, "Watch it. I don't want any accidents." With Tim Prister and a beat writer from the *South Bend Tribune* in earshot, he followed that with, "Though some people may not believe it, I'm concerned about *your* welfare."

While Willingham was subtle before practice, he was anything but when he addressed the media afterward. In the early part of the season, Willingham met with the press in front of the tunnel that led from the stadium. The very second the small gaggle of reporters had gathered around him, he scanned the group as a whole, making eye contact with each, letting them know he was about to drop something gravely serious. Clearly annoyed, he spoke tersely. "You guys have been clamoring for access on Sunday, on Monday, and the eighth day," he said. "Yesterday, after a *Wednesday* practice, there were only *two* questions asked."

He paused to scan the group again. "*Two.*"

Then he flashed a friendly smile and stuffed his hands in his pockets. "Okay, my point is well taken," he said. "What questions do you have for me today?"

Prister nervously broke the tension. "Uh, what about that red-zone offense, Coach?"

The scene was brief and intense, but it set the tone for the rest of the season. Willingham made it clear that while his job description included a daily address to the media, it wasn't necessarily the highest of priorities. Later, reflecting on that, he said, "It's not that I don't like talking to the media. That's not necessarily true. When people ask you questions, you have the opportunity to shape their answers, to shape the image and the message you want to get out there. Now, nine times out of ten, the media is spreading a message I want to get out there."

But in speaking to the media, Willingham had made it clear beyond the shadow of a doubt that while he was friendly and consistently polite, there had to be certain limits placed on that interaction. No one had to explain to Willingham that kindness could be mistaken for weakness or that there was always a chance that good-natured humor, when placed into the wrong hands, could easily degenerate into a minstrel show. That's why his dealings with the media had been so consistently focused. "I just don't have time to joke around and give people quotes to play with. For what? That sort of thing has nothing to do with winning."

At Thursday's practice, while his teammates were stretching, John Crowther, the long snapper, saw one of his teammates walking toward him and offered him a loud and hearty greeting. "Courtney Watson!" he yelled. Watson's long gray T-shirt hung off his shoulders, and his legs were much thinner than usual. With one year of eligibility left, Watson had spent the entire off-season adding mass to his 232-pound frame, but in just two hellish weeks of illness, he had dropped 17 pounds.

Trent Miles walked up to him. "Hey, man, can I get that diet you're on?" They both laughed, each knowing it was a bad joke, but it was just good to have Watson upright again. Now, in the second week of the season, Watson faced the prospect of yet another comeback, another reinvention of himself. It had become old hat for him.

Watson, a big, solid running back with decent speed and great natural vision, had come to South Bend from Sarasota, Florida. But Notre Dame had very little depth behind the then All-America Anthony Denman, so linebacker coach Kirk Doll smoothly coaxed Watson into playing the middle linebacker spot. Cold, lost, and pissed about getting no run, Watson spent his freshman season in misery. But by the time he had concluded spring ball in his sophomore year, Watson had discovered that his vision, lateral quickness, and short burst made him a natural for his new position. He discarded self-pity and resigned himself to becoming a legitimate baller at linebacker.

That first season, he made some plays on the kickoff and punt teams, and by the time he embarked on his junior year, he was fully prepared to stake a physical and spiritual claim as the starting middle linebacker. That his junior debut would come in Lincoln, Nebraska, was fitting. Where else could a football player discover if he had the goods? Watson had 18 tackles that day, 17 solos, against a quick and violent Cornhuskers option attack.

As the season progressed, Watson's growth was lost amid his team's overall poor performance. While he blossomed into an explosive middle linebacker, finishing that season with 76 tackles and a pick for a touchdown against Tennessee, Notre Dame football was in a tailspin.

But ever since Willingham's arrival, things had been different. Watson knew that Willingham valued senior leadership, and he could provide that. He also knew he would be challenged to make plays, and he could provide those too. Before camp, he sat down and listed three goals for the season: (1) lead the team in tackles; (2) become a finalist for the Butkus Award; and (3) make the All-America team. "I wanted to do the same things LaVar Arrington did during his senior season in 1999," said Watson. In the process of achieving those things, Arrington earned himself a spot as the second pick in the 2000 NFL draft.

Before the Kickoff Classic, as summer camp segued into the regular season, everything was as it should have been. On the Wednesday practice before the Kickoff Classic, Watson was moving well, driving on the ball, and looking especially quick. His team reenergized and the whole program renewed, Watson also felt good about what lay ahead for him personally.

After practice, Watson returned to his room at Zahm Hall. He went to bed feeling okay — not great, but okay. But when he awoke the next morning, his head was throbbing. Watson was one of those guys who never got sick, not so much as a cold, and had never even popped a Tylenol. But having watched his mother suffer from migraines, he knew instantly what he had.

With the team scheduled to fly to New Jersey on Thursday, Watson went to the trainer Jim Russ. In addition to the migraines, his stomach churned with nausea. Russ diagnosed a viral infection and gave Watson something to induce vomiting. By Thursday afternoon, he was strong enough to travel with the team, and by Saturday morning, he felt normal again. He asked to play in the game, but was told that if he played while still sick, he might miss the next two to three weeks.

On Saturday night, Watson stood on the sideline in a white polo shirt while sophomore Brandon Hoyte, making his first ever collegiate start, played with the reckless and confused abandon of one who didn't fully grasp the defense but who knew enough to fly everywhere and hit everyone. Hoyte finished with nine tackles.

Immediately after the game, the team flew back to South Bend, and by Sunday morning, Watson woke up feeling worse than he had throughout the four-day ordeal. The migraine had returned, and unbeknownst to him or to anyone else, he was suffering from encephalitis, or swelling of the brain. Only later did Watson learn that the flight home, during which he spent a couple of hours at 30,000 feet, had caused the swelling.

Early Sunday evening, unable to keep anything down, he dialed his girlfriend, Christina Trieweiler, who drove him to the infirmary. The doctors there, upon seeing his condition, immediately sent them to St. Joseph hospital in South Bend. But at St. Joseph, the doctors still couldn't tell him what kind of viral infection he had.

After checking him for the West Nile Virus, they gave him a spinal tap — a truly heinous procedure. Using a four-inch needle with a sinister hook attached to the tip, a doctor plunged it into Watson's spine. Only half-conscious, he vaguely felt the odd sensation of having someone lightly dig into his spinal cord. But still, when it was done, the doctors couldn't tell him what kind of virus he had.

For a few days, Watson lay in bed, wasting away as the team embarked on what was already turning into a special season. Each day, Christina came by to visit him, and Willingham called him. Bob Simmons, despite his dislike of hospitals, illness, and uncertainty, came by, too, and prayed for Watson.

Then suddenly, in the middle of the week, Watson took a turn for the better. By Thursday, to everyone's surprise, he was well enough to leave the hospital. For the rest of the season, the Notre Dame medical staff would refer to his illness as a "viral infection" because Watson's symptoms vanished as quickly as they had appeared. On that Thursday afternoon, when he walked onto the field, his frame had shrunk, but his hunger for success had grown.

One of the things Willingham most enjoyed about coaching at Notre Dame was revealed on Friday night before the Purdue game — his first pep rally. His excitement that evening stemmed from his first chance that season to address the students. The lights dimmed, and as he strolled across the arena floor on a dark-blue carpet, Willingham was bathed in a huge spotlight. Dressed in a dark suit, white shirt, and dark solid tie and bearing a calm, fixed expression, Willingham looked like a lighthearted minister taking in a sporting event. It was the first official meeting of the football season between coach and student body, and the scene carried the appropriate gravity. The second he entered the arena, nearly 12,000 fans, including students wearing fluorescent T-shirts bearing the names of their residence halls, screamed like savages.

Senior offensive tackle Jordan Black was the appointed team speaker. At 6'6", 305 pounds, Black was the largest member of the offensive line and one of the team's most articulate members. He was a good-looking, gregarious kid, with excited eyes and a quick wit about him. A preseason honorable mention All-

America, he was entering his fourth year as a starter and was clearly a team leader. Back in February, only a month into the Willingham era, Black was the first to proclaim that this team "believed in Coach Ty."

It was clearly evident that Black, in his final season, had mixed emotions about his previous three years on the team. From Rowlett, Texas, he was among a generation of players that Bob Davie had recruited from the state. While none of the players on the team would openly criticize their former coach, they all exuded a fresh energy that had been completely absent a few months earlier.

After he adjusted the mike, Black looked at his audience, then back down at the podium, and, with all sincerity, remarked, "I haven't seen it this rowdy in a long time." His sincerity stemmed from the fact that this evening was clearly something the upperclassmen, both players and students, had never experienced, and what the freshmen had probably expected all along — the special tradition of Notre Dame football. But Black said pep rallies in the past had been perfunctory at best. "People would file into the gym, do some clapping, do a few cheers, and go home," he said. "Back then, everyone was just going through the motions."

But that evening, the enthusiasm was real. What took place on Friday night, September 6, was a living, breathing, active resurgence in Notre Dame football. And the most endearing aspect of the 2002 season was the relationship between the student body and the coach.

As Black ended his address, saying that the team had the best backs, receivers, linemen, and quarterbacks, he took the appropriate dramatic pause. "And we certainly have the best coach." After a thunderous applause, Black sat down and let the suspense mount. Chuck Lennon, the executive director of the Alumni Association, was the emcee for all pep rallies. After Lennon introduced Willingham, the band began to play the *1812 Overture*, and the students unveiled their special greeting. With thumbs placed together and index fingers extended, each student made a W.

Leprechaun Mike took it a step further, combining his hand

gesture with a sort of genuflection toward the podium. Sure it was only a pep rally, but the cultural significance was much larger. When 12,000 students unleashed an unbridled rapturous cheer for a dignified black man, it was nothing short of moving. "We love you, Coach Ty!" came a cry from the rafters.

Before speaking his first words, Willingham stood at the podium and for a few seconds clapped along with the students. "This moment has been a long time coming," he began.

For just a second, the building fell absolutely silent. What did he mean? Was Willingham, at the most inopportune moment, alluding to his being the first black head coach at Notre Dame? Less than 24 hours before his first home game, he was finally making his statement now?

The suspense mounted as he said, "When I was hired, a lot of people asked me questions. Some wanted to know about the offense. Some wanted to know about the defense. But most people wanted to know this: 'What are you gonna say at the first pep rally?'"

With the tension broken, the crowd erupted, and Willingham continued, "As you may know, I'm a man of very few words. So I'll start with these." He then slowly recited the chorus of the Notre Dame fight song: "'Cheer, cheer for old Notre Dame / Wake up the echoes cheering her name / Send a volley cheer on high / Shake down the thunder from the sky.'"

The students cheered, but in a somewhat reserved fashion, not quite sure what to make of their new coach. Before the season, Andrew Soukup, a sportswriter for *The Observer,* the student newspaper, said, "We were all excited about the possibility of getting Jon Gruden. When we heard it was Tyrone Willingham, we were like, 'We don't know anything about him.'"

That evening, it was as though the students weren't expecting the new coach to be so dedicated to *their* tradition. A black face in a place of authority was a novelty to this predominantly white crowd, and they were probably expecting the "hip quotient" to rise. They wanted to learn something about him, about where he came from and what he stood for, but instead, by teaching them about Notre Dame, he was reminding them of what *they* stood for, who *they* were.

Willingham, looking over at Chuck Lennon, remarked, "You said to 'raise the roof.' That's old school!" The students cheered at his obvious reference to the hip-hop culture. "Well, I'm old school too," he said. "So I'll go along with that!" He raised his arms in the traditional "raise the roof" gesture, and the rapturous crowd followed suit.

He then reminded the students of their role in the game. "I want you to really come down on Purdue tomorrow," he told them. "I don't want them to be able to think at all, let alone think about winning. Let's go, Irish!" Willingham stood, clapping with the crowd as the sounds of Handel's *Messiah* pierced the air.

Before he sat down for good, there was one more gesture, one more hint that Willingham had come to Notre Dame with a mission. As they had discussed beforehand, Chuck Lennon started him off by recognizing each residence hall in attendance. "Let's hear it for Alumni Hall," he yelled. The students in that section erupted.

"All the students in Dillon rise," he shouted, and they all stood. Once he had finished honoring the students in this way, Lennon handed the mike back to Willingham, who introduced the players from each hall.

"From Zahm Hall, Courtney Watson." It was then that Willingham made clear one of his primary objectives — to form a bond between the team and the student body. In the past, the coach had only introduced the offensive and defensive starters, but on Willingham's watch, the students were going to be a part of the show. There were no "jock dorms" at Notre Dame, and because of that, Willingham wanted his players to be acknowledged as part of the student body, not as separate entities whose presence only mattered on Saturday afternoons. As he gathered the team and led them from the arena, the students stood in unison, cheering a new coach and a new era. It was unbridled enthusiasm mixed with hope and relief, because after that brief introduction, they still didn't know much about Willingham, or about his team, but they were obviously happy to have a reason to cheer.

On Notre Dame's first offensive drive against Purdue on September 7, 2002, the students still had reason to cheer. The week before, against Maryland, the tight end was virtually nonexistent, and Gary Godsey and Jared Clark had combined for just two catches. To get away from Maryland's All-America linebacker E. J. Henderson, they had relied heavily on the quick slant game outside, rather than attacking the middle. But this day, from the get-go, Bill Diedrick went right at the heart of the Purdue defense.

On the first play, Holiday drilled the ball to Godsey in the middle of the field for nine quick yards. Two plays later, Ryan Grant got six in the middle. Picking up two quick first downs, the offense looked better than it had the previous week.

Holiday sprinted to his right on a play designed to hit Omar Jenkins on a deep comeback. But seeing Jenkins was blanketed, Carlyle Holiday calmly pulled the ball down and ran for 11 yards and another first down. Three plays later, after two successive dive plays with Rashon Powers-Neal, it was third-and-10 when Holiday, waiting for Battle to get free on a curl route, calmly threw the ball away.

It would prove to be one of Holiday's better decisions that day. Upstairs in the coaches' booth, Bill Diedrick knew he'd made a mistake with the game plan. After their success against Maryland in the opener, Diedrick wanted to build on it. But he had given Holiday way too much to think about. "We should have just let the kids have confidence and play," said Diedrick. "We were always trying to get into the ideal play or ideal protection instead of just letting the system work."

On several occasions, Holiday got stuck holding on to the ball, trying to determine if the safety was blitzing, or if the defense was in two deep zones or man. "We gave Purdue more credit than they deserved," said Diedrick. "And Carlyle froze because of it."

While the offense was struggling, trying to establish some kind of identity, the defense, particularly the secondary, took another step toward establishing itself as the real deal. The previous week, they had canceled any semblance of a passing game. But facing Purdue, they were up against a young, talented natural passer named Kyle Orton. People around West Lafayette were already saying that Orton, though only a sophomore, was better than former Purdue quarterback Drew Brees, who'd been a second-round pick for the San Diego Chargers in the 2001 draft. Orton was 6′4″ and about 220 pounds.

Notre Dame defensive coordinator Kent Baer knew that in Purdue's spread offense, one that was heavy on three- and four-receiver sets, Orton could make any throw, whether it be the out, curl, or deep ball. "When they spread you out on the field, it's like basketball on grass," he said. "And they do a better job of running the ball than people give them credit for. *That's* a real concern of mine."

Every team has that one coach of whom the players are a little afraid, who intimidates in that tough-love sort of way, and for Notre Dame, Kent Baer was him. While friendly, Baer exuded a bottom-line let's-cut-the-bullshit kind of air. Even his look set him apart from the rest of the staff. Whereas Diedrick could pass for an accountant and Willingham a professor, Baer, with slicked-back hair and a round face, had a blue-collar texture. He was born and raised in Utah, but he had a gritty edge that resembled a neighborhood mechanic or factory worker with a penchant for dropping real-world knowledge on the sheltered, affluent teenager. In fact, that's one thing he did while serving as defensive coordinator for Stanford.

"When summer break began, most of the kids wanted to stick around and work out and take it easy," he said. "I remember asking twelve of my kids, How many of you have ever had a job before? You know how many said yes? One. One freakin' kid. Well, I sent them all home, and when they came back they all thanked me and said how much they had learned."

As Stanford's defensive coordinator, Baer not only built a unit that led the conference in rushing defense (for only the second time in school history) but also gave the defense some credibility, which was a fleeting thing for a program that, having been coached by Bill Walsh and Denny Green and led by players like Jim Plunkett and John Elway, had always been associated with offense. Because of that accomplishment, and his 29 years of experience, Baer had been a candidate to take over the program after Willingham took the Notre Dame job. But after Buddy Teevens got the Stanford job, Baer joined the rest of Willingham's staff at Notre Dame. Now, with Notre Dame's rapid ascension predicated on his defense, Baer and his unit had the perfect opportunity to rise to another level.

Although Orton was a big, strapping Midwestern corn-fed specimen and could throw the ball as well as anyone they would face all season, he was still a youngster. And any time a defensive coordinator gets a youngster under center, he'll blitz his young ass. That's exactly what Baer did. Beginning with the third play of the game, he sent a variety of players after Orton, from a variety of angles.

When the defense played nickel, using five defensive backs, Shane Walton lined up over the slot receiver, into a position from which he had already proved he could either cover the receiver or drop into a zone. Against Purdue, he was often in that position when they ran their "Money" blitz package. On the third play, Walton lined up over the receiver, but just prior to the snap he crept toward the line of scrimmage and sprinted off the edge, chasing Orton out of the pocket and forcing him to throw the ball away. On the next play, Purdue running back Joey Harris was stopped for no gain. At fourth-and-six, Purdue punted, and it looked as though things were going according to plan.

But on their very next series, Purdue's coach Joe Tiller made it clear he wasn't going to allow all this blitzing. If Notre Dame was going to finesse them with a nickel package, then he was going to ram it down their throats with an old-school Big Ten power game. The first play began with Harris gashing the Irish for nine yards on a dive. Three plays later, he got seven off the tackle.

As the first quarter ended, Purdue was still scoreless, and five blitzes had kept Orton from establishing his rhythm. But Purdue's offensive line was starting to overpower Notre Dame's front four, in particular end Kyle Budinscak. While the secondary was clearly the strength of this unit, the defensive line was a very close second. Ryan Roberts, Cedric Hilliard, and Darrell Campbell, all seniors, were solid, if not spectacular, players. But the unit had lost defensive ends Grant Irons and Tony Weaver, to the

Buffalo Bills and the Baltimore Ravens, respectively. Budinscak, a junior, was in only his second game as a starter, and Purdue was beginning to exploit his inexperience. Midway through the first quarter, with the game still scoreless, the tackle had got underneath Budinscak, driving him off the ball as Harris broke off runs of seven, 11, and 14 yards. Because of the heat, almost 90 degrees, Hilliard and Campbell were tiring.

The second quarter began with Purdue's running back Montrell Lowe gashing the middle for 23 yards, and for a minute it looked as though Purdue was about to get the defense on the ropes. But two plays later, the secondary collectively stood up and asserted itself as a force, squashing a screen play. After Lowe caught the ball, Walton held off the left tackle long enough to make Lowe change direction. As Lowe tried to get around his teammate, his left hand grazed the tackle's shoulder, and the ball spilled onto the ground. Irish senior Gerome Sapp smoothly scooped it up, sidestepped one potential tackler, cut back, and took it 54 yards for a quick score, making it 7–0.

Eleven seconds later, Willingham got the kind of decisive game-turning play for which he yearned. On the ensuing kickoff, the returner bobbled the ball, and sophomore strong safety Lionel Bolen caught it midair and quickly dashed into the end zone. The score was now 14–0, as members of the kickoff team piled on Bolen in the end zone. Lost in the celebration was the fact that the Irish offense had yet to score a touchdown. But Willingham hadn't forgotten, and at a time when they were feeling good and confident, he'd remind them of it.

After Purdue's next series, which ended with an incompletion by Orton, Willingham gathered his offense on the 30-yard line. After posting two quick scores, the Irish had Purdue in a corner. But Purdue was fighting back and still had life, and that troubled Willingham. He leaned in close and spoke evenly, loud enough to be heard over the band. "There comes a time when you have to put a team away," he said. "You're up fourteen-oh, and they're on the ropes. Now let's execute!"

On the second play of the drive, it looked as if they would do just that. Ryan Grant broke a tackle in the backfield, ran over the safety, then reversed field, and with a smooth, elongated stride, galloped down the sideline for 36 yards. It was the kind of run Buzz Preston had been stressing since camp. At practice, each time a back was hit, or even held up by defenders, Grant had to finish the run, taking it all the way to the end zone. Grant didn't quite make it to the end zone, but it was the longest run of his career and easily the most aggressive play by any offensive player of the young season.

On the next play, Holiday hit Godsey for five; then Powers-Neal got six on a run, and Holiday hit Campbell on a screen for nine yards. Moving the ball down to the six-yard line, the offense finally had some rhythm. But after Grant was dropped in the backfield and Holiday threw the ball behind him on a swing pass, it was third-and-goal from the seven. Holiday ran a quarterback draw, darting to his right, then lunging forward, and he really looked as though he would get in. But even after stretching out his body, he got no farther than the two-yard line.

As Willingham spoke into his headset, calmly conferring with Diedrick, receiver Carlos Campbell pleaded for him to go for it. "Come on!" he screamed from the middle of the field. "Let's get this!" But Willingham stuck to his conservative guns and sent in Nicholas Setta to kick. After a 19-yard field goal, the score was 17–0, and the offense had yet to make it to the end zone. Setta was proving himself to be Notre Dame's most reliable source of production. In the previous season, Setta had made 15 of 17 field goal attempts, and was eight-for-eight from beyond 40 yards.

Upstairs, Diedrick was pissed. They were winning, but the offense hadn't scored. The next evening, Willingham, Diedrick, and the rest of the offensive staff would promise themselves never to overthink a game plan again. They would decide that next week, against Michigan, would be the time to open things up.

But at the moment, Willingham's team lacked more than offense. With a little more than three minutes left till the half, Purdue's Anthony Chambers took a punt at the 24-yard line, broke two tackles, cut across the field, and accelerated, taking the ball 76 yards for a touchdown. The play did more than just put Purdue on the board; it exposed the Irish special teams — the punt coverage unit in particular — as another area that had considerable room to grow.

Eight minutes into the third quarter, Notre Dame had once again driven to the red zone. But on third-and-seven, Holiday was sacked by Purdue defensive lineman Kevin Nesfield, and he gave up the rock. Ten plays later, after Purdue running back Jerod Void scored from the three, it was 17–14. And a few seconds into the fourth quarter, a 35-yard field goal tied it.

Midway through the fourth quarter, the secondary once again rose to prominence. Purdue had the ball on the Purdue 25-yard line. It was crunch time, when coaches are prone to recite the time-honored mantra *Somebody make a play!* In bracket coverage, Shane Walton and Gerome Sapp converged on the ball. On Orton's release, Sapp drove hard toward the receiver, looking for the knockout blow. But as Sapp came forward, the ball glanced off his fingers and landed gently in Vontez Duff's hands. With quick little baby steps, Duff took off, and Orton, with a good angle on him, chased him downfield. When they reached the goal line, Duff rose and Orton went low. Orton caught Duff at the ankles and upended him. But Duff, airborne, stretched the ball over the pylon to give Notre Dame the go-ahead score.

A few minutes later, after the defense had stopped Purdue on its final drive, Willingham walked down the sideline, holding up four fingers. There was 1:44 left in the game, and he was giving the signal for the four-minute offense, time to run down the clock. Behind him, someone casually remarked, "Oh, I guess that means we won the game, then, right?"

Throwing his head back and opening his mouth wide, Willingham laughed. It was the first time since taking the job that he had openly shown himself to enjoy his new gig. And it was the first time a national audience saw him so animated while on the sideline. It was caught by the NBC telecast and replayed several times as proof positive that Willingham possessed another face. It was the nation's first clue that he did indeed own a sense of humor. And he had reason to laugh. Not only was his team 2–0, but they had risen from unranked obscurity to a No. 23 AP ranking.

On Monday night, Willingham sat on the tan sofa in his office. He reached into a box and picked up a football, read it, and paused. "Okay, this kind of thing scares me." He held up a white game jersey with a handwritten note attached. "I've enclosed this jersey signed by Devine, Parseghian, Holtz, and Davie. I've also enclosed a self-addressed, stamped envelope and a hundred dollars."

"Why is he sending me one hundred dollars? To me, it sounds like he's going to sell this on eBay." He shook his head and gently laid the jersey back in the box, recoiling from it as if it were made of plutonium. Two weeks into the season, Willingham wasn't about to take part in anything suspect or controversial. "I'm gonna just leave that one alone," he said.

The same conservative practicality applied to his sideline demeanor. When he was told that his big grin at the end of the game had been as much a topic of conversation as the dramatic win itself, Willingham laughed. Just like after the Maryland game, when he refused to smile for the photo, there was a reason for his public disposition. He knew that he was always being watched, always being critiqued by people who just might hold him to another standard. So he launched a preemptive strike and held himself to his own impossible standard, and that standard didn't have much room for public mirth.

"See, people always think if you laugh you're not being serious," he said. "But you know there are times when something happens during the course of a game that makes you laugh. And that was just one of them. In fact, my wife and I were watching something on ESPN the other night, and there was some segment in which they said I never smiled." He shrugged in a way that suggested it was the most ridiculous notion he'd ever heard. "My wife knows that's not the case at all. I'm always laughing and joking."

About the time Willingham was leaving his office, Shane Walton and Arnaz Battle were leaving their apartment to go to a place called Studes, a little hole-in-the-wall bar and grill about two miles from campus. During the fall, Monday Night Football made it one of the featured hangouts for students. Both Walton and Battle had been regulars there the year before, but things were different now. Willingham hadn't exactly ordered his players to stay away from local hangouts; he had merely expressed to all of them his concern that they take care of themselves.

"I don't want them to get off their training schedule," he explained. "It may be one beer or two beers, but everything counts."

But it was more than the physical effects of a couple beers that concerned Willingham. In light of a rape scandal involving former players that had broken loose the previous spring, Willingham had told his team that if he got wind of any players being involved in *any* shady dealings, there would be consequences and repercussions on Sunday morning. That Sunday punishment was called the "Breakfast Club," and it wasn't just the endless series of sprints and push-ups that scared the players. It was the threat of being absolutely punked by the head coach, who was more than twice their age, but still just as fit as they were and five times as disciplined. During those sessions, Willingham would drop to the ground, sometimes putting his face only inches away from a player, challenging him to keep pace with his coach.

It wasn't just the nightlife that concerned Willingham. His oversight extended to class attendance as well. Carlyle Holiday flatly stated that the year before, classroom attendance hadn't been a top priority, but this year was different. "I won't lie," said Holiday. "We didn't always go, but this year we're afraid to miss class." Actually, they were afraid to miss any appointments or commitments. Whether it was a class or an interview with a reporter, if they had agreed to it, Willingham saw to it that the commitment was honored. His goal manifested itself in a motto that applied to him as well as to his team: "Be amazingly consistent."

But Willingham's intent, by getting his team to think about their behavior at all times, wasn't to be some all-controlling tyrant. South Bend was a small town, and they were high-profile guys.

In many ways, the flat, sleepy blue-collar town was even smaller than its 100,000 people. The main street was Grape Road, which was marked by strip malls, car dealerships, and chain restaurants. There was an Olive Garden, a T.G.I.Friday's, a Chili's, and Outback and LongHorn steakhouses.

Closer to campus, there was a pair of college bars with the requisite Notre Dame paraphernalia plastered on the walls.

About 500 yards from the stadium was a dingy, low-ceilinged joint called the Linebacker and a stone's throw from it was the more "upscale" Coach's.

Notre Dame athletes were highly visible, and when that's the case, perception is often reality. A regular Notre Dame student sipping a beer was a harmless gesture. But for a Notre Dame football player, drinking a beer could easily be interpreted as getting drunk. Both Battle and Walton liked to have a drink, but early in the season, each watched his step. Willingham had made it clear to all the players that they were being watched especially closely that season. He also made it clear that everything they did and everywhere they went would eventually get back to him.

After Battle and Walton came into Studes, they walked past the big screen, where the New England Patriots were beating up on the Pittsburgh Steelers, and the pool table, where a couple of brothers were shooting eight ball. After shaking hands with a few people, making the rounds as if casing the joint to see who might be casing them, both Battle and Walton went back outside. While the DJ began to move the sparse but lively crowd, the two players stood outside, casually conversing with a small group of girls. They had accomplished one goal by getting out of the house, so now they just chilled outside for a while. Neither was risking anything. There was too much riding on this season.

7

MICHIGAN

TYRONE WILLINGHAM WAS an electric presence. There was no doubt about that. Not since the Lou Holtz era, which resulted in a national championship in 1988 and nine straight New Year's Day bowl games from 1987 through 1995, had there been such a positive feeling around campus. But now the program once again possessed a personality whose mere proximity to the field made players, fans, and alums hold their breath in constant anticipation that something exciting was about to go down.

Early in the week of the Michigan game, Willingham was upbeat and optimistic. Talking about the upcoming game he said, "Oh, I know this is a big rivalry. And their coaches will always do or say something to keep it a heated rivalry."

In 1887, when the Irish started playing collegiate football, their first opponent was Michigan. Since then, the matchup had become one of the most heated and exciting series in all of college sports. And it was a rivalry based on not only proximity but also college football dominance. Notre Dame's .7495 winning percentage ranked them number one in college football history, and Michigan, at .7453, was ranked number two. Because he'd once played for Michigan State, Willingham brought his own Wolverine issues to Notre Dame. He didn't particularly care for Michigan; he found them rather arrogant, to tell the truth. But, as was his style, he revealed his feelings in a typically veiled fashion. Over gold-rimmed glasses held by a long black rope that hung down and brushed his shoulders, Willingham expressed his take on the Michigan rivalry with a sly grin and a knowing glance. "Oh, I'm not into all that, but at the same time I'm *all into it. This* is one of the great contradictions of life."

Just as Willingham predicted, the very next day, at the weekly press conference, a caller informed him that Lloyd Carr, Michigan's head coach, had said playing teams like Notre Dame could hurt Michigan in the BCS standings. Carr didn't elaborate on what he meant, but it was assumed that Michigan, which entered the game ranked No. 7 in the nation by the AP, could drop several points in the BCS standings because Notre Dame was ranked so low at No. 20. Shaking his head, Willingham smiled. There clearly wasn't a whole lot of love between him and Lloyd Carr, but he played it cool. He told the caller, "That sounds like gamesmanship on that coach's part, so I'll just leave that one alone."

Of course he left it alone. He didn't engage in that sort of thing. He had neither the time nor the energy to invest in such trivial conversation. At least he didn't just then. There would be time for talk about the BCS much later, but for the time being it could wait. Willingham had other things on his mind.

That week, the Notre Dame campus exuded the kind of commotion, the kind of great expectation, that hadn't existed since Rocket Ismail had done his thing. Ismail was always exciting and always unpredictable, but there was one spectacular performance — against Michigan in 1989 — that made Ismail a Notre Dame legend. On the second day of September, No. 1 Notre Dame was trailing No. 2 Michigan 7–6 when Ismail lined up to receive the second-half kickoff. He took the ball on the 12-yard line and exploded through the wedge. At about midfield, Michigan corner Corwin Brown was closing in on him from his right, but in shifting to overdrive, Ismail disregarded and juiced him, leaving him with nothing as he took it to the end zone from 88 yards. With almost 13 minutes left in the game, he did it again, this time breaking three tackles, going 92 yards, and solidifying his place in Irish lore.

So it was entirely fitting that the seed for the glorious scene that would take place that upcoming Saturday was planted on Wednesday, the day Ismail showed up at practice for the second time since Willingham had taken over the program. Ismail had ruptured a disk in his neck that August and was out for the season. He had come back to shoot a segment for ESPN on the "luck of the Irish," and since their season was going so remarkably well, he was excited for another visit.

The normally staid atmosphere of midweek was pierced when Ismail came bounding onto the practice field. When he walked over to Willingham, embracing the coach as if he'd known him his whole life, it was obvious why South Bend had suddenly become a stop on his itinerary. Notre Dame had played Michigan seven times since Ismail's departure. But the 2002 game marked not only the renewal of the series but also the first time Notre Dame would play Michigan under the direction of a black coach.

Like most major universities, Notre Dame is predominantly white. But that alone is not an adequate description. Whiteness is a mere surface condition. Notre Dame, in its tradition, and in its execution of that tradition, wasn't just white — it was hopelessly *Caucasian.* Wearing a gold Notre Dame jersey with a number 1 on it and sporting a small afro, Ismail was anything but colorless. In many ways he had been the ideal Notre Dame athlete, the type who in one breath could expound on the lyrics of Tupac Shakur and in the next compare a scene from a football game to a Salvador Dalí painting. But until Tyrone Willingham showed up, he had little to connect him to his alma mater.

In front of the stadium, in front of the huge cast-iron gates, with an embrace and a brief, simple exchange, two diminutive, charismatic black men offered striking evidence that Notre Dame and, more important, the football program that defined Notre Dame's public image were undergoing much-needed change. The old excitement had returned, but in a new way, in a way that was unique, fresh, and, for lack of a better word, more colorful than ever before.

When Willingham said he wanted to make every player who had worn a Notre Dame jersey proud of the program, it had an especially poignant effect on former black players. One of Ismail's former teammates, on hearing that Willingham was hired, had started wearing his championship ring again. Prior to Willingham's arrival, he really hadn't wanted to be associated with Notre Dame, feeling that the school didn't think much of its black athletes. But shortly after Willingham's arrival, that feeling began to change. Once Ismail had offered his congratulations to a pleased Willingham, he turned to his right, where Omar Jenkins was waiting his turn to speak to Rocket. Wearing a loud striped shirt and sitting atop his mountain bike, Jenkins looked much younger than his 21 years. Normally upbeat, he was subdued that day and had been all week. The most versatile receiver on the team, he had been excited to play in the new wide-open West Coast offense. After three years of blocking, he was all set to start *catching* the ball. He had caught some balls in the first two games, but overall the offense as a unit looked disastrous. Jenkins was understandably glum, but when Rocket saw him and humbly walked over and introduced himself, Jenkins's mood instantly brightened.

"What's up with my Cowboys?" asked Jenkins. A Dallas native, he wanted the inside scoop on America's team.

"Oh, you know the deal," said Ismail. "Business is business. But things will be all right."

But by quickly changing the subject, Ismail made it clear he wasn't there to discuss his own future with the Cowboys. He was there to discuss a much larger picture.

"Enjoy your time here," he said. "This is a special time in your life. You'll look back on it and say, 'Man, what happened? That went by so fast.'"

Jenkins, smiling now, nodded. "Okay, I hear you," he said. Sometimes it was hard to slow things down amid all the pressure, but here was a man, a hero to Jenkins, who had been through it all. When he and Rocket were done talking, Jenkins rode away, looking like he normally did — upbeat and optimistic.

One of Tyrone Willingham's first tasks on arriving at Notre Dame was to cast himself headlong into the Notre Dame tradition. At heart, he was a teacher, so he took more than a passing interest in familiarizing himself with every aspect of student life. As one who always had great respect for tradition and who was ruled by a historical perspective, Willingham spent the winter and spring going to the dorms and introducing himself to the student body. Like any college coach, Willingham was a symbol of the university. But at Notre Dame, the football coach was more than that — he was the shining emblem of the school's history and spirit.

Willingham wanted to connect with the students, and his personal appearances in their dorms that spring had been a great start. But the real connection, the lasting one, was made through a green T-shirt. Each year, there was one shirt — in recent years it had been light blue and navy blue — that the students were encouraged to wear to every football game. They usually complied, but only for the first home game of the season. Afterward, the shirt was usually discarded like any other T-shirt in a college kid's wardrobe. But like some other lifeless traditions at Notre Dame, this too would be revived that season.

It just so happened that Michigan's primary color, like Notre Dame's, was blue. The garment of choice for the 2002 season was a bright, bold green T-shirt, so it only made sense for the student body to use it to distinguish themselves from the Michigan fans.

The slogan printed on the back of the green T-shirt, "Return to Glory," wasn't a suggestion, or even an expectation; it was a *destination,* and Notre Dame fans considered that destination — that place of glory — their rightful home. By accepting the coaching job, Willingham acknowledged that he would take them there. It was typical of him to take any idea and pour it through his own personal filter. And his filter wasn't like most people's. Tyrone Willingham saw life through a prism in which any and all things could be spun into a positive light. He didn't view that slogan as something that placed undue pressure on him; he saw it as the perfect way to form a relationship. Just before the Michigan game, Willingham told the students to make Notre Dame stadium a "sea of green"; it was his way of getting everyone involved with what was happening on the field.

After being on campus for a few weeks, Willingham made one observation, and from that he devised a very simple plan. "There's a lot of energy at this place," he said at the time. "But it all seems to be going in different directions." That observation and that statement would be the cornerstone of Willingham's plan for that season. He took it upon himself to funnel that energy into one central area. Of course, the most convenient place to do this was at the weekly pep rally. And the rally prior to the Michigan game was an ideal place for him to introduce the students to a little exercise in unity.

It was a slightly corny exercise, which his team had already mastered. It went like this: Willingham would tell the team to clap their hands a certain number of times, in unison, on his command. Willingham and the team provided an example. Willingham barked, "Hit!" and immediately every single person on the team clapped one time. The crowd laughed, obviously interested. It was one thing to get his team to do it, but it was truly ambitious to attempt such a stunt with 12,000 people. But then again, that was the point.

Willingham told the crowd, "Okay, on my command, one clap." When there was absolute silence, Willingham said, "Hit!"

The crowd answered with a single sound. Willingham nodded.

"Okay," he said. "Now, two times." But before Willingham gave the command, he did the unexpected. With his hand raised in the air, Willingham looked up into the stands and said, "I need you, Dickie V."

From the middle of the bleachers tumbled ESPN college basketball analyst Dick Vitale. At the sight of his round face, huge grin, and gleaming bald head, the crowd, all of whom were familiar with the severity of Vitale's enthusiasm, exploded. In one typically frantic motion, Vitale bolted to the middle of the floor, hugged Willingham, grabbed the microphone, and began to yell. It was a brief, breathless stream-of-consciousness sort of thing.

"The other day, I was sitting at home when I got a call," said Vitale. "The guy says, 'My name is Tyrone, and I'm the head coach at Notre Dame. I was wondering if you would come speak to the team.' I said, 'I'd be honored.' I wasn't good enough or smart enough to get into Notre Dame, but I love it. My daughters went here, and I live vicariously through them. This is a wonderful place, a spiritual place."

Vitale then told them how much he was looking forward to the game against Michigan. Before he left, he turned around and spoke directly to the team. "Oh, and one more thing," said Vitale. "I saw Tyrone play in college. If you guys can get everything from yourselves, get everything from your bodies like this guy did, then I guarantee you'll win the national championship!"

As Vitale returned to his seat, his message was met by a lusty ovation. And Willingham was pleased. While he waited for the crowd to simmer down, he nodded and smirked. Regarding Vitale's address and the crowd's response to it, he would later say, "See, that's the sort of energy you get with this place. We're trying to create a positive flow here. They've been fighting themselves for a while. We're trying to get on the same page. We're trying to get *one . . . positive . . . energy.*"

Of course, Willingham got directly involved in the flow. On the morning of the Michigan game, while the team went through pregame warm-ups, Willingham stalked the field wearing a navy-blue polo shirt, the interlocked ND just above his heart. But at 1:00 P.M., when the team emerged from the tunnel to start the game, Willingham led them out wearing a green shirt. When the rowdy throng of students saw the coach bearing their colors, they roared.

The Irish started the September 14, 2002, game intent on scoring an offensive touchdown. They had begun the season 2–0 and had risen to No. 20 in the nation despite failing to do just that. Beginning with its opening drive, the offense asserted itself with the kind of confidence that comes from having absolutely nothing to lose. Still pissed at the stifled game plan they had taken into the Purdue game, Bill Diedrick wasn't going to keep his quarterback under wraps anymore. He wanted Carlyle Holiday to throw the ball downtown early and often.

Michigan won the toss, and Lloyd Carr flipped the script on Willingham. Carr deferred to the second half, and the Irish offense took the field first. On the first play, Carlyle Holiday threw long to Arnaz Battle, who had beaten his man. But the pass sailed out of bounds. The Notre Dame fans stood. They knew something was different. They knew this wasn't the offense they'd seen the previous week.

After the second play from scrimmage, when Holiday chucked the ball 41 yards to Maurice Stovall, it was painfully clear that the coaching staff had more in mind than carefully installing this new offense and transforming Holiday from option quarterback to passer. Each time Holiday took a snap and dropped five steps into the pocket, they wanted to make it clear to Notre Dame fans, to college football fans, and most of all to Michigan, that it was *on*.

After Stovall's catch in the middle of the field, the offense exuded an air that suggested moving the ball this way, with an unfettered nonchalance, was what they always did and what they always expected to do. Nine plays and 80 yards later, when Ryan Grant took a toss and jogged into the end zone from the one, Willingham's first Notre Dame team had finally scored an offensive touchdown. Willingham was relieved. But his reaction was his standard postscore response. He stood, statuelike, index finger in the air, telling the offense to go for one.

With the offense having come to life, the defense raised its game to an even higher level. Michigan's first offensive drive ended when Irish nose tackle Cedric Hilliard smacked Wolverines receiver B. J. Askew. Of course, there was an Irish defender who was waiting there when the ball came free. And it was no surprise who it was. Three weeks into the season, Shane Walton was finding every way possible to get his hands on the ball. After Walton recovered the ball, the Irish offense had another chance to establish itself. But a few minutes later, when Nick Setta's field goal was blocked, they lost that opportunity.

On their next offensive series, all the momentum they had gained was lost on second down. Holiday wanted to hit Omar Jenkins with a slant. Michigan was playing a zone, meaning the defensive backs had to drop into coverage and read the quarterback's eyes. And disguising his motives still wasn't one of Carlyle Holiday's strengths. After taking the snap, Michigan corner Marlin Jackson took his drop and let Holiday's gaze take him to Jenkins. On Holiday's release, Jackson stepped in front of the ball and zipped into the end zone to tie the game at seven.

Midway through the second quarter, Courtney Watson began to feel his strength return. It was his first start of the season, and while he'd had a decent week of practice, he still felt weak for much of the first half. But at the nine-minute mark, when Michigan tried to run a reverse, Watson was overtaken by a surge of energy.

Michigan quarterback John Navarre handed the ball to receiver Braylon Edwards, who was looping around behind him. But the second he saw Edwards headed to the backfield, Watson bolted upfield and dropped him for a 10-yard loss. Watson would finish the game with nine tackles, but it was that play that brought him back from the abyss.

In the next two series, the Irish D continued to flow. With Michigan backed up on its seven-yard line, sophomore defensive end Justin Tuck, who was becoming the team's best pass rusher, beat his man and roared into the backfield. But before Tuck could drop Navarre, a Michigan offensive lineman grabbed Tuck's jersey. The referee called holding, which resulted in an automatic safety.

Barely three minutes later, after Navarre completed a pass to receiver Tyrece Butler, both Big Head and Little Head teamed up to make a play. Shane Walton hit Butler and knocked the ball loose. After Vontez Duff jumped on it, the Irish had the ball on the Michigan 28-yard line with a minute and a half to get into the end zone. Four plays later, on a quarterback draw, Holiday took the snap, blasted upfield, and ran over Marlin Jackson for the score.

At halftime, Notre Dame led Michigan 16–7. As the two teams ran to the locker room and were about to collide in the tunnel, Carr began yelling at the referee and the Irish team. Carr loudly reminded them that the visiting team was supposed to go in first. The Irish players kept their cool as they stepped aside and let the Wolverines run by.

In the third quarter, Michigan came roaring back. With just under three minutes left in the quarter, they kicked a field goal to make it 16–10. And after Arnaz Battle fumbled the ensuing kickoff, it took Michigan just six plays to take a 17–16 lead.

At the start of the fourth quarter, it was time for Notre Dame to score another touchdown. When the kickoff return team broke the huddle and Willingham clapped his hands and walked briskly up the sideline, it was a celebration of sorts. Willingham was celebrating the fact that regardless of the outcome, his team was playing *together*. The offense was making its way into the end zone, and the defense was establishing itself as one of the best in the country. But it didn't end there.

When any coach takes over a program, his primary objective is to get his team on the same page, to get them to buy in to his philosophy. Willingham's team had already done that. His desire for unity extended beyond just the team. It applied to the students, alums, and subway alums. As he would point out throughout the season, his team didn't always *execute* properly, but they always played together. And right then, in the heat of a physical game against a hated rival, with a thundering soundtrack provided by Tchaikovsky and the students wearing green, Willingham's primary directive had come to life — "There should be one voice, one mind, and one goal."

The immediate goal was to score another touchdown. Notre Dame lined up to receive the kickoff, and Battle fielded the ball and gutted out a modest 16 yards. Then they drove the field in five plays, the biggest play coming on first-and-15, from the Michigan 49-yard line.

Holiday took a five-step drop. Split 10 yards from the Michigan sideline, Omar Jenkins took off and headed toward the Notre Dame sideline. Holiday reared back and threw. As Jenkins crossed midfield, he did something a punt returner normally does. The man covering Jenkins, safety Cato June, one of the fastest players on the Michigan team, was closing on him. But briefly calculating the distance between himself and the defender *and* himself and the sideline, Jenkins slightly turned his head. Seeing that June was still a yard away, Jenkins looked up, found the ball, made the catch, and kept his feet in bounds at the two-yard line.

Two plays later, Ryan Grant burst off the right tackle and into the end zone, and Notre Dame was winning again.

They kept winning because Shane Walton kept making plays.

With a little more than three minutes left and trailing 25–17, Michigan had driven the ball down to the Notre Dame eight-yard line. On third down, quarterback John Navarre fired a strike to his tight end Bennie Joppru, who had run a slant right in front of Irish linebacker Courtney Watson in the end zone. Just like that, it was 25–23, and Michigan went for the two-point conversion and the tie. They set up for the conversion with receivers B. J. Askew and Braylon Edwards lined up on the same side. Kent Baer, the Irish defensive coordinator, spoke into his headset, discussing the deal with Trent Walters, the secondary coach.

"What do you want to do?" asked Baer.

"Let's go zone," he replied.

"You sure?"

"Yeah, zone it," said Walters.

They lined up in cover two, with Walton and nickelback Preston Jackson set up between the receivers. They'd shown this formation before, but in a bracket coverage. On two occasions, Michigan had sent a man in motion, close to the formation, making it harder to double-team the receiver because the two defenders were so far apart. But on the five-yard line, that wasn't a problem.

Walton lined up between the two receivers, in a place where he could easily cover his zone. Navarre dropped back but didn't really disguise where he was going to throw, giving Walton a chance to read his eyes. When Edwards ran inside and tried to spin back out to the flat, Walton easily burst to his left, stuck out his left hand, and knocked the ball down. He sprinted to midfield, his teammates chasing him, trying to congratulate him.

But the celebration was short-lived. After failing to run out the clock on their next possession, Notre Dame had to punt. Once again, they had failed to put away an opponent. With 1:25 left on the clock, 72 yards separated Michigan from the winning field goal. Willingham walked up to Carlyle Holiday on the sideline and, over the din of the crowd and the band, told him, "When we get the ball back, kneel."

With 22 seconds left, Michigan had advanced to midfield. But Shane Walton, on a pass deflected by Cedric Hilliard, plucked the ball from the air for his fourth pick of the season, bolted a few yards upfield, and did a little hook slide to end the play.

After he took the snap, Holiday kneeled.

A second after Holiday's knee hit the turf, something happened. The student section, in the single-minded way of lemmings, began to furiously spill onto the field. They jumped over the pale brick wall, each one more reckless than the last. The security guards quickly gave up trying to keep the students in the stands. It was tradition to storm the field after a big win, a *significant* win, and everyone in the house knew that this game was special. They had been starving for something to celebrate, and Willingham's first win over Michigan was like manna from heaven.

A round heavyset blond girl nearly came out of her jeans as she stumbled onto the turf. Underneath the goalpost, a small wiry black kid had ripped off his shirt, exposing his bony chest and ribs, and sat precariously on the shoulders of his classmates, waving his shirt over his head. The students, all of them wearing the green shirts, meshed with the players in a frenzied circle. A diminutive brown-haired girl ran up to defensive tackle Ryan Roberts and hugged him; inside linebacker Mike Goolsby hugged his coach, Bob Simmons; and Shane Walton did a Jim Valvano impression, running around looking for someone to embrace.

Done with his postgame interview with NBC announcer Lewis Johnson, Tyrone Willingham found himself in the wrong place. He was standing at ground zero of a bona fide revival. It was a revival that he had deftly and thoughtfully orchestrated, but when it threatened to physically engulf him, he froze. His face was, as usual, placid, but his thoughts were panicked. *Help!* he thought. He saw an opening in the tunnel and took off, sprinting just ahead of the crowd.

At about 5:30, the students began to exit the stadium through the same tunnel the team had. As they made their way up the ramp, the students serenaded themselves with a chant of "Here come the Irish! Here come the Irish!" Near the top of the tunnel, inside the bowels of the stadium, with the drumbeat bouncing off the walls, their chant was deafening. At a little after 6:00, when Lloyd Carr came from his postgame interview, his face worn, ashen, and beaten, the students were still going and still chanting as he waded across the river of kids.

Afterward, Willingham, his Oakley shades resting atop his head, was pleased. "It was great to beat those guys," he said. He hadn't seen what happened as the two teams ran into the tunnel at halftime, but he was fully expecting Carr to tell him about it sometime the following week.

"Oh, he'll call me," said Willingham. "And probably tell me to do something with my team. But you know, my guys weren't even doing anything."

Nothing but winning.

8

MICHIGAN STATE

IN 1973, THERE WEREN'T a whole lot of big-name schools looking for quarterbacks who stood 5'7" and tipped the scales at a buck forty — let alone *black* quarterbacks of that size. And they sure weren't roaming around Jacksonville, North Carolina. Though not one recruiter found his way to the Willingham living room, and not one school offered him a scholarship, he still considered playing Division I football a realistic dream. Willingham sat down and mailed 100 handwritten letters to colleges, asking for the chance to try out for the team as a walk-on. Only two wrote back — Toledo and Michigan State.

Why Tyrone Willingham chose Michigan State in the fall of 1973 was equal parts pragmatic reasoning and the magnetic pull of some powerful social and cosmic forces. One reason was that the Michigan State program had a good reputation for its treatment of walk-ons. "Unless you were just so bad that you made everyone wish you'd leave, they treated you pretty well," said Willingham.

Another reason was the 5,000 black students on campus. "That was more black people than some *black* colleges had at the time," said Willingham. "When I first got to East Lansing, I was *country*. There were more people on campus than in my whole hometown."

But the one element that not only lured him to East Lansing

but also brought Willingham's collegiate experience full circle was the splendid legacy of Jimmy Raye.

In 1964, Raye had been the first black quarterback in Michigan State history. But even more significant was that he'd been the quarterback for the second-ranked Spartans team, coached by Duffy Daugherty, that played in the most memorable game in school history. It was the famous 10–10 tie in the 1966 season — against top-ranked Notre Dame. To this day, college football purists still refer to the low-scoring, brutally violent contest as the greatest college football game ever played. That was also the day when Ara Parseghian made perhaps the most hotly debated decision of not only his career but also Irish history.

With 1:24 left in the game, Notre Dame had the ball on its own 36-yard line. There were two timeouts left, but rather than try to throw the ball downfield to get in a position to score, Parseghian elected to run the ball four straight times. When he did attempt to throw, quarterback Coley O'Brien (who had replaced an injured Terry Hanratty) was sacked by Michigan State defensive end Bubba Smith. It was second-and-17 when the clock ran out.

Of course, Parseghian was vilified for his decision to play for a tie, but only for that week. The following Saturday, after Notre Dame beat USC 51–0, Notre Dame was named No. 1.

But around North Carolina, especially for 13-year-old Willingham, the legend of Jimmy Raye eclipsed Notre Dame's title. That Raye had grown up in Fayetteville, North Carolina, about 80 miles from Willingham's hometown, gave Raye legendary status around the state. "There weren't too many people who *didn't* know of Jimmy Raye," said Willingham.

Willingham's legacy as a player would never be as great or as distinguished as Raye's. He had some success though. A physical education major, he received the Big Ten Medal of Honor as the best scholar-athlete in the league during his junior year. By the time he graduated, he'd received three letters in both football and baseball.

Whereas Jimmy Raye had trailblazed a path for the black quarterback, Willingham found himself the latest in a long line of black ex-quarterbacks. Ironically, Willingham's arrival to East

Lansing coincided with the arrival of Charlie Baggett — the second black quarterback in MSU history.

When Baggett was injured, Willingham actually started four games as a freshman in the 1973 season, winning three of them. He was only 10 of 19 for 124 yards and a touchdown, but the worst part wasn't his three interceptions. No, the worst part came his senior year, when new Spartans coach Darryl Rogers, who had replaced the retired Dennis Stoltz, moved Willingham from quarterback to receiver and kick returner.

But Willingham handled it like he handled all things — with dignity. And Rogers, rather than defending his decision, praised Willingham instead. "I never had to worry about how Tyrone was going to react to the move," said Rogers. "A lot of guys, as seniors, would have had problems with that. Not Tyrone. The team was always first. He just wanted to help however he could."

Willingham's character was evidenced by his resolve to perform under any circumstance. The Michigan State players, led by Baggett, made a pact to all run wind sprints without giving their best effort. To prevent the coaches from catching on, everyone agreed to run together. Well, almost everyone.

"Ty wouldn't do it," said Baggett, now the receivers coach for the Minnesota Vikings. "He'd be out in front, and the coaches knew he wasn't the fastest guy on the team. We'd tell him to slow down, but he wouldn't. He'd look at us like we were crazy."

Several years later, when Darryl Rogers was the head coach at Arizona State, he offered Willingham a job on his staff. But in 1980, Willingham had returned to Michigan State to coach the secondary and special teams. He declined the offer, and his reason for spurning Rogers would become the foundation for his coaching career. "I believe in loyalty," he said.

Actually, loyalty is a difficult virtue to maintain in the coaching profession because one can only gain experience and knowledge by exposing oneself to a variety of programs. As coach of the secondary, receivers, running backs, and special teams, Willingham broke his career as an assistant coach into three-year tenures at Michigan State, North Carolina State, Rice, Stanford, and the Minnesota Vikings. But only one of those tenures ended badly — and even then, Willingham put a positive spin on it.

After the 1985 season, in which the Wolfpack finished 3–8, head coach Tom Reed resigned from North Carolina State. Still, Willingham said, "It was a good experience. I was around some good people there. But obviously we didn't win as many games as we wanted to, or needed to. But it was a very positive experience."

That was also the first and only time Willingham was out of work for an extended period of time. But it did nothing to unravel his passion for the profession.

"I've never had those doubts," he said. "Now my wife probably has. When you're unemployed, she's asking, 'Where's the bread coming from? We got to eat.' But your spouse questions that more than you do. It was only a month or two, but it did seem like an eternity."

Willingham's next job, coaching receivers at Rice, coincided with one of his greatest opportunities. In 1987, 49ers coach Bill Walsh established the National Football League's first Minority Coaching Fellowship program. The summer of 1988, at the 49ers training camp, Willingham, along with Cal State Fullerton offensive coordinator Jerry Brown, enjoyed a 49ers fellowship that provided room, board, a car, and several weeks of personal involvement with 49ers coaches.

That was the summer Willingham met Dennis Green. Green, who was then the 49ers receivers coach, was taken by Willingham's charismatic presence. "I was immediately impressed," said Green. "Ty is an extremely demanding coach. He's concerned with more than his own goals. He's one who knows how to help players reach their own goals."

Willingham was similarly impressed by Green's commanding presence — and Tyrone Willingham isn't very easily impressed by *anyone*. Although Green didn't have a great record as head coach at Northwestern, his experience made him the dean of black football coaches. "Denny has a clear vision of what he wants his program to be and his players to be," said Willingham. "And he has a way of communicating, of conveying that vision to everyone in and around the program." It was just what Willingham would strive to do when he became a head coach.

The following year, after the 49ers won the Super Bowl, Green was named head coach at Stanford. Green immediately put Tyrone Willingham in charge of the Stanford running backs. Willingham's loyalty extended beyond the programs he chose to the people he cared about; he would follow Green to his next job, with the Minnesota Vikings.

And in 1999, when Michigan State, his alma mater, was looking for a head coach, both kinds of loyalty were in play when Willingham turned down the offer. "I have a wonderful job here at Stanford," he said. But it turned out to be a good thing that Willingham stayed put. Had he taken that job, it could have possibly closed the door on another black coach in the Division I-A ranks.

Willingham remained in Palo Alto, and his good friend Bobby Williams, at the time Michigan State's associate head coach, got the job in East Lansing.

On Monday night, five days before his return to East Lansing to play his alma mater, Willingham found on his desk a short story on the BCS. It stated that because Notre Dame's first game of the year, against Maryland, was technically considered part of the preseason, it didn't count in the BCS standings. That meant Notre Dame had to win seven more games, rather than six, to be eligible for a BCS bowl game.

Willingham looked annoyed as he squinted at the paper. "Oh, when there's no story, you just make one up," he said. He shrugged and tossed it aside. "So I guess our goal is clarified then."

This was the week of the one game on Notre Dame's schedule that would turn the focus from football to race. With Michigan State being coached by his good buddy Bobby Williams, Willingham knew what all the talk would be about. "Of course there will be two African-Americans going against each other," he said matter-of-factly. "And it's my first time back since I coached there. Yeah, it's an exciting atmosphere, but you know the goal."

The week before, Michigan State, a team that featured the most explosive receiver in the country in Charlie Rogers, had their butts kicked 46–22 by California — at home. But Willingham was all too familiar with the mind-set of any team preparing to play Notre Dame. After all, he had seen the view from the other side.

"Oh, we won't see *that* team," he said. "We'll see the one that's been told that in order to be an All-America you have to play well against Michigan, Ohio State, and Notre Dame. I know this because it's what I was told as a player. So I *know* Bobby is telling them that now." Nodding his head and briefly conceding that this was a battle between two competitive black men, he smirked and couldn't contain a laugh when he infused a little black colloquialism to his enthusiasm: "Oh, it's gonna be *on.*"

His mood changed when the topic switched to the student-athlete ideal. Because his parents had been teachers, he deeply valued education. But when he got to Michigan State, he was suddenly surrounded by young black men who hadn't been taught the same things he had. He saw guys who were content to play ball and go through the motions in class. It was then that he realized a one-dimensional coach had the power to enable one-dimensional athletes.

"You have to look at these guys as people, not just athletes," he said. "There are more black men in prison than in college." He stared ahead, driving home the point that this sobering reality disgusted him.

"There are always two people at fault," he said. "The system and the individual." By sticking to his guns as a private, God-fearing man, Willingham had already established himself as the most visible component of the "system." As such, he was in a position to directly influence the performance of his players. While he was in charge, Willingham would do all he could to ensure that none of the Notre Dame players wasted their opportunities the way some of his teammates had done while he was a student-athlete at Michigan State.

"I remember guys would play cards, bid whisk, spades, go to lunch, go to practice, and come back and repeat the process. Then they'd flunk out of school. What are you gonna do with that? I mean, you have no skills. No skills! What are you gonna do?

"There was one guy when I was coaching there who I think was dyslexic. When you told him to raise his right hand, he'd do this" — Willingham raised his left hand, then continued — "but he really wanted to graduate. You know what he did? He graduated. He had a problem and he graduated. The other guys, who didn't have a problem, they didn't graduate." He sat silent, staring for another several seconds. "The system . . . and the individual."

The next morning, at his weekly press conference, Willingham kept his fire under wraps. He strolled in, wearing a tie and a dark blazer, and assumed his normal stance at the WNDU news desk. This week, more than any other, his blackness made him and Notre Dame the center of attention. Well, that and the fact that he once played at Michigan State and that the Irish owned a five-game losing streak against the Spartans.

After Associate Athletic Director John Heisler did his dry rendition of "*Heeeere's* Tyrone," Willingham sat down, folded his arms, and leaned onto the desk, not so much awaiting the first question as *daring* someone to ask it. For several seconds, there was silence.

It was silent because everyone knew what was coming. Everyone knew that Michigan State was coached by Bobby Williams and that on Saturday, exactly one half of the total number of black coaches in the NCAA would be on the field at Spartan Stadium. They knew that Willingham was purposefully vague and reluctant on the topic of race, but they didn't really know why.

Willingham's technique for dealing with race has mirrored Bill Cosby's approach throughout his career. Cosby's comedy was nothing like Richard Pryor's or Redd Foxx's. In standup shows that focused on everything from parenthood to drinking, he never did anything to set himself apart from a white audience. His material was always heavy on human interest and light on *blackness.* It was significant that comedy was the vehicle of Cosby's message because even if he did tackle race, it could be addressed in a manner that was nonthreatening, always inclusive, and rarely divisive — thus the success and subsequent criticism of *The Cosby Show.*

Black people cried that the show wasn't "black enough," and that because of that, the characters weren't "believable." But the Huxtables offered an alternative to the standard black TV character. They offered a household full of smart, loving people who faced the same trials any upper-middle-class family would. The people who lived in the house just "happened to be black."

One of the few times the show dealt overtly with race was in an episode that aired on or about the day the country celebrated Martin Luther King Jr.'s birthday. And even that episode was handled with subtle brilliance. The TV was on, and Dr. King's voice echoed throughout the living room. Rudy, the youngest child, was sitting by herself on the sofa, trying to make sense of the words. Slowly, one by one, each member of the family came in and joined her on the couch. The scene ended without any-one on the sofa saying a word. All the audience heard were the haunting words of King's "I Have a Dream" speech. When it came to the topic of race, Cosby let the most powerful voice of all speak on his bchalf.

Throughout his 25-year coaching career, whenever the topic of race was raised, Tyrone Willingham had tried to let wins and losses tell his story. When you're a highly visiblc black man, what-ever your message, it has to be delivered in a way that doesn't necessarily make people forget that you're black, but that always steers the focus away from it. Since his job each week was to pre-pare his team for a football game, Willingham wanted to make it clear that, regardless of race, he was just like every other coach in America. The South Bend media had already grown weary of hearing him say, "My only goal is to win," often rolling their eyes in anticipation of it.

But on Tuesday morning, as he awaited that first question, he knew the topic wouldn't be winning. He knew it would center on Bobby Williams. A writer from the Associated Press stood up: "Coach, it seems like you're avoiding the issue of race."

Willingham, remaining calm, addressed him. "Oh, to be very honest about it, I don't think I've ever avoided the issue. I think I've put it into perspective of the way I view it, which may be less than some others look at it."

With that statement, that brief address on a potentially volatile topic, Willingham reeled in the conversation and deftly steered it back to thc game.

It was fitting that the story line for Michigan State week was about refocusing because after Tuesday's practice, the team sorely needed to do just that. About two thirds of the way into the workout, Willingham blew his whistle and brought the team to the middle of the field. He reminded them that they needed to rededicate themselves to the task at hand.

The next day, the coaches went the extra mile to ensure that the team had life. Buzz Preston walked up and down the row of stretched-out players, filling the air with playful yet encouraging words. "What's up, Jay Sapp?" he said to Jason Sapp, a defensive tackle. And to defensive tackle Ryan Roberts, he shouted, "What's up, big booty? Heard you strained a hamstring!" He walked over to Carlyle Holiday and shouted, "What's up, Doc Holiday!" It got a giggle from the normally reserved Holiday. In typical hands-on fashion, even Willingham lent himself to the effort of re-energizing a tired team. "Oh, I see some wiggle there," he shouted as they sprang to their feet after stretching.

Wednesday and Thursday's practices were much better, and on Thursday afternoon Willingham was in a good mood. After his daily address to the media, he lingered outside the stadium, speaking to reporters for another 20 minutes. After someone asked him if he remembered his stats as a kickoff returner, he told him, "I don't really keep up with that. I told you, I'm not one to reminisce about the past."

But the past must have been on his mind a minute later as he silently pried a wad of pink bubble gum from the stadium wall. With his fist, he absentmindedly rolled it around on the brick surface. Lightly pounding the gum back into the wall, he reminded himself of his objective. "We've *got . . . to . . . beat . . . Michigan State*," he said.

It was the first time all year that Willingham had allowed himself to be so open about wanting to beat a particular opponent. Whereas the game against Michigan had been a big one because of the history between the schools, this one was meaningful because of the social and personal ramifications. For Willingham, it was the biggest game yet.

On September 21, 2002, Tyrone Willingham made it back to his alma mater. He and his team came to remedy the longest losing streak in the series since Michigan State won eight games from 1955 to 1963. But there was more than just that.

It was as though the game couldn't be contained to the field. There were exactly 10 yards between the field of play and a big concrete wall. The players were cramped, and the area for the coaches to roam up and down the sideline was virtually nonexistent. About an hour before kickoff, Willingham walked out with his son, Nathaniel, and sat down on one of the narrow wooden benches. Never one to dwell on the past, he had remarked to a friend that "a little meditation is good." That was one of his rules. That's why he seldom spoke about the past, and only when pressed for details would he reluctantly provide sketchy examples. But there was a lot to reflect on that day.

On the team bus to the stadium that morning, Willingham had sat in the front seat and reflected on his journey there. He thought about the day he, his brother and sisters, and his parents had piled into the Buick and driven to East Lansing from North Carolina 29 years earlier. As the bus rolled past Kalamazoo Stadium, he thought about having committed 20 errors in 20 games in one season on the baseball team. But once inside the football stadium, he didn't want to dwell on anything for too long. So for all of one minute and 12 seconds, he sat next to Nathaniel in silent meditation. Then, as if snapping himself from a trance, he sprang to his feet and briskly walked to midfield to meet with the officials.

The first offensive series of the game served two purposes. First, the Irish proved that they could score on the opening drive, just as they had against Michigan. Second, they gave their next opponent, Stanford, something to think about when they watched the film. On a first down, Carlyle Holiday handed off to Arnaz Battle on a reverse, and Battle, showing his quarterback skills, threw downfield to Holiday. It was a play called Cardinal Special, a play that Bill Diedrick, while at Stanford, had run against Notre Dame the previous year. With Stanford as their next opponent, there was little doubt why they ran it on the opening drive. It's just common practice among coaches to give their next opponent something to ponder.

Battle's pass looked as though it would sail over Holiday's head and into the turf. But proving that his athletic gifts transcended just running, Holiday stretched out and snatched the ball for a 30-yard gain. Three plays later, Ryan Grant walked in from six yards out for his third touchdown of the year to give Notre Dame a quick 7–0 lead.

But after that series, the offense seemed out of sync. The fullbacks didn't attack the backers on running plays, and the tailbacks just weren't explosive. With each game, Ryan Grant had gained more confidence and run with a greater sense of purpose. But there were still times when he hesitated to hit a crease. So Buzz Preston stayed on him. "Come on," Preston told Grant, "you've got to *believe* when you hit that hole."

Perhaps the reason the game was so sloppy was that there were just too many emotional subplots, which manifested themselves in several crucial moments. Whenever that's the case, it's virtually impossible to maintain the delicate balance between heart and mind.

That's exactly what happened when Rhema McKnight mixed it up with Spartans cornerback Cedrick Henry. It was a running play in which McKnight had to block Henry, and after the play was over, neither of them wanted to let the other one have the last lick. McKnight slapped Henry upside the head, and both received 15-yard penalties. McKnight was immediately pulled from the game, and he walked to the sideline. If there was anything that went against the philosophy of a Tyrone Willingham football team, it was fighting in a game. "Whenever that happens," said Willingham, "it means you're putting yourself ahead of the team."

The offensive coaches, Diedrick, Trent Miles, and Preston, were so infuriated with McKnight that they were late signaling in the next call. "What were you thinking!" screamed Miles. Holiday waited in front of the huddle as the play clock ran, but by the time Diedrick sent the signal, it was too late and Holiday had called timeout.

In McKnight's defense, the Spartans' defensive backs had made extracurricular activity a priority all day. Normally, Omar Jenkins was as cool as a fan. But throughout the game, he was involved in shoving matches with Michigan State defenders. In the third quarter, when Holiday was pushed out of bounds on the Notre Dame sideline, cornerback Preston Jackson screamed at the defender and had to be restrained by teammates.

With 11 seconds left in the second quarter, the offense rediscovered its rhythm when Holiday found freshman Maurice Stovall on a seam route. On second-and-10 from the 15-yard line, Stovall got a step on the corner, then used his 6′5″ frame to shield the ball. It was the polished move of a veteran receiver. That made it 14–3, and it looked as though Notre Dame had taken control of the game.

But at 3:19 in the third quarter, the team's momentum ceased, and things looked bleak. That was when the offense ran a play the offensive coaches had put in earlier that week. While they were actively developing Holiday as a passer, his skills as a runner were just too hard to ignore. So they inserted a quarterback sweep, in which Holiday, behind a block from the fullback on the safety, was supposed to get to the edge and go one-on-one with the corner.

But on third-and-two, Rashon Powers-Neal and Jordan Black blocked the defensive end, leaving Holiday alone with Michigan State safety Jason Harmon. As Harmon rode Holiday out of bounds, Holiday landed on his left shoulder — *hard*. He didn't lie on the ground for long, so Willingham and the rest of his staff weren't particularly concerned.

Why should they be? Holiday was as physically tough as anyone on the team. In the games against Purdue and Michigan, he had taken more than a dozen hard shots from each team. His toughness had already been well documented by the harshest of critics. Jordan Black, during winter conditioning, openly marveled at how hard Holiday attacked weight-training sessions.

But as he came to the sideline, it was fairly apparent that Holiday wasn't going back into the game anytime soon. For the first time that season, the lack of depth at quarterback was suddenly an issue. Chris Olsen wasn't ready to play, and Holiday's backup, Pat Dillingham, had absolutely no game experience.

As trainer Jim Russ sat Holiday down on the end of the bench and began to remove his shoulder pads, Nicholas Setta was lining up to kick a 39-yard field goal. After the usually reliable Setta missed the attempt, Notre Dame still led by 11 points, but the feeling on the sideline was panic as well as concern at having lost Holiday. Willingham watched stoically from the sideline. Directly behind him, Pat Dillingham warmed up, ready to see the first action of his career.

That was about the time Michigan State receiver Charles Rogers decided it was time to get busy. Rogers was a Heisman Trophy candidate and easily the best receiver in the nation. He was tall, 6'4", rail thin at 190 pounds, and had legitimate 4.2 speed. It was the kind of package that begged for Randy Moss comparisons. But Irish fans were well aware of him because the year before he had beaten them after he caught a pass, ran through Vontez Duff's tackle, and took the ball to the end zone.

But he hadn't done much in this game. Safeties Glenn Earl and Gerome Sapp had created such a presence in the middle of the field that when Rogers had ventured there, he had done so cautiously, dropping a pair of catchable balls in the process. But on Michigan State's first drive of the fourth quarter, Rogers blasted upfield, running by a double-team, and caught a 38-yard touchdown, bringing the Spartans within four points. Then, with less than six minutes left in the game and Notre Dame leading 14–10, Rogers declared ownership of the field, the game, and the Notre Dame secondary.

On first down, from the Michigan State three-yard line, Vontez Duff had Rogers cut off down the sideline, but Rogers, while hovering, torqued his torso and reached down, behind, and over Duff to pluck the ball off the small of Duff's back. Four plays later, Spartans quarterback Jeff Smoker hit Rogers on a 17-yarder in the middle of the field for another first down. Feeling the crowd, feeling the offensive rhythm, and feeling himself, Rogers stood up, stared at Gerome Sapp, and ferociously banged his heart. Then, five plays later, after a sack by Justin Tuck and a false start temporarily halted the Spartans' momentum, Rogers got truly Heisman on their asses.

With 1:45 left in the game, on fourth-and-11, Shane Walton and Sapp had Rogers in bracket coverage. Walton had him to the outside, and Sapp had the deep middle. But when Smoker started scrambling, Sapp's attention went to the tight end, who was running a shallow crossing route in the middle of the field. That's all Rogers needed.

While Sapp crept toward the middle of the field, sensing the chance for a pick, or at the very least a big hit, he lost sight of Rogers, who drifted toward the back of the end zone. Walton still maintained perfect position on Rogers's shoulder, but there was no way he was going to reach the ball from there.

Smoker's throw was so high that the ball looked as though it might actually hit the crossbar of the goalposts. But with Walton draped on his shoulder, Rogers rose, and like a long, black, lanky hawk, he plucked the ball from the air and floated gingerly back to Earth. But before he rolled out of the end zone, he had the presence of mind to lightly drag his right foot through the colored grass. Touchdown.

Walton rolled helplessly out of the end zone and then bounced to his feet to see what had happened. Sapp, Glenn Earl, and Courtney Watson circled the ref and argued that Rogers had landed out of bounds. Walton ran over to join them. But they argued only halfheartedly, the way one argues when he knows something bad has happened but is powerless to change it. Michigan State had gone ahead 17–14.

With 1:41 left, Notre Dame fans across the country groaned. How could their team lose to Michigan State for the sixth year in a row when they had just bested powerhouse Michigan? It felt like a recurring nightmare.

On the sideline, Pat Dillingham prepared to go back in. His last throw, with just under six minutes left in the game, had ended up in the hands of Spartans safety Thomas Wright. When Dillingham came to the sideline after that interception, Willingham told him not to worry, that the pick was just like a punt in that it pinned the Spartans on the three-yard line. But after Michigan State had gone 97 yards, Charles Rogers had made his seventh reception of the game, and the Spartans had taken the lead, Willingham's rationalization lost its currency.

But as he jogged out to the field, Dillingham looked carefree and cool. Why shouldn't he? He was Michael Dillingham's kid. His pop was the orthopedic surgeon for both Stanford and the

San Francisco 49ers. Hell, Dad's scalpel had sliced into the sacred flesh of both Joe Montana and Steve Young, prolonging the careers of two Bay Area bona fide demigods. If he had chosen to, Pat Dillingham could have ridden the wave of "advantage" that surely accompanies such an impressive pedigree. But he didn't.

Having grown up in the affluent hills of Portola Valley, about two miles from the Stanford campus, Dillingham attended St. Francis High School and was classmates with Cassidy Willingham, his coach's daughter. He had been a star quarterback at St. Francis, but after his final football season, the big school recruiters weren't offering him scholarships. Determined to be his own man, Dillingham bolted the Bay Area and headed to Notre Dame, where he assumed the title and role of walk-on. His bald head, accentuated by short black stubble, combined with his pale blue eyes and slender pink legs made him look even younger than his 19 years.

At 1:41, Dillingham got under the center and went to work. All he needed was something easy and high-percentage to get things going.

Diedrick had him hit Gary Godsey for a six-yard curl on first down. On the next play, Dillingham tried to hit Maurice Stovall on a slant, but he had stared him down and the play was broken up by the cornerback. But an interference call gave the Irish another first down. After Dillingham underthrew Arnaz Battle, Diedrick went right back to the playmaker. From day one, and especially in the past two weeks, Diedrick and staff had tried to make Battle the focal point of the attack.

On second-and-10, with 1:15 left, the corner lined up in bump-and-run position, so Battle prepared to run a fade. But then he noticed the strong safety creeping down into the tackle box, preparing to blitz. With that void created by the safety, Battle changed his route to a slant and hoped Dillingham had seen the same thing.

He had. Battle caught the ball in front of the corner and took a step upfield, causing the cornerback and the safety to collide. Then he accelerated. He glided down the sideline, not really pulling away *from* anyone. There was no one there. Instead, he was running *toward* something — toward his first touchdown of the season, toward credibility as a big-play receiver and validation as Notre Dame's playmaker. He ran with a swaybacked stride, his head erect and torso tight, with feet just scraping the ground, the profile of someone riding a bike. His 60-yard sprint completed, and with the score 21–17 and 1:09 left, it looked as though the game was over.

On the sideline, with the Notre Dame players going wild, Willingham appeared calm. Actually, it was the first time all day he had allowed himself to relax. The day had been emotional, and he had been uncharacteristically animated. How could he not be? This was his alma mater and the field where a self-proclaimed country brother got his first chance to run things, and with his good friend Bobby Williams across the sideline, there were some seriously strong emotional undercurrents that day. At one point in the first half, Willingham had even sacrificed some cool points when he got a sideline warning for walking onto the field to protest a call. And now, after his guys had taken another step toward establishing themselves as a legitimate team, Willingham was still emotional. But the Spartans still had one last chance.

After the kickoff, Smoker hit running back Dawan Moss for seven yards; then he hit receiver Eric Knott for 11. But after Smoker completed another seven-yard throw, he was sacked by Irish defensive end Ryan Roberts. On third down, Smoker was looking for Charles Rogers. He heaved the ball downfield one last time, but Rogers, who was bracketed by Gerome Sapp and Glenn Earl, had no shot at the ball.

Sapp came down with the ball, and Willingham calmly, slowly, and methodically removed his headset and sipped some water from his Gatorade cup. The game ended 21–17 and, to the relief of Notre Dame fans, so ended the Michigan State curse.

As Battle jogged past him, Willingham pulled him aside. He leaned close and said, "I knew, when it was time, you would step up. I never stopped believing in you."

A few minutes later, as ABC announcer Jack Arute interviewed him, Willingham motioned for Arnaz Battle to join him.

"I want everyone in the nation to see this man," he said. "He's a battler and a champion." As they walked toward the locker room, Willingham said, "You were a great example today." Battle, physically tired and emotionally spent, whispered, "Yes, sir."

Afterward, Willingham addressed the media. "If we win every game like this, I know it creates a little more heartache for a lot of people, but I'll take thirteen like that," said Willingham.

A few feet away, Arnaz Battle spoke to a small group of reporters. With his slow bayou drawl, he confirmed that this year's team bore no resemblance to the 2001 team. "The difference is, we used to lose games like this," Battle said. "Now we're finding a way to win games like this."

On Sunday morning, Buzz Preston was well into the fourth quarter of the game tape. "Oooh," he said as Ryan Grant missed an opening on a dive. "If I can just get him to believe, he'll hit that and be gone."

A few minutes later, having just watched the film, Trent Miles walked into Preston's office. Miles had a big grin on his face, and Preston immediately knew it was because of Maurice Stovall's touchdown in the second quarter.

"Looks like big man is getting some confidence," said Preston.

"And I ain't mad at him because of it," said Miles.

"Your boy is gonna be all right if you don't screw him up!" Preston joked.

Sunday mornings after a game, the coaches' office took on the air of a gossip circle. The consummate workaholic, secondary coach Trent Walters usually arrived first, at about 8:00 A.M., to start grading tape, and Buzz Preston would arrive a half-hour later. Over the next hour, the other coaches would trickle in, each preparing to watch the game tape. Often, as they watched, one would see something that either excited or bothered him, and with the idea fresh in his mind, he'd run to another coach's office with a question or comment about a specific play. On that particular Sunday morning, there was one consensus topic — the play that led to Carlyle Holiday's injury.

Bill Diedrick poked his head in the door. "How far are you into it?" he asked.

"I'm just about done," said Preston, fully aware why Diedrick was asking. He turned down the stereo, temporarily muzzling a crooning Al Jarreau.

"How did it look?" asked Diedrick.

"You really couldn't see it from this angle," said Preston.

Diedrick solemnly nodded and walked into his office next door. Preston had watched the play over and over. As Holiday glided toward the sideline, he would slow down the tape. "Right *there*," he said. He could just barely see where Holiday went out of bounds. Just then, offensive line coach John McDonell came in and stood by the door.

"That was my bright idea," McDonell said with a sheepish smile. Like Preston, McDonell was also a former offensive coordinator. And like all the members of the staff, he was free to provide input on the game plan. He tried to joke about this particular idea, but he wasn't convincing himself.

"Slow it down again," he said. He watched, squinting, unable to see the end of the play, just able to see that Rashon Powers-Neal hadn't blocked the right guy. Players make mistakes. But in this case, McDonell and the rest of the offensive staff felt as though they hadn't given their guys enough time to work on that particular play. Shaking his head, McDonell walked silently back to his office.

A minute later, the mood brightened when Trent Walters came bounding into the room, holding a piece of paper. "Look, we're at number ten," he said. Without looking away from the screen, Preston smiled. They were a Top 10 team, and even though they still had miles to go before they were a polished team, their current standing was a source of pride. "From nowhere to tenth in the nation in four weeks," said Walters.

A few minutes later, as he began watching the kickoff return team, Preston wondered aloud about Bobby Williams. "The fire birds are out in East Lansing," he said. "Yeah, they've lost two in a row, and they're struggling." He fell silent for a moment. The black coach's community is a particularly small one, and although they competed against one another, no one likes to see another coach get the ax. But Preston knew the reality.

So did Willingham. But ever practical, Willingham was relieved to have such an emotional game behind him and to be 4–0. Later that afternoon, as he and Bob Simmons walked over to the stadium for the team meeting, he tried to joke about having won a game in the last second like that over his good friend. "Better we feel bad for Bobby" — he sighed — "than Bobby feel bad for us."

But no one was joking in November. Two days after a 49–3 loss to Michigan dropped the Spartans to 3–6, Bobby Williams was fired. In his office, Willingham, who remarked on many an occasion that he wasn't a phone person, sighed when he said, "I'll have to give him a call."

9

STANFORD

O N SUNDAY, SEPTEMBER 15, Trent Walters was hunched over his laptop, watching game tape and dishing out grades. On the 20-inch television behind him, the Indianapolis Colts were trailing the Miami Dolphins 21–13. While CBS announcer Solomon Wilcots chastised Colts running back Edgerrin James for failing to get out of bounds and stop the clock, Walters was trying to decide whether to give Shane Walton a minus for allowing a catch. The receiver outleaped Walton for the ball but came down out of bounds.

"How would you grade this?" Walters asked aloud. "He had good position and cut him off okay, but the guy still made the catch." Finally, he decided to give Walton a minus. *"Get some vertical!"* he wrote on his grade sheet. He laughed and distractedly whipped around to see what was happening on the TV behind him.

Walters was a huge Colts fan. Not just because he was a close friend of Indianapolis coach Tony Dungy, with whom he coached while the two were with the Minnesota Vikings, but because the kid who wore number 86 for the Colts just happened to be his son Troy. Just a few minutes earlier, when another Colts receiver left the game with a concussion, Troy went from kick returner to the third receiver in the Colts offense.

Troy Walters had been one of Willingham's most prolific

players during his seven-year tenure at Stanford. After catching 74 balls for 1,456 yards in 1999, he had won the Fred Biletnikoff Award as the nation's best receiver. The 1999 season, the year Stanford had gone to the Rose Bowl, had begun with Texas beating Stanford 69–17 in Austin. Like a lot of folks who spent any amount of quality time with Willingham, Troy insisted a substantial slice of the Willingham legend was carved from that afternoon. After the game, Willingham stood before the team in the locker room, and without hesitation, irony, doubt, or humor told them, "There's a champion in this room."

"That he could look at us, and after that game tell us that . . . that's easily my best memory," said Troy Walters. At 5'7" and 172 pounds, he had no business making it this far in the NFL, but Troy was entering his third NFL season mostly because he embodied the one concept endemic to any Willingham player — fight.

"Regardless of the situation you're in, he gives you a belief in yourself," said Troy. "And he cares about you not only as a player but as a person. Oh, he was definitely the most demanding coach I had, but demanding in a good way. You just want to play well for him. And that desire to please him goes beyond football."

At that moment, however, it was all about football for Troy's dad. The most difficult part of his job was trying to simultaneously grade game tape, watch the TV, and field calls from his wife, Gail, who would keep him updated throughout the day on their son's progress. Each time he left the office to consult another coach or to use the bathroom, he would sprint back in to call his wife. "What did I miss? What did he do?"

Walters stood about 5'6" and, in his mid-50s, still maintained the cut physique of a young man. He had once been a competitive bodybuilder — he won both the Mr. Indiana and the Mr. Louisville title — and he still trained feverishly. He had an easy smile, accentuated by a gold tooth, and was quick to tell you how proud he was of all of his kids. On his desk was a photo of him and Troy taken while he was the outside linebackers coach for the Vikings and Troy was a rookie receiver after being picked by the Vikings in the fifth round of the 2000 draft.

Like Willingham, Walters was a coach whose interest in his players extended beyond the field, simply because many of the kids he saw at work looked like the kids he saw at home. Walters's other kids, Trent, an advertising exec, and Vanessa, soon to graduate from the University of Washington School of Medicine, were also on the fast track to professional success. For a man like him, for whom successful kids are the norm and not the exception, it was harder to see a college football player as some mercenary on a four-year mission. Having raised three upwardly mobile professionals, Walters wasn't one of those coaches who would gladly bail a kid out of a holding cell on Friday just to get him on the field on Saturday.

A self-proclaimed workaholic, Walters was glad all of his children were grown now. He was always in a rush to get home when they were kids, but now he could take his time. He was routinely the first to arrive at the office and the last to leave.

He leaned forward to watch the TV. It was third-and-seven with 24 seconds to go. "Oh, don't throw it to that little man," said Walters facetiously. "He might mess around and score a touchdown on you!" A few minutes later, Troy caught a short pass and got out of bounds to stop the clock. From down the hall came shouts of "Get the ball to Troy" and "Come on, Troy!" A second later, offensive coordinator Bill Diedrick bounded into Walters's office. On his heels was Kent Baer, the defensive coordinator. "Of course the little kid from Stanford is smart enough to get out of bounds!" said Diedrick, laughing.

Diedrick had been Troy Walters's coach at Stanford in 1998 and 1999, and he and Baer came in to share the moment with his dad. They hadn't come in just to ease the tension of a nervous father — since they, too, had once coached Troy, they considered him one of *their* kids. The coaches watched as the Colts, with really poor clock management, failed to get off a play. The game ended 21–13, and Diedrick and Baer quickly filed out of the room and back to their offices. And Walters, disappointed by the outcome but pleased with the "little man's" effort, went back to grading tape.

*   *   *

On the Monday night of Stanford week, Willingham sat in his office watching another game tape. With just under 120 hours to go before his new team teed it up against his old one, Willingham was already wearing his game face. The tape he watched wasn't a coach's copy, which is shot with a wide lens and shows both the offense and the defense. It was the ABC copy, complete with commercials. "I like to watch the network copy first," he said. "I like to get a feel for what's going on, what the conditions are, what the announcers are saying."

On the screen, Stanford already trailed Arizona State by three touchdowns, and Willingham's mood was equal parts somber, contemplative, and just plain pissed. "I spent ten years at Stanford," said Willingham, without taking his eyes from the screen. "I recruited all of those guys. I've been in their homes and met their parents. Of course I have some ties there." He tried to joke about the story line for the week. "I guess I'm the one supposedly caught in the middle." He shrugged.

From an emotional standpoint, that was partially true. How could it not be? There was history between the coach and the school. There was a time when Stanford, like Notre Dame, hadn't even pondered the idea of a black head coach. That was odd because Stanford's reputation had never been tethered to conventional wisdom. In the late 70s, when Native American groups objected to the sports teams' "Indian" nickname and mascot, Stanford listened and renamed itself the Cardinal, a loose mockery of Harvard's Crimson moniker. But it wasn't until after the 1988 season that Stanford applied that unconventional wisdom to its football coach. Playing a key role in that process was a woman who would later become one of Tyrone Willingham's best friends — President George W. Bush's national security advisor, Condoleezza Rice.

Long before she advised the folks in the Pentagon about a new direction for Palestinian authority, Rice, a die-hard football fan who has long stated that her dream job would be NFL commissioner, played a pivotal role in redirecting the Stanford football program. In the winter of 1988, soon after head football coach Jack Elway was fired, Stanford's athletic director, Andy Geiger, put together a search committee. The committee consisted of Rice, a political science professor; Stanford baseball coach Mark Marquess; and several other professors. From the very start, Rice assumed leadership of the group.

Over a two-week period, each candidate was led into a small conference room in the Hoover Building on the Stanford campus. After each one was interviewed, Rice not only summed up their present positions but also, in almost every case, accurately predicted their futures. First was Dave Wannstedt, then the defensive coordinator at the University of Miami (Fla.). After fielding questions about who his staff would consist of and what his offensive and defensive philosophies would be, one of his final questions centered on the issue of classroom discipline. "What would you do if you found out one of your players was skipping class?" he was asked. Without hesitation, Wannstedt, well aware that he was on the campus of Stanford University and talking to a bunch of professors, answered, "Bench him."

Afterward, Rice was unimpressed by his response, though sympathetic to the reason behind it, and quickly foretold Wannstedt's future. "I think he was telling us what he thought we wanted to hear on that classroom issue," she said. "But he's definitely a pro coach." Several years later, after four years as the defensive coordinator for the Dallas Cowboys, Wannstedt became head coach of the Chicago Bears and later the Miami Dolphins.

Next was Pete Carroll, who was, at the time, a defensive back coach for the Minnesota Vikings. He regaled the group with a story about the most exciting game he had ever coached. It was while he was at the University of the Pacific, and the game had been decided in the final seconds. As Carroll related the story, he exuded an infectious energy that Rice said would make him a great college head coach one day.

Then there was Dennis Green. Having been the head coach at Northwestern and a Stanford assistant under Bill Walsh in the late 70s, Green was well versed in the Stanford tradition and well known by this group. In speaking about the university, he was forthright and focused, and commanded an instant respect. Roughly 15 seconds after Green had departed, Rice, looking first at Andy Geiger, then scanning the rest of the room, said with a smile, "I think we have our new coach." Two days later, Dennis Green became the first black head coach in Stanford history.

One of his first actions was to hire Tyrone Willingham to coach the running backs. Green had met Willingham while Willingham was part of the 49ers minority coaching program, and he had instantly noticed the young coach's intensity and discipline. After the 1991 season, when Green left Stanford to take over the Minnesota Vikings, he asked Willingham to join him. The man chosen to replace Green was none other than Bill Walsh, whose three Super Bowl rings made him a legend in the Bay Area.

In the winter of 1995, the legendary Bill Walsh announced his retirement. Condoleezza Rice, as she had back in 1988, suggested that Stanford athletic director Ted Leland at least explore the option of hiring another black head coach. Willingham's primary competition for the job was Chicago Bears offensive coordinator Ron Turner, along with Terry Shea, who was Stanford's offensive coordinator. Both men had a distinct advantage over Willingham. They had both been head coaches at San Jose State. On paper, either would have been a great choice.

At the time, Leland was looking for someone to inject energy and discipline into a program that was hungry for both. It didn't matter if the new coach had experience as a head coach or a coordinator. Leland needed someone to challenge the players, the fans, and the university. An aging Bill Walsh still maintained his mastery over offense, but Stanford needed a coach who could crawl up into his team's ass when necessary. They needed the kind of coach who could reach his team, the kind who could lead them not just by standing in front of them but while running alongside them. In 1995, Tyrone Willingham left his job coaching the Vikings running backs to become the second black head coach in Stanford history.

Willingham gazed solemnly at the television as Arizona State continued to whip his former Stanford team. He had hand-picked each one of the kids on the roster and had pushed them and molded them into a rare combination of top-level athletes with sincere academic interests. They were clean-cut, disciplined, and did nothing to tarnish the school's reputation.

The ABC camera highlighted offensive tackle Kwame Harris. At 6'7", 300 pounds, Harris was the Cardinal's best offensive lineman. He was said to be even better than Bob Whitfield, Stanford's last great offensive lineman, who was the eighth pick of the 1992 draft and currently in his eleventh year with the Atlanta Falcons. But Harris was not only a dominant blocker and bona fide first-round material but also a modern Renaissance man. A refined concert pianist, Harris could have probably entered the draft after his junior year, but he loved Stanford and loved being a college student, so he stayed put. The combination of all those factors made him the quintessential Willingham guy. When Willingham watched him, his mood momentarily turned from combative to wistful. "I really like that kid," he said. "Man, I really like him."

But Willingham's bond with quarterback Chris Lewis was even deeper. He admired Harris and had a deep respect for him, but his relationship with Lewis was more paternal. When announcers Keith Jackson and Dan Fouts rather flippantly mentioned that Lewis had been ineffective in the first half, Willingham's mood switched back to combative. "Hmm," he said, obviously annoyed. In the second quarter, Kyle Matter had taken over for Lewis.

Willingham was obviously pained by the way new Stanford coach Buddy Teevens alternated Lewis and Mather. The irony was that Teevens, having served as the assistant offensive coordinator at Florida under Steve Spurrier, had essentially adapted Spurrier's technique for handling quarterbacks. From week to week, the starter and the backup rarely knew who would assume either role.

Willingham had carefully groomed Lewis for two years, and now that Willingham was gone, Teevens seemed to be undoing his work. "I don't like what's happening with that kid," said Willingham. "He may not recover from that. And that's too bad because I really think he could play on Sundays."

But it was more than that. The team he was watching wasn't

playing to the standard he'd set for them, and he was visibly pained by it. When fullback Casey Moore fumbled the ball, Willingham winced. "Come on, Casey," he said. "You're much too good for that." As the tape rolled, he got even more animated, dropping some science on fumbling. "See, he's carrying the ball too far away from his body," he said. "If you're holding a dumbbell, where can you lift the most weight? Away from your body or in close?" He answered his own question. "In close, that's where you should carry the ball."

The Stanford defense, put in bad position all day, couldn't keep Arizona State from scoring. As a Sun Devil running back sauntered into the end zone, Willingham muttered, "I hate bad football." And it was pretty bad. The Cardinal had five turnovers in the first half, four of them occurring within their own red zone.

Willingham often mentioned casually that a coach couldn't allow ego to interfere with his decisions to run a football team. But he hinted, more than once, that perhaps Teevens's ego played a large part in Stanford's demise that season. Just one year after finishing 9–3, Stanford was on its way to a 2–9 season.

"If Bob Davie had left everything here in place for a winner, I wouldn't have changed anything," said Willingham. "I wouldn't have had to make changes."

He shrugged and flashed a look that suggested he didn't understand why any coach would change a system that was already successful. "It's all about winning for me," said Willingham. "I changed things that I thought would help my team win."

But Willingham was thinking more about the future than he was about the past, and his competitive fire was fully ablaze. "I know these guys better than the new guy does," he says. "I know their strengths and weaknesses." It was that familiarity that would give him a competitive edge this week.

"This is like playing against your brother," he said. "You love him, but afterward, when you walk into his house and look him in the eye, you want him to know you won." Willingham, looking toward the future, already had his sights set on the next time Notre Dame would play Stanford — in Stanford's house, in the second to last game of the 2003 season.

But that night, Willingham was just looking toward Saturday, and his angst about Stanford didn't end with the players. One member of Stanford's coaching staff, Tom Williams, had been a starting linebacker during Willingham's stint as a Stanford assistant on Denny Green's staff. After his playing career, Williams had been a graduate assistant at Stanford. He'd also coached linebackers at Hawaii and was the defensive line coach at the University of Washington before returning to Stanford as a member of Buddy Teevens's staff.

While pleased to see one of his coaching protégés enjoying some success, Willingham was bothered by Williams's title as Stanford's co–defensive coordinator. It irritated him because he felt that a hyphenated title could only lead to hyphenated credibility. At 32, Williams was among the brightest of college football's promising young coaches, and Willingham wanted him to be viewed as such.

"I don't like all that 'co' stuff," said Willingham. "If you're going to give a man responsibility and authority, then give him the responsibility and authority. But when you have 'co-this' or 'co-that,' when it comes time to make a decision, who do you think is going to make that decision?" He arched his eyebrows suspiciously, leaned back, and returned his eyes to the TV.

Several minutes later, Willingham's mood lightened as he talked about his new surroundings. He had enjoyed his time at Stanford, but football culture was different in the heartland. "No offense to California, but this is football country," he said. "On Thursday, you can almost smell a football weekend coming." That wasn't the case in the Bay Area, where football was a legitimate "attraction," but hardly the focal point of a fall Saturday.

At Friday night's pep rally before the Stanford game, special guest Regis Philbin, a 1953 Notre Dame grad and host of *Live with Regis and Kelly*, would join Willingham. As he had been doing for each pep rally, Willingham would urge the fans to once again create a "sea of green" — but this week it was a little more personal. Willingham would send a message all the way back to Palo Alto. He wanted the folks at Stanford to see what real school spirit looked and felt like.

In fact, school spirit and how it was defined had been a tangible source of contention between Willingham and Stanford athletic director Ted Leland. Willingham thought school spirit was taking a school to its first Rose Bowl in 28 years — and that as a result of the financial windfall afforded the school, the football team should get lights for the practice field. But the athletic director thought otherwise. Leland's stance had undoubtedly fueled Willingham's jump to Notre Dame.

"Tyrone has been quoted in the paper as saying he's happy to be at a school where football is king," said Leland. "Well, football is king at Notre Dame, and it will never be king here. So if you're a football guy, it is a good move." Willingham *was* a football guy, and at least for that season, football *was* king at Notre Dame. As he leaned back in his leather chair, his eyes boring into the TV screen, Willingham seemed especially pleased to be part of that royal tradition.

The next morning, at his weekly press conference, Willingham walked into the WNDU studio eager for that afternoon's practice. He seemed even more prepared than usual, more excited about fielding questions. And after the local media had finished their questions and it was time to take phone calls, it became clear that he'd been expecting one caller in particular.

"Hello, Tyrone. It's Glenn Dickey from the *San Francisco Chronicle.*"

In 1995, when Willingham was hired by Stanford, Dickey had said they'd made a mistake and openly called it a "minority hire." Seven years later, after Stanford hired Buddy Teevens, Dickey had written another column. The headline read: "Teevens seems to be a perfect fit at Stanford."

Dickey said Teevens's credentials were perfect. A Dartmouth graduate, he had an Ivy League education. He also had a picture-perfect family, including a 13-year-old son who was a surfer. And lastly, wrote Dickey, "He coaches a wide-open offensive system that emphasizes passing. It isn't difficult to be successful at Stanford, and it's easier if the coach understands the importance of the passing game."

As he sat in the cold studio that morning, Willingham was poised because he knew at some point Dickey's phone call was coming. And at about 11:30, when it came, Willingham was even cooler. "Hello, Glenn," said Willingham with a smile. "How are you?"

"I'm fine," said Dickey dryly, before continuing. "What do you miss most about Palo Alto?"

Willingham sat up, folded his arms, and smiled. He clearly relished the opportunity to subtly clown this guy. "I'd have to say my hot tub, Glenn."

"Your hot tub?" asked Dickey.

"Yeah, I have a hot tub, but it's not working right now."

When he had finished killing him with kindness, Willingham pleasantly thanked him for calling. "Nice to hear from you, Glenn." There were some things about California Willingham didn't miss at all.

On Friday night, while Willingham and the team were holed up at the Holiday Inn in downtown South Bend, their normal spot the night before a home game, there were two significant pregame parties. At 6:30 P.M., Kim Willingham held a reception for a small group of Stanford alums at the Willinghams' home in Granger. Before the guests arrived, she sat in the living room, chatting with a friend.

About 5′6″, her skin a shade darker than peanut butter, with soft eyes and a round face, Kim combined a Midwestern sensibility with a cool, earthy charm. She had grown up in southern Michigan, only 40 minutes from South Bend, and had met Tyrone while the two were students at Michigan State, he a senior and she a freshman. They met at a Spartans basketball game. Having been born and raised in Covert, Michigan, she, too, acknowledged that Bay Area football fell beneath the standards of the heartland. But that was all she offered on the subject because each evening, when her husband jumped into his big green Yukon for his drive home, he left football in the Joyce Center.

Though his home office contained some football effects — photos of the coaching staff at Rice, a few game balls, and the *Sports Illustrated* with Maurice Stovall on the cover — the living room was barren of such memorabilia. The most colorful photo was of Willingham wearing an oversize hat on the golf course, a huge floppy brim and shades hiding his eyes as he completed his backswing. Other than that, it was light on football and heavy on family. "When he comes home, we usually talk about the kids," said Kim.

In fact, on the night of the biggest game of his career, the night Notre Dame played Maryland, Kim wasn't at Giants Stadium. She was in Colorado with their oldest child, Cassidy, who was about to begin her freshman year at the University of Denver. At St. Francis High School, where Pat Dillingham quarterbacked the football team, Cassidy had been a highly regarded gymnast. The night of August 31 found her in the midst of Denver's orientation week. Her friends knew she couldn't be there for her pop and understood the magnitude of the event, and that evening, they had thrown a party while they watched the game.

At about 6:40, a busload of 20 or so Stanford alums arrived at the Willinghams' home. Among them were Laura Wilson, the chief of Stanford's campus police department; Stanford business school professor Jerry Porras; and Kirsten Teevens, wife of Stanford coach Buddy Teevens. They filed into the kitchen, greeting Kim, telling her how good it was to see her and asking how she and her husband were adjusting to life at Notre Dame. Then they hung around the kitchen, eating hors d'oeuvres, sipping wine and beer.

At 7:30, after a five-minute drive from the Willinghams', the same group of Stanford alums rolled up to Kevin White's house. Like the Willinghams', it was a sprawling Midwestern mansion with enough large open rooms to hold a few hundred guests. But inside there was a different vibe from the earlier party. It was a much more lively scene because a couple hundred people, plus the Notre Dame Glee Club, were in attendance.

Inside the three-story home, there was an undercurrent that suggested both Notre Dame and Stanford wanted to "claim" Tyrone Willingham as their own. It was understandable because, for the moment, his success gave both schools just a little more juice than they'd had in recent years. Since the black coach issue was a major topic that season (there were two major stories in *USA Today* on minority coaches, with Willingham appearing on the front page in October), both Notre Dame and Stanford got automatic cool points for kicking it with the most popular Negro in America. He may have had ties to Stanford and may have been in the process of bonding with Notre Dame, but the claim of complete ownership was presumptuous on the part of both schools.

"Don't believe the hype" had been Willingham's mantra that week. He said it to his team, but it also applied to the hype surrounding him that evening and that season. It certainly applied to Kim. She stood in the basement at White's house, the party swirling around her. To her left, Ted Leland leaned against the bar sipping a cocktail, while all around her, small cliques of alums who had worked their way onto the list through random hookups were getting their drink on as if there were no tomorrow.

Whenever anyone approached Kim, she was warm, friendly, and genuine. She knew the deal. Her husband was South Bend's most popular resident and, at the time, maybe the most important man in sports. Standing next to the bar, watching people celebrate the season, she wore a peaceful expression. She seemed content and pleased, but not especially overwhelmed. She left early.

In the kitchen, Father Malloy walked up to a small group of people and introduced himself. "Hello, I'm the president," he said. He was very charming and relaxed as he chatted about the lakes on campus, which were surrounded by running trails for students and faculty. He joked about the preponderance of duck feces and how the swans, while breathtakingly beautiful, were natural enemies of the Canada geese. When the talk turned to football, and specifically to Tyrone Willingham, Malloy's tone softened, a delighted smile accompanied his speech, and he gazed at the ceiling.

"We're very happy to have him," he said. "He has brought a whole new energy to the place." He was right. That night, as folks from two rival camps joined in seamless fashion, it was fairly clear that Willingham's concentration on unity and synthesis had effectively shaped the scene. And five games into the season, Malloy and crew had realized that what they had in Tyrone Willingham was more than just the hottest coach in football. What they had was the ideal representative for their university.

*   *   *

A half-hour before kickoff on October 5, 2002, coaches from both teams gathered in the north end zone for a brief pregame re-union. Preston, Miles, Denbrock, McDonell, Baer, and Diedrick had joined Willingham in South Bend. But Dave Tipton, Stanford's defensive line coach, had remained in Palo Alto. Preston walked up to him, offering a handshake and huge grin. As one who had been doing it for many years, Tipton knew teaching college kids special teams could be an adventure, and he was glad to have Preston back in the little fraternity.

"How are those special teams treatin' you?" Tipton smiled.

"Oh, you know how it is," said Preston. "Just gotta get 'em lined up. The players are the ones who win the games; we coaches just can't lose it!"

Knowing that was only partially true, especially when it came to special teams, both men laughed.

Other than Willingham taking on his old team, the other less intriguing plot twist centered on who would play quarterback for the Irish. Carlyle Holiday had practiced that week and didn't appear to be in too much pain from his shoulder injury. But with plans to start Pat Dillingham, Willingham hadn't given Stanford any clues. It wouldn't matter. Notre Dame was a much better team than Stanford. After Willingham's departure, the Cardinal had become less disciplined, and it showed on the field. Though they were only 1–2 for the season, they looked nothing like the team that had finished 9–3 the season before.

But that wasn't apparent in the first quarter. Stanford had come ready to play. They wanted to beat their old coach as much as he wanted to beat them. It was a natural sign of respect for each party to give the other its absolute best. And the defense gave its best. After the Notre Dame offense effectively moved the ball on its first series, the Stanford defense stiffened. In their next possession, after loss of yardage and an incomplete pass by Pat Dillingham, the Irish punted.

When Stanford had the ball, the offense wasn't polished, but they were determined. With two minutes left in the first quarter, they made it to midfield before having to punt. Vontez Duff retrieved the ball at the eight-yard line and skated 92 yards for an apparent touchdown. But Notre Dame was called for roughing the center. In college football, the center, while his head is down, cannot be blocked. But that's exactly what happened on that play, and Stanford got the ball back at the Notre Dame 37-yard line. Chris Lewis wasted little time as he hit receiver Teyo Johnson on a 14-yard slant for a touchdown.

It was 7–0, and Willingham quietly stalked the sidelines. Notre Dame had come out flat. And that was because they still didn't get it. They still couldn't match Willingham's intensity. Once again, just like against Michigan State, the game carried a personal significance, and Willingham took the team's lackluster effort personally. He calmly paced, patiently waiting for the moment his new team would ignite and bury his old team.

Willingham would have to keep waiting though. On the last play of the quarter, Stanford outside backer Jared Newberry came from the opposite direction and dropped Dillingham for a five-yard loss. In the next series, defensive tackle Matt Leonard hit Dillingham in the chest, and Newberry came again, this time knocking the ball down. After each play, Stanford co–defensive coordinator Tom Williams leaped up and down on the sideline, screaming, "That's it, D! That's it, D!" And after the last play, he bent over and flexed as he made a guttural "Yeeaaah!"

Midway through the second quarter, Shane Walton, draped all over Cardinal receiver Nick Sebes, turned and dropped what would have been an easy pick. As was the rule in practice, Walton dropped down right there on the 40-yard line and did 10 push-ups for his crime. Not one to be outdone, and because all the young guys did what Shane did, a few minutes later, Preston Jackson, after a deflection, also performed 10 push-ups.

As Walton did his push-ups, Willingham watched, neither pleased nor upset by the impromptu display. In fact, some fans had wondered why the Notre Dame players spoke so confidently and carried themselves with such arrogance. They were winning games, but they still weren't *that* good. It was true. They were pretty far removed from being a polished team. But Willingham wasn't hearing that, and he didn't want his team hearing it either.

Willingham's plan, in addition to giving them discipline, was to build their confidence. In many ways, he agreed with Joe

Theismann's comments before the Maryland game. While they were out there competing, he did want his guys to be those cocky Notre Dame players. He wanted them to be those players other teams hated, and he wanted other players to have a reason to hate them. As he led his team into the locker room trailing Stanford 7–3, Willingham was pissed. Contrary to popular belief, Willingham didn't seek total control of every situation on the field; he wanted his *team* to do that. And 11 minutes into the third quarter, that's just what they did.

About two minutes after Rashon Powers-Neal dragged a defender into the end zone to take the lead, 10–7, Courtney Watson and Shane Walton tag-teamed the Cardinal offense and, in a little more than three minutes' time, completely broke its spirit. And they did it without really moving from one spot on the field. On the first play, Lewis hit Teyo Johnson on a curl. As Johnson turned, Watson bore into him as if he were attempting to cave in his chest, dropping Johnson at the spot he caught the ball. It was your classic "woo lick." As coined by Hall of Fame defensive back Ronnie Lott, it was one of those hits that makes everyone say *"Woo!"* The second Johnson went down, the Notre Dame sideline came to life.

On the next play, Lewis rolled to his right. Mike Goolsby, who was covering the fullback, came roaring from the flat to take a shot at Lewis. Rushing his throw, Lewis never saw Walton, who had been deep. Not having a threat, Walton ran to the flat, snatched the ball, and returned it 18 yards for a touchdown. It was Walton's fifth pick of the season.

On the next drive, Courtney Watson, after taking his drop in the middle of the field, once again drove on the receiver. This time, rather than laying the wood on him, Watson turned bully and just punked the kid and took his lunch money. As Stanford tight end Alex Smith tried to pull the ball into his body, Watson wrenched it from him, pushed him over, and returned it 34 yards for another score.

Ryan Grant's one-yard touchdown run at the beginning of the fourth quarter made it 31–7 and punctuated Notre Dame's best offensive performance to date. With 103 yards, Grant had his best day of the season. Rashon Powers-Neal also had more than 100 yards as he gained 108 on 13 carries.

When the clock ran out, Willingham made his way to midfield. After briefly shaking hands with Teevens, Willingham was speaking to NBC's Lewis Johnson when he saw Chris Lewis walking toward him. Willingham's face softened. In an instant it went from impenetrable coaching mask to protective guardian. He looked at Lewis with an expression that seemed to say "I hate what you're going through, and I hate even more that we had to put it on you like we did. But you know how I feel about you." Willingham grabbed Lewis, and they locked in a tight embrace.

Lewis had likened Willingham's departure to the man of the house leaving. "I never dreamed that he wouldn't be there for all four of my years," he said. "But I knew it was important for him and important for all black coaches for him to take that job."

But for the time being, Willingham was genuinely concerned with getting his old team back to its normal level of play. Willingham told Lewis to "rally the troops, get 'em back on track" so that they could still salvage their season. After that, one at a time, each of Lewis's teammates quietly sauntered up to their ex-coach, each of them seeking a brief yet meaningful audience with someone who had obviously left a lasting impression on them. Willingham chatted with Luke Powell, laughed with Teyo Johnson, and caught up with Kwame Harris.

When they were done, and he and his former players had reassumed their current roles, Willingham left midfield and bolted toward the tunnel. As he passed beneath the goalpost, the Irish fans, some hanging over the railing in the tunnel, reaching down to touch him, let out a cheer: "Five and oh!"

As he ran by them, Willingham tightly pumped his fist in that familiar conquering fashion of his. He didn't look up at them, though. He had just beaten his brother, and for the moment, he wasn't quite prepared to look anyone in the eye.

10

PITTSBURGH

B Y THE SECOND WEEK of October, Willingham's team was 5–0 and ranked No. 8 in the nation, and Willingham had joined Jesse Harper, Frank Leahy, and Ara Parseghian as the only Notre Dame coaches to win their first five games. But in the 5–1 Pittsburgh Panthers, they were up against their toughest opponent yet, and they still needed to establish a definitive personality. After last-minute wins over Michigan and Michigan State, Willingham was still waiting for that to happen. "We just keep winning this way, and in those types of games," he said. "You look for an identity in a team, but the way we're winning . . ." Trying to make sense of it, Willingham shrugged. "Maybe that's just who we are."

Willingham's seniors knew who they were. Courtney Watson, Shane Walton, and Arnaz Battle began to assert themselves both as players and as people, and they gave the team its strength as they embarked on the toughest part of their schedule. Battle had been steadily progressing all season, and perhaps because of that, by midseason he felt comfortable enough to leave his apartment and risk being seen in public.

On Monday night, he went to Studes to watch the game. Dressed in the outfit of choice for most Notre Dame football players — blue-and-gray Notre Dame sweats — Battle sat next to the big screen, where the Green Bay Packers were playing the

Chicago Bears. While he sat, a couple of local girls, one dark haired and the other a peroxide blonde, both in perilously snug jeans, sauntered into his line of vision. But for the moment, Battle was content to just chill. A fan came up to him and said, "Glad to see it's finally happening for you, man." Battle smiled and shook his head. "I just hope it keeps on happening."

It was happening because Battle was no longer just lining up at receiver; he was beginning to actually *play* the position. At the time he had only 11 catches for 177 yards — hardly extraordinary numbers for most big-time receivers. But considering where he had started, those numbers were large. "I feel like a receiver now," he said. "Last year, it helped being in an option offense. I think being out there on the corners and blocking on the running plays helped me a lot. But this year, I'm taking it to another level. I'm running routes, catching the ball, tucking it away. All the things you should do in the passing game."

Near the midpoint of his final season, Battle was beginning to fulfill a dream that had begun five years earlier. "One thing with my parents," he said. "Once you start something, you finish it. I never gave up. Not once did I think of leaving this university, even when times were tough. If I had to do it all over again, I would. If I had the chance to be recruited out of high school and had the choice of all the same schools, I would still come to Notre Dame."

His whole family would come too. His grandmother had been there when he had surgery on his wrist. And this season, his mother, his grandmother, his sister, and his aunt made the trip whenever possible. Shane Walton loved to tell stories about Battle being too close to his family. Once, Walton came home to the apartment to find all five of them lying on Battle's bed watching television. "You guys must really be from the South," said Walton.

Battle laughed at that. "Yeah, he calls us country because of that." But the truth was, Brandon's death and Arnaz's journey had unified Battle's family to the point where they were inseparable. Walton may have joked about how country they were, but he clearly appreciated it.

"It's great to see a family like that," he said.

As the Notre Dame players continued to grow and mature, the same could be said for them. In many ways, the same blend of hardship and great expectation was molding them into a family as well. And there was no one more suited to be the point man in their evolution than Arnaz Battle. Said Battle, "Sometimes things have to get worse before they get better."

On Wednesday afternoon, October 9, right before they took the practice field, the receivers huddled next to the seven-foot wooden retaining wall. With Arnaz Battle in the middle and Maurice Stovall standing on the outside, reaching his impossibly long arms over the group, they put their hands together and collectively shouted, "Wideouts!" They did this before every practice. It was a gesture designed to foster unity within the group, a model of inclusion.

A few minutes later, through a ball drill, Trent Miles reminded his group that everyone would be held to the same standard. Like every coach on the staff, Miles recognized no hierarchy when it came to fundamentals.

They were catching balls from the JUGS machine, a four-foot-tall light-blue tripod that spit footballs at varying speeds. Miles had each receiver stand with his back turned to the machine while one of the student managers pulled the lever and squirted a ball at him. On the word *go*, each whipped around a half-second before the ball hit him in the face mask. They were having a bad day. First Carlos Campbell had one fly off his fingertips; then Ronnie Rodamer slapped at a ball headed for his face. Even Omar Jenkins, the most consistent member of the group, bobbled one.

"Okay, from now on, everyone who drops the ball, or even bobbles it, we do up-downs." Fear of a new punishment firmly in place, the concentration level increased as they made it through five people without another drop.

But on the next drill, Bernard Akatu ran into trouble. Akatu was a senior from Lagos, Nigeria, who hadn't seen any action in a game. Quiet and good-natured, he went about his business, working with the other seldom-used reserves, known as the scout team. On this drill, each man stood about six feet from the

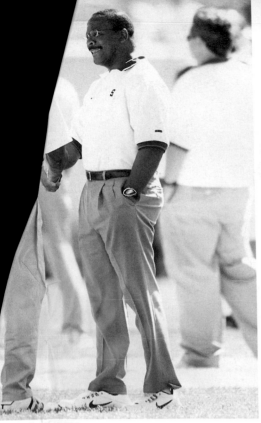

Willingham greets Michigan State coach Bobby Williams before the game

Willingham consults with backup quarterback Pat Dillingham during the Michigan State game while receivers coach Trent Miles looks on

Receiver Arnaz Battle scores the winning touchdown against Michigan State

machine and came forward as the ball hurled toward him. The difficulty factor for this particular drill was extremely high, but there was a practical use. It was an exercise designed to simulate those times when a receiver has to sprint back toward the quarterback, effectively eluding the man who was covering him. Third in line, Akatu came forward, and as the ball came toward his chest, he jumped to catch it.

"If you don't need to leave your feet, then don't leave your feet, Bernard," said Miles.

Two repetitions later, Rhema McKnight leaped sweetly in the air, and although he made the catch, it still didn't sit well with Miles. "Okay," said Miles. "The next time someone leaves his feet, the whole group does up-downs!"

Akatu came forward, and once again, force of habit told him to jump for the ball. When he did, the ball slipped through his hands and loudly smacked him in the chest.

"Okay, everybody down!" shouted Miles.

After 10 up-downs, they continued. And a few minutes later, after Akatu's next rep, when he jumped again and dropped the ball, the group hit the ground for a fresh round of calisthenics. "We're doing these because of you, Bernard," said Miles.

A few minutes later, when the horn mercifully sounded, signaling it was time to move to the next station, Miles jogged beside Akatu. Miles wanted to make sure he knew that anyone who came out on the field, regardless of his spot on the depth chart, had to maintain a certain standard of performance, and anyone who suited up was going to be *coached*. "We're gonna get you to break that habit one day, Bernard."

At Friday night's pep rally, Courtney Watson nervously leaned over the pulpit and prepared to deliver the most sincere of all the Friday night addresses that season. Standing before a crowd, eager to offer his ideas, he was noticeably excited. "We all could have gone to other schools and won football games. But everyone came to Notre Dame because it was special." As emotion and nerves made him scramble for his words, the members of Zahm Hall, his residence, held up 8-by-10 black-and-white photos of him. Who knew where they got them, but the gesture was symbolic of the significant position that Watson occupied on the Notre Dame campus.

Every week, each of the dorms was introduced at the pep rally. Whenever one of its members was singled out, that dorm was always quick to get behind that player and proud to claim him as their own. But in Watson, their claim went significantly further than the immediate cachet a starting football player afforded them.

The previous spring, some of his friends had suggested to Watson that he run for Zahm Hall senator. They thought his passion for speech and love of politics would serve him well in the senate. His initial reaction was to think of it logically. And with a daily four-hour commitment to football, it seemed unlikely he'd have time to legislate campus law. But the more he considered it, the more he realized what it could possibly mean for him, his image, and his life after football.

Several months earlier, Watson and Gerome Sapp had had lunch with Willingham. As they got up to leave, Willingham told them, "Don't let anyone pigeonhole you." As usual, Willingham's words were smart and focused. But on Watson, they may have been wasted. Courtney Watson was the last person who ever needed to be told that he could be more than a football player. He disdained the whole "dumb jock" image, and in everything he did, he tried to distance himself from it. He was a young man with a focused desire to change the world.

He had actually acquired a taste for politics two years earlier. During his freshman year, he was at a party in Zahm Hall when he made the acquaintance of one Christina Trieweiler. A senior at Saint Mary's College, Christina was the daughter of Montana Supreme Court justice Terry Trieweiler. She had dark-blond curly hair, expressive blue eyes, and the sinewy upper body of a runner. During a lively conversation, with topics ranging from rapper Tupac Shakur to the virtues of the Jeep Cherokee, Christina engaged Watson on the issue of campaign funds. It was an election year, and Christina's father was in the midst of a race for chief justice against Karla Gray.

After a few hours of animated banter, Watson was hooked on

Cornerback Shane Walton celebrates after knocking down a two-point conversion to preserve a 25–23 victory over Michigan

Students in their green T-shirts celebrate after the victory over Michigan

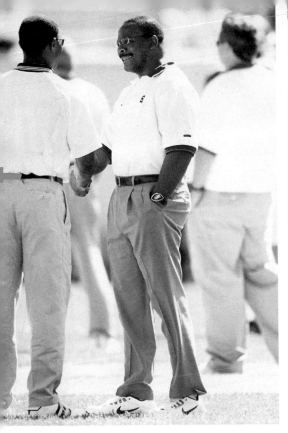

Willingham greets Michigan State coach Bobby Williams before the game

Receiver Arnaz Battle scores the winning touchdown against Michigan State

Willingham consults with backup quarterback Pat Dillingham during the Michigan State game while receivers coach Trent Miles looks on

Cornerback Shane Walton celebrates after knocking down a two-point conversion to preserve a 25–23 victory over Michigan

Students in their green T-shirts celebrate after the victory over Michigan

symbolic of the significant position that Watson occupied on the Notre Dame campus.

Every week, each of the dorms was introduced at the pep rally. Whenever one of its members was singled out, that dorm was always quick to get behind that player and proud to claim him as their own. But in Watson, their claim went significantly further than the immediate cachet a starting football player afforded them.

The previous spring, some of his friends had suggested to Watson that he run for Zahm Hall senator. They thought his passion for speech and love of politics would serve him well in the senate. His initial reaction was to think of it logically. And with a daily four-hour commitment to football, it seemed unlikely he'd have time to legislate campus law. But the more he considered it, the more he realized what it could possibly mean for him, his image, and his life after football.

Several months earlier, Watson and Gerome Sapp had had lunch with Willingham. As they got up to leave, Willingham told them, "Don't let anyone pigeonhole you." As usual, Willingham's words were smart and focused. But on Watson, they may have been wasted. Courtney Watson was the last person who ever needed to be told that he could be more than a football player. He disdained the whole "dumb jock" image, and in everything he did, he tried to distance himself from it. He was a young man with a focused desire to change the world.

He had actually acquired a taste for politics two years earlier. During his freshman year, he was at a party in Zahm Hall when he made the acquaintance of one Christina Trieweiler. A senior at Saint Mary's College, Christina was the daughter of Montana Supreme Court justice Terry Trieweiler. She had dark-blond curly hair, expressive blue eyes, and the sinewy upper body of a runner. During a lively conversation, with topics ranging from rapper Tupac Shakur to the virtues of the Jeep Cherokee, Christina engaged Watson on the issue of campaign funds. It was an election year, and Christina's father was in the midst of a race for chief justice against Karla Gray.

After a few hours of animated banter, Watson was hooked on

machine and came forward as the ball hurled toward him. The difficulty factor for this particular drill was extremely high, but there was a practical use. It was an exercise designed to simulate those times when a receiver has to sprint back toward the quarterback, effectively eluding the man who was covering him. Third in line, Akatu came forward, and as the ball came toward his chest, he jumped to catch it.

"If you don't need to leave your feet, then don't leave your feet, Bernard," said Miles.

Two repetitions later, Rhema McKnight leaped sweetly in the air, and although he made the catch, it still didn't sit well with Miles. "Okay," said Miles. "The next time someone leaves his feet, the whole group does up-downs!"

Akatu came forward, and once again, force of habit told him to jump for the ball. When he did, the ball slipped through his hands and loudly smacked him in the chest.

"Okay, everybody down!" shouted Miles.

After 10 up-downs, they continued. And a few minutes later, after Akatu's next rep, when he jumped again and dropped the ball, the group hit the ground for a fresh round of calisthenics. "We're doing these because of you, Bernard," said Miles.

A few minutes later, when the horn mercifully sounded, signaling it was time to move to the next station, Miles jogged beside Akatu. Miles wanted to make sure he knew that anyone who came out on the field, regardless of his spot on the depth chart, had to maintain a certain standard of performance, and anyone who suited up was going to be *coached*. "We're gonna get you to break that habit one day, Bernard."

At Friday night's pep rally, Courtney Watson nervously leaned over the pulpit and prepared to deliver the most sincere of all the Friday night addresses that season. Standing before a crowd, eager to offer his ideas, he was noticeably excited. "We all could have gone to other schools and won football games. But everyone came to Notre Dame because it was special." As emotion and nerves made him scramble for his words, the members of Zahm Hall, his residence, held up 8-by-10 black-and-white photos of him. Who knew where they got them, but the gesture was

Willingham and Stanford coach Buddy
Teevens share a laugh before the game

Cornerback Vontez Duff in his stance

Students from Zahm Hall salute linebacker Courtney Watson at a pep rally

Defensive line coach Greg Mattison

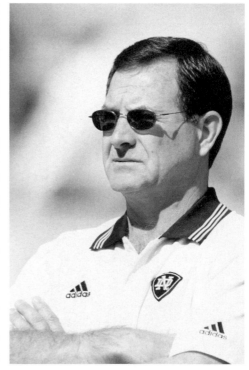

Running backs coach Buzz Preston

Secondary coach Trent Walters

Offensive coordinator Bill Diedrick

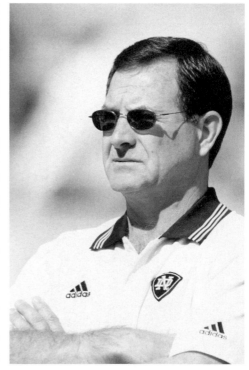

Defensive coordinator Kent Baer

Linebackers coach Bob Simmons

Offensive line coach John McDonell

Offensive line coach Mike Denbrock

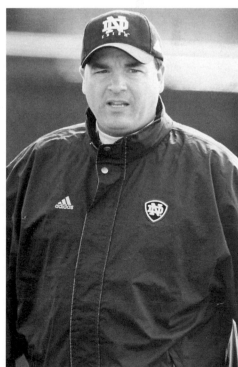

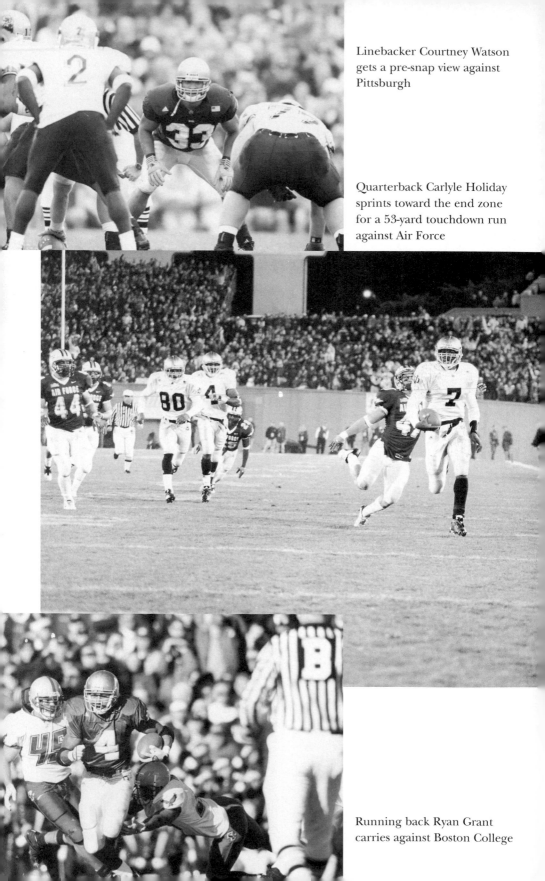

Linebacker Courtney Watson gets a pre-snap view against Pittsburgh

Quarterback Carlyle Holiday sprints toward the end zone for a 53-yard touchdown run against Air Force

Running back Ryan Grant carries against Boston College

Athletic Director Kevin White and President Edward Malloy before the Navy game

Willingham chats with National Security Advisor Condoleezza Rice after the victory over Navy

Safety Gerome Sapp speaks at the Senior Night pep rally

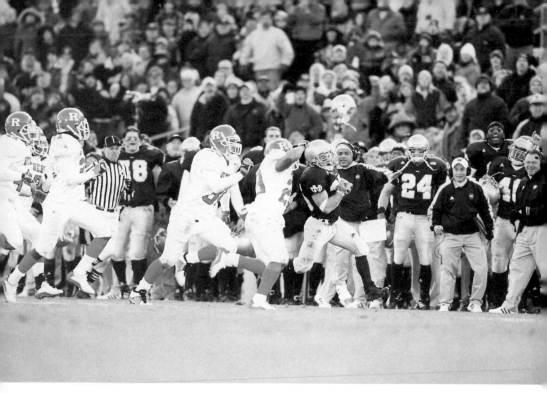

Reserve tailback Tim O'Neill breaks a long run against Rutgers to the delight of his teammates and coaches

Quarterback Carlyle Holiday separates his shoulder as a result of this hit by North Carolina State's Dantonio Burnette during the Gator Bowl

both Christina and politics. He had grown up in a house where he was taught to believe his vote didn't count, so he had never had an interest in politics or in politicians. But the topic that night piqued his interest. He began to study and follow issues that intrigued him. And during the Democratic convention, when he saw outgoing president Bill Clinton address his party and noted the power and influence he commanded, Watson got a glimpse of his own future.

At that moment, he realized that football could pave the way for his own political aspirations. Watson discovered he could use his name as a Notre Dame football player, much like Oklahoma representative and former Sooners quarterback J. C. Watts had done. Although Watson was hardly a fan of the ultraconservative Watts, this was an example he could follow.

With that in mind, in the spring of 2002, Watson decided to run for dorm senator. At first it was a joke; he didn't really think he had a chance to win. Part of his campaign consisted of walking up and down Zahm Hall for a good half-hour, shouting into a bullhorn. "Vote for Courtney Watson! Don't vote for the other guy!" But after getting 75% of the vote, he had his first victory, and a political career was born.

That Friday night was the first time, aside from the weekly Student Senate meetings, that Watson got a chance to address people in the dual role of political agent and football player. He knew a large portion of the pep rally crowd was composed of subway alums, and he reached out to them as if they were his constituency. "There are people who never went to this school, who never set foot on this campus, but they continue to support us," he said. This got a predictably thunderous applause from the subway crowd.

Watson was clearly in his element as his voice grew louder and more confident. He represented more than just his team. He represented the students in Zahm Hall, and he represented Notre Dame. And by their actions, by their sincere enthusiasm, it was obvious the crowd felt him. He motioned to his teammates seated behind him. "We all could have gone to other schools and just won football games," he said. "But we chose Notre Dame because we all wanted to do more with our lives. That's why people come here — to make something of themselves while they're here and after they leave."

That also held true for Watson's teammates, especially Brandon Hoyte, Watson's backup at linebacker. Hoyte, a sophomore from Parlin, New Jersey, was a double major in premed and psychology. "Today, a lot of people think football players have to be one-dimensional," said Hoyte. "I think our job is to show that we're more than just ballers. When we get on that field, don't be mistaken, we give it one hundred percent. But that's the thing that was always stressed to me — education. That's why before choosing Notre Dame, I looked at Ivy League schools like Princeton and Brown. Education has always been important to me because that's the way I was raised. And it was like that on every team I ever played for. I think a lot of guys on this team have that background."

Hoyte also expressed a particular concern for the image of other black athletes. He knew that when most people listened to him speak, they were usually taken aback. "Unfortunately, the word is *shock* to society," he said. "You look at young black men on TV, you always see how young black men are portrayed. I think it's my duty as a young black man to prove them wrong. Every day I leave my room, I know I can leave a different impression. I feel it's my duty to shape that image."

In politics, as in many arenas, image is everything. Later that season, another issue concerning a politician's public image took hold of Courtney Watson. It brought his passion for politics to a boil. Senate Majority Leader Trent Lott, while attending Strom Thurmond's birthday party, had taken the opportunity to praise Thurmond's Dixie Campaign from 50 years earlier. Lott had said that if Thurmond had been president, "we wouldn't be in the mess we are today." But Lott hadn't elaborated on what that meant, and he didn't have to. The foundation for Thurmond's campaign had been segregation, and it seemed that he and his supporters still clung to that doctrine.

Watson, like all others who knew the depth of the situation, knew it wasn't the words but the sentiment behind them that made them ugly. "You look at his history and some of the things he's done in the past, and you know the things he said were things he had in his heart," said Watson, speaking of Lott. "How could he remain in office that long believing in the things he did?" A few weeks later, amid the racial firestorm, Lott would resign as the Senate majority leader.

Discussing the Lott episode made Watson speak even faster than he usually did. This was exactly the sort of thing he hated. Certain issues, like drilling in Alaska, gave him reason to fight. But this wasn't an issue or topic for debate. This was the sort of principle that gnawed at his gut, making his face taut, his voice strained. But Watson had to be careful.

Passion is a good thing. But Watson was one of those young men often too consumed by his passion to be aware that others just might not *get it* like he did. It was good that his boys at Zahm Hall had realized that he had more to offer than just football. It was good that they respected him enough to push him to run for Student Senate. It was good that they saw him as a person.

But one evening at Coach's, while he spoke, his voice saturated with emotion, it was clear Watson still had things to learn in terms of reaching the masses. He would eventually learn that when someone who looked like him — muscular and black — offered *opinions* and *suggestions* in a wonderfully animated way, some folks might not recognize his passion. Outside the controlled environment of academia, most folks were ruled by fear instead of curiosity, and they might confuse his *passion* for *anger.*

Seated next to him, Christina was pensive. Young, vibrant, idealistic, and in every way just as passionate as he was, she balanced him well. Whereas he always questioned people's hearts and motives, she looked for the good in people. She leaned forward, opening her eyes wide and tilting her head to one side to emphasize her point. "But don't black men need to show that they're angry about some things?" she asked. "Don't people need to know certain things that upset them? Isn't that what's needed to change things?" It was a hopeful question.

Christina realized that there were some people, including some with whom she attended classes, who probably wouldn't react too kindly to any kind of emotion from a black man. She had already seen and been hurt by how some of her classmates failed to see Courtney as a human being. She was troubled that they couldn't or wouldn't see all the great things about him besides his skills as a player or the mere color of his skin. She'd heard how some of the Saint Mary's girls thought her being with Courtney made her less than what she was. And she had heard there were some people who had called her unflattering names after they discovered she was dating a black football player.

She also knew that her voice and point of view, like her boyfriend, differed from the "majority." They were both on record as being Democrats, and that didn't sit well in the conservative environs of Notre Dame. Getting tired, she shrugged and put the conversation to rest. "Maybe I have been discriminated against," she said. "And I just haven't realized it."

On October 12, 2002, a sleepy, overcast South Bend day framed a subdued first half by both the offense and defense. Pittsburgh's first offensive series began with a pair of long runs by running backs Lousaka Polite and Raymond Kirkley. Pitt's offense didn't do anything fancy, just gashed Notre Dame between the tackles. But three plays later, Shane Walton allowed them the opening they needed.

One of the secrets to Walton's success as a big-time playmaker was that the game was never bigger than he was and nothing ever intimidated him. He was always cool, always loose, and always enjoying himself. But there came a time in each game when he got bored. And when boredom set in, he would get careless in his alignment.

On a Pittsburgh third-and-10, Notre Dame ran a blitz, meaning neither Gerome Sapp nor Glenn Earl would be anywhere near the middle of the field. Because of that, Walton was supposed to line up on the receiver's inside, refusing him access to the middle. But peeking into the backfield, anticipating that the quarterback would recognize the blitz and change the play, Walton favored the receiver's outside shoulder. On his release, Walton, his attention on the quarterback, stood as if stuck in mud while the receiver blazed past him and up the field. He gave chase and, 52 yards later, caught him, but the damage was done.

On the sideline, Kent Baer was starting a slow boil. The defensive line wasn't getting off blocks, and the normally disciplined secondary had already made two big mental errors. But the first drive did have one saving grace — the only saving grace a defense has when it gives up long gains on a drive. They kept Pitt out of the end zone and made them kick a field goal.

The first offensive series for the Irish, though sluggish, was successful in one way: Carlyle Holiday, starting his first game since the injury, survived two nasty shots on blitzes. Willingham, maintaining a stoic pose, cringed slightly on impact. But after each shot, Holiday bounced up without hesitation. Nonetheless, when he badly overthrew Omar Jenkins in the flat, it was apparent that those two weeks he had missed had left him terribly out of sync.

After the Notre Dame defense forced another punt on the next series, Bill Diedrick called Cardinal Special. Pitt had by far the best defense the Irish had faced all season, and they had already shown that they were capable of stopping just about anything. Only six games into the season, the Pittsburgh defense already had forced 21 turnovers, and their middle linebacker, Gerald Hayes, was an absolute beast. Quick and explosive, Hayes had been unblockable against the run that season. Eight of his 56 tackles had come from behind the line of scrimmage. It was especially early in the game for Notre Dame to go reaching into their bag of tricks, but Hayes and company would not allow them to run the ball that day.

If Notre Dame had any chance of getting Pittsburgh off them, they would have to make the Pitt defense *think* instead of *react*. The only way they could do that was through a gadget play. On second-and-eight, Holiday handed off to Arnaz Battle, who rolled out and threw downfield to Omar Jenkins. But after the pass was underthrown and intercepted, it looked as though the entire offense, not just Holiday, had chosen the absolute worst time to take a step backward. Playing against a defense with so much speed, their margin for error was almost nil.

But in the second series of the second quarter, for some reason known only to him, Arnaz Battle started to feel it. It was the right time for him to start feeling it, of course. Whenever the offense needed life or needed someone to make some noise, Battle was always more than happy to oblige. He made three successive plays, the last of which was nothing short of spectacular.

On third-and-eight, Holiday lofted a ball down the sideline, which Battle snatched over the corner's shoulder for a 23-yard gain. Three plays later, on third-and-two, he caught a simple hitch. It should have been a nice five-yard gain, the ideal goal for such a play. But that day, Battle proved that his 60-yard run against Michigan State had stirred something feral in him. His athletic ability had never been doubted, but the jury was still very undecided on his skills as a genuine receiver. Battle made the catch, and after a half-spin, a quick wiggle, and a burst, he squirted from the corner's grasp and exploded down the sideline for 22 yards.

But the one play that signified his arrival — as a receiver, as a football player, and as a legitimate professional prospect — came two plays later. Holiday threw a fade into the left corner of the end zone. The ball floated, looking as though it would land about three yards out of bounds, right in the laps of the Pittsburgh band. Battle took one second to rise, one second to hover and rotate his torso to the left, and another to catch the ball. By the time he landed, he had taken another significant step toward becoming a bona fide receiver. But then again, that was something he already knew he could be. And it was something his brother, Brandon, probably knew as well. After he duckwalked in the end zone, Battle gently ran a gloved hand over his left shoulder. Battle finished the day with 10 catches for 101 yards — both career bests.

Battle's teammates knew he had skills, and they lived that moment with him as well. Courtney Watson certainly knew. He had been a senior in high school when Battle had that terrible day against USC, but he had watched as Battle struggled through his painful debut. He had seen Battle fight through injury after injury. He had seen him fight through people saying he couldn't play quarterback at Notre Dame, saying he was overrated coming out of high school. The fact that Battle was so hardworking and determined wasn't lost on Watson. "He's getting everything he deserves," said Watson.

By the time the fourth quarter began, with Notre Dame leading 7–6, Courtney Watson was ready for his team to get what they deserved. And after having missed the first two games, he'd been getting his own game back to the place it belonged. Since his illness, Watson had been steadily progressing, and after a solid week of practice, he was playing as well as he ever had. He would finish that day with nine tackles and renewed energy.

With 9:28 left in the game, Pitt had the ball on its own 10-yard line when Watson felt something. On second-and-10, Watson got hyped and darted toward the line of scrimmage, where he began screaming at Pittsburgh quarterback Rod Rutherford. Watson was the self-appointed leader of the defense, and when he started to "feel it," he usually let the others know. In the huddle, after getting Shane Walton to quiet down, Watson called the defense and would often start yelling: "This is where we make our money, D! Come on, this is where we make our money!"

At that particular moment, Watson knew the next play was going to be a quarterback draw, and he was moved to tell the opposing quarterback as much. While Rutherford called the signals, Watson charged the space in between the center and guard. "It ain't gonna happen! It ain't gonna happen! Not today! Not today!" he screamed.

Rutherford looked up at Watson with eyes the size of saucers. He took the snap and bolted between the guard and tackle. But the instant he cut back toward the middle of the field, Glenn Earl met him and popped him in the earhole. Upon impact, the ball fell softly at Earl's feet, where he cradled it. Five plays later, Ryan Grant took a toss and scored from the one-yard line to make the final score 14–6.

After the game, Willingham was pleased. At the time, Willingham knew the victory carried a lot more weight than most people thought. With Miami far and away the class of the Big East conference, Pittsburgh and Virginia Tech ran a close second. And by beating Pitt, the Irish had established that they were indeed a credible team. In addition to that, Pittsburgh was the first of Notre Dame's three Big East opponents. Notre Dame needed to beat those teams to justify its sacred independent status in college football. In each of its other varsity sports, Notre Dame *was* a member of the Big East, but the football program had remained fiercely independent.

Michigan may have been the most highly ranked team they had beaten that year, but at the time, Pitt, with its quick defense and talented corps of receivers, was the best overall team they had played. But Willingham still had some concerns. "We still haven't exposed who we are totally," he said. "We still haven't established a complete identity. There's still some more offense there."

11

AIR FORCE

THE WEEK BEGAN with Notre Dame ranked No. 7 in the AP poll. The team was rolling, and it was reflected in their mood. After Wednesday's practice, defensive tackle Darrell Campbell and noseguard Cedric Hilliard came into the media room fussing like a married couple. "You're supposed to take your shoes off before coming in here," said Hilliard.

"Who are you to be telling people that?" replied Campbell.

"All I know is, the rule is that you're supposed to take your shoes off before coming in here!"

They were joking, but the scene was reflective of the light-hearted environment that season. Offensive tackle Jordan Black said that Willingham had instilled a family atmosphere in the team shortly after his arrival. They were more relaxed than they had ever been and seemed to be enjoying themselves more than they ever had. Three days before meeting Air Force, the loose, carefree attitude was equal parts enthusiasm at being undefeated, optimism at staying that way, and the overall freedom of just enjoying the experience.

In the past, they had been Notre Dame football players, period. The pressure to be that and only that had eroded their spirit — football had become a job for them. But now Hilliard and Campbell's jovial mood reflected the whole team's. They were undefeated, on a roll, and having fun again. And it was

hard to deny that the upbeat, relentlessly positive coach bebop-
ping around campus was responsible for it.

Sitting in his office one night that week, Willingham was
especially relaxed. He seemed wickedly confident and ready to
play the game at that moment. He dripped sarcasm when referring to that week's topic — the Air Force offense. He had already
studied the film and had said, almost sneering with contempt,
"Their offense is *awesome.* Just *unstoppable.*" He looked a little
more tired than he had in previous weeks, but his tone and his
smirk provided clear evidence that he already knew they would
be all over Air Force on Saturday.

Behind him, from a small Sanyo speaker, Jackie Wilson's
"(Your Love Keeps Lifting Me) Higher and Higher" bathed his
office. The sound moved him, the upbeat tempo forcing a tight
smile to form on his lips. He lightly bobbed his head and listened
for a minute. "*This* is good music. You know the best lyricists
come from R-and-B artists and country and western," he said. "In
rap and hip-hop, there are no classics."

The next voice from the speaker was James Brown's. The
hoarse, screechy voice of the Godfather of Soul created a different mood. Willingham became more animated, recalling the
days when Brown's musical black pride was outlawed on the airwaves. "They didn't play James Brown on the radio when I was
young," he said. "Oh, no, are you kidding? Shoot. 'I'm black and
I'm proud'?"

The mixed CD he was listening to, which had been mailed to
him by a fan, didn't contain any jazz. And that's the music Willingham liked most. He preferred contemporary jazz artists like
Joe Sample. Willingham was particularly fond of a song Sample,
while a member of the Crusaders, had done with the British
singer Joe Cocker. It was called "I'm So Glad I'm Standing Here
Today." Willingham loved both the title and Cocker's presentation. "Cocker had a gruff voice, just a terrible voice," he said,
laughing. "It was like he wanted to scream but couldn't scream."

He acknowledged that John Coltrane, Thelonious Monk,
and Charlie Parker were fabulous musicians, but he enjoyed Joe
Sample because he appealed to a wider audience. "The thing
about jazz is that it's never offensive," said Willingham. "If you

put on country music or rock music, someone is gonna get offended. If you play rock, there'll be someone who can't stand the lyrics or the guitar. Either way, someone is gonna get pissed off." He shrugged. "It's because different forms of music alienate different people. But jazz alienates no one. With jazz, you can just listen and tap your foot along to it."

Six games into his first season at Notre Dame, Willingham's relationship with the university could be described in terms of an unlikely jazz ensemble. On the surface, there were two radically different instruments — Willingham, the slight oboe with the resonating tone, and Notre Dame, the haughty brass section. The self-proclaimed country boy from North Carolina had stepped into the most conservative Catholic institution in the country — but the coach, his team, and their fans were already jamming to the same simple beat. And the rest of the nation was beginning to tap its collective foot as well.

Willingham's face was everywhere. His wife, Kim, told him earlier that season, "I'm tired of turning on the TV and seeing your face." But that was the time for him to be seen. With recruits due to sign letters of intent in February, the September to December season was like college football's sweeps week. For any college football coach, there's no such thing as too much exposure.

Midway through the season, when Notre Dame and Florida State were said to have the best recruiting classes lined up at that point, Willingham got some great exposure when he appeared on CNN on October 17. It was Aaron Brown's report. Segment 7 was the final portion of the broadcast, and for it to feature Willingham and his team offered proof that what was taking place at Notre Dame had exceeded the confines of the sports world.

After showing black-and-white photos of the neighborhood where Willingham grew up, they flashed shots of him as a player at Michigan State, and then cut to the man himself, who sat straight-backed in front of the camera. Of course, Brown, like everyone else, wanted to know what kind of player Willingham had been, but when it came to his athletic skills, Willingham was consistently self-deprecating.

"I was terrible," he said.

Brown laughed. "Why?"

"I just had no athletic ability."

When Brown asked him questions about race, Willingham was just as forthright. "Young people just need to hear a positive message. And it doesn't matter if it's coming from someone black, red, yellow, or green."

By the time the national segment ended, Willingham had gained just a little more momentum in his ceaseless effort to get the attention of prospective recruits. Just two weeks earlier, the university had received a verbal commitment from Trevor Laws, the top defensive tackle in Minnesota. He had come for a visit during the Stanford weekend and had made his decision the following day. On Sunday morning, after watching the film from that Saturday's game, Greg Mattison had rushed over to Trent Walter's office to break the news.

"We got him," said Mattison, doing a little happy dance, which consisted of tilting his pelvis and pumping his fist. "He's coming here. He just committed." It was a welcome addition to the defensive line, which was, at the time, about to play its best ball.

Thursday's practice took place in a steady frosty drizzle. Willingham was buzzing with positive energy as he rode in on his bike, the grass sloshing beneath his tires. The Air Force game would be the first time since Michigan, back in September, that the Irish entered a game as three-point underdogs. Some coaches in Willingham's position would have resented taking a backseat to a school — an *academy,* no less — currently ranked No. 18 by the AP. But it was obvious that Willingham relished the underdog label. How could he not? He had been doubted his entire life.

Willingham had entered the Notre Dame job search as an underdog, his team had begun the season as an underdog, and after eight weeks, he and his team were still underdogs. Since he was practiced at keeping people at bay, artful at making them guess his thoughts and motives, why not privately convey to his team that he loved that image of underdog and publicly be a relentlessly positive bundle of energy? It wasn't that he just relished proving people wrong; he relished proving people wrong without having to say "I told you so" afterward. In conveying his feelings through a relentless aura of invincibility, he always implied that you were wrong for underestimating him and that he was right for making you look bad. Underneath his good cheer and positive vibe beat the heart of a competitive killer. And as he prepared to take on Air Force, that supreme confidence was beginning to rub off on his team.

This was the first time Notre Dame would face an option team in the Willingham era, and all the questions about the upcoming contest centered on how they'd stop an offense that had been averaging 300 yards per game. Year to year, the Air Force teams were always the same. They relied on small athletes who beat people by utilizing speed on both sides of the ball, swarming and biting at an opponent's scheme until he quit. Because of that, they rarely had that one stud athlete who wreaks havoc on both the college and professional level.

In Air Force, the Notre Dame defense was issued its first public challenge. After beginning the season with a shutout and scoring three touchdowns at a point when the offense couldn't get into the end zone, the defense had proven itself as the real deal. But public sentiment proclaimed that the Irish defense wouldn't get any love unless it stopped the intricately potent option offense.

Baer and his crew knew that the real secret to Air Force's success was speed and deception. Chance Harridge was the typical cadet quarterback. He was listed at 5'11" but was closer to 5'9" and quick as hell. In many ways, he resembled former Air Force quarterback Dee Dowis, who finished sixth in the 1989 Heisman Trophy race. Harridge was also a shit-talker and had brazenly stated that Notre Dame couldn't stop the Falcons' running game and that he would throw the ball at will against their secondary.

Air Force's running game centered on using the quick dive to tenderize the middle of the defensive line. And after that had been accomplished, after the interior linemen had been cut blocked and chopped to death, the Air Force offense would attack the edges with a relentless option attack that got its pace from Harridge's superb swiftness.

It's difficult for a defense to prepare for such a strong offense without getting people hurt at practice. During the week, Notre Dame's scout team simulated blocking low, around the defensive linemen's legs. Darrell Campbell, Cedric Hilliard, Ryan Roberts, and Kyle Budinscak would have to get their hands down and leapfrog oncoming offensive linemen. Greg Mattison, the defensive line coach, had Campbell and Hilliard play a G technique. That meant they would spend the entire game stacked directly over the guards, effectively clogging up the inside running lanes, which Air Force had been relying on. When the game turned to the outside, Notre Dame would lean on strong safety Gerome Sapp, who played like a linebacker, to come up and force the pitch by stoning Harridge.

Greg Mattison was the one holdover from Bob Davie's staff. He had been the Irish defensive coordinator for the previous five seasons, and his daughter, Lisa, was a standout on the Notre Dame softball team. Tall, outgoing, and personable, Mattison also served as the Irish recruiting coordinator. He had hand-picked some of the guys on the defensive line. That week, Mattison was even more fired up than usual. He knew that to stop Air Force, his unit had to play an outstanding game.

With the game plan in place, Mattison went to work on his players' psyches. "Play like a bunch of thugs!" he screamed at them. At practice, Mattison wore a little blue skullcap cocked to the side — pimp style — perhaps to give him some credibility and to bolster his thug-life exhortations. "Throw some people around. Be thugs in there!"

Saturday arrived, and the game, which was scheduled for an 8:00 P.M. kickoff, would be Notre Dame's first night game since Maryland. And though it was only mid-October, it was already cold in Colorado Springs. It was 38 degrees, and the frosty air had an aftertaste that smacked of gunmetal. Perhaps that was because of the unmistakable military presence among the 56,409 fans.

Minutes before kickoff, the cadets, many dressed in camouflage, assembled silently on the field. When they broke formation, they made a frenzied dash to the stands, yelling and screaming as if possessed. While it's true there have been too many tired and worn clichés comparing football to war, the delicate balance of icy discipline and rabid enthusiasm displayed at Falcon Stadium created the ideal battlefield that night in Colorado Springs — especially for the Notre Dame defense.

All the questions about how they would handle the Falcons' offense were answered fairly early. On the first two plays, both options, Chance Harridge managed to get around the corner and pick up a quick first down. But that first series, and any spark from the Air Force offense for that matter, turned out to be nothing more than a tease. That night, the Irish defense, particularly the defensive line, played with white-hot intensity that screamed for national credibility.

After those first two series, Cedric Hilliard was gasping for air. He came to the sideline, slumped down on the bench, snatched the oxygen mask, and sucked. He was moving with every ounce of quickness he had and was playing his best game of the season.

On the next Air Force drive, ESPN analysts Lee Corso and Kirk Herbstreit wandered over to the Notre Dame sideline. "Wow," said Corso, impressed by Hilliard's speed, "they haven't blocked that number fifty yet." They hadn't. Hilliard was knifing through blocks, jumping over linemen, and getting in the backfield on just about every play.

On one play, when Harridge attempted to throw and the ball was tipped by Roberts, Hilliard, tracking the ball in the air and watching it float toward the Notre Dame sideline, went airborne, his short, compact fire hydrant of a body stretched out like an Olympic diver. The ball fell just out of his grasp, but the portrait of him laid out and fully extended told the story of that night.

The defense was out to earn some respect and to make people recognize the real depth of their hunger and talent. And they were doing it the only way a defense can — by beating the offensive linemen off the ball and beating the crap out of the quarterback.

With his defense asserting itself as the real deal, Willingham urged on his offense. He realized they were still searching for an identity, but in the meantime, he worked on their sense of urgency. On a few occasions, they barely snapped the ball before the play clock expired. At one point, Willingham pushed Holiday after he came to the sideline. "Come on," he said. "We can't move faster than that?"

But for the most part, Holiday and his teammates demonstrated the kind of hardheaded resilience that had come to define the team that college football fans and media loved to doubt. After the shoulder injury, Holiday had taken a lot of hits, but he hadn't given in to caution.

On the sixth Irish play of the game, when Holiday was drilled in the back by a Falcons linebacker, he gave up the ball. Then, four series later, he was smacked in his blind side by a defensive end, and the ball was caught in midair and returned for a touchdown, giving Air Force a 7–0 lead. But on the very next series, Holiday, acting as though none of that had happened, took off and got positively freaky on the Air Force D. As he ran, his body language stated, rather matter-of-factly, "Let me do a little somethin' to get these nonathletic cats off me." He swerved back and forth, making at least four defenders look *bad* on his way to a 53-yard touchdown, tying the score at seven.

But on the next series, a crisis arose. After a 10-play drive took them to the Air Force 24-yard line, Nicholas Setta jogged out to kick a 41-yard field goal. When it sailed to the right, it was official. Setta was in a slump. On Notre Dame's next offensive drive, while they pushed downfield, Setta solemnly kicked into the net on the sideline. He knew he might be called on again, and he wanted to be ready. A few feet away, Darrell Campbell, his bald brown head steaming from sweat and frost, watched Setta. "You got that thing ready, man?" Campbell asked. Setta, obviously happy to get the support, nodded at his teammate.

But the offense didn't need Nick Setta just then. In the simplicity of trench warfare, both the offensive and defensive lines were engaged in a competition. Beginning with the opening game shutout of Maryland, the defensive line had established itself, but against Air Force, their offensive counterparts made significant strides.

In the middle of the second quarter, they mounted a 12-play drive in which seemingly every Irish back on the roster took bites from the Air Force defensive line. Holiday got 18, Marcus

Wilson got seven, fullback Mike McNair got 12, Ryan Grant got 10, and Tom Lopienski got five. On second-and-10, Ryan Grant exploded for an 18-yard touchdown, putting Notre Dame up 14–7 and taking control of the game.

At halftime, the cadets performed a show that suggested two things: (1) it was really easy to poke fun at Notre Dame, and (2) it was even easier to poke fun at Notre Dame now that they had such a high-profile black man leading the football team. A short black kid, presumably one of the cadets, skipped onto the field dressed as a leprechaun. He wore lime-green hose and plaid knickers, and carried a small pot of gold. The announcer's voice echoed over the stadium. "Uh-oh, ladies and gentlemen. It looks as though a leprechaun has made his way into Air Force stadium. This looks like a job for Big Bird and Minibird."

A second later, the two Air Force mascots came onto the field in a mock-menacing manner. The larger bird rolled a large silver container. "Looks like they're trying to tempt the leprechaun with a keg," said the announcer. The crowd roared, while Mike the Leprechaun, Notre Dame's mascot, wore an expression that suggested it had never occurred to him that people around the nation weren't especially enamored with any part of the Notre Dame tradition.

The two birds managed to lure the little black leprechaun close enough to "assault" him. The little bird jumped on the leprechaun, sat on his chest, and began whaling away with make-believe haymakers. The bizarre skit ended when another cadet, bare-chested and dressed in running tights, ran onto the field and joined the other characters in a strained rendition of *Riverdance.*

A month later, the Naval Academy would also perform a half-time show at the leprechaun's expense. This was not an original concept, of course. But in the Naval Academy's version, the leprechaun was pummeled by a sailor in a fictitious boxing match. It was cleverly executed and cute enough to get laughs from even the Notre Dame fans, but the production in Colorado Springs — one of those remote settings ideal for militiatype lunacy — smacked of something else. The proverbial drunken Irishman being seduced by sweet alcohol, coupled with a little black man getting beat down by white folks in blue uniforms, made the Air Force Academy seem a little too eager to harness every stereotype they could into one sinister presentation. Perhaps it was best Willingham missed the show.

The second half opened with disaster, with the kind of play that could have torn the spirit from the team and halted their season's-worth of momentum. After receiving the kickoff, Vontez Duff found a seam and was just starting to accelerate when an Air Force defender stripped him of the ball. Air Force recovered on the Notre Dame 16-yard line. It was the first time the Air Force offense had been anywhere close to scoring position. In the battle of momentum, it was exactly what they needed. But the defense still made them work for it. It took Air Force six plays to go 16 yards, but after Chance Harridge slithered in from the one-yard line, the game was tied at 14.

Undaunted, the Irish offensive line used the next drive to mount another assault on the cadets' front four. It took them 11 plays to move downfield. On first-and-goal, they lined up on the four-yard line. Once there, they smelled blood. O-line coach Mike Denbrock ripped off his headset, took a few steps onto the field, and screamed at his guys, "Finish! Dammit, finish!"

That was no problem for Jeff Faine, who specialized in finishing blocks, steering his man like a go-cart around the tackle box, then driving him into the ground long after the whistle. Faine's MO was simple and often personal: "I want to make the other guy think maybe he's chosen the wrong sport."

But that night, Faine wasn't alone; everyone followed suit, especially Ryan Grant. In many ways, Grant came of age that night, running through people after contact, toting the rock 30 times, and finishing the game with a career-high 190 yards. After Grant was stopped at the one-yard line, Holiday took it from there, putting them up 21–14.

With less than six minutes left in the third quarter, Shane Walton halted the Falcons' next drive. Harridge, attempting to throw deep in front of his own sideline, never saw Walton drifting from the hash mark. Walton rose and plucked the ball from the air for his sixth interception of the year.

A little later, when Notre Dame's running game hit a lull, Arnaz Battle took over. First, on a hitch, he stuttered the cornerback and slipped through his grasp like a greased pig for a gain of 15 yards. But the most astonishing play of Battle's night, and perhaps of the entire season, came at the 12-minute mark of the fourth quarter. It was second-and-26 from the 42-yard line. It was Battle's play — the hitch screen. He caught the ball on the numbers, exploded into the middle, and shifted to a higher gear. After about 20 yards, the Falcons defenders converged on him — the safety had him around the waist; the corner jumped on his neck, wrapping his arm around Battle's throat as if he were performing a choke hold; and both linebackers attacked his ribs. Battle dragged all of them for another five yards. It was third-and-one, and Battle staggered to the bench, winded and exhausted, his legs cramping. While he was doubled over, sucking on oxygen, his offensive teammates committed one of the worst sins in team sports — they wasted the great individual effort of a teammate.

With the score 21–14, they had a chance to put Air Force away, to destroy their will, to score another touchdown and run the clock out. But once again, they either failed to recognize the moment or just didn't have what it took to deliver the blow. On a play called 45 Escort, Grant followed his fullback, Tom Lopienski, off the left tackle. Lopienski was supposed to block the linebacker, but as he tried, the backer drove him backward into Grant. On contact, Grant's legs stopped churning, and he fell for a loss of two in the backfield.

The Falcons defenders partied, leaping in the air and celebrating — they still had life after all. Battle, bent over, dropped the oxygen mask and looked up from the bench to see Nick Setta running onto the field. He looked up at Carlos Campbell. "We're kicking a field goal?" he asked breathlessly. Campbell nodded. "Aww fuck!" he said in disbelief. Making things worse, Setta's 36-yard attempt sailed right.

Willingham, arms folded, was expressionless. His team was playing well, exceeding all the expectations most fans had in the preseason, but he wanted more from them. They still hadn't developed that killer instinct, and they couldn't put a team away when they had the chance. At least his offense couldn't. But he knew the defense had given him a foundation upon which to build that night.

With 6:19 left in the game, Air Force began its final series on its own 10-yard line. Harridge had done nothing to back his pregame shit-talking; he had thrown for just 29 yards and rushed for a paltry 31. But true to his reputation as a bona fide baller, he hadn't backed down yet and was still intent on winning the damn thing. He completed two quick passes to make it to the 33-yard line. But once there, the Irish defense, in one final, decisive instant, squashed all doubt and answered all questions about themselves. And much to Willingham's delight, they did so right in front of him.

As Harridge tossed the ball to his tailback, the receiver tried to block Vontez Duff. But Duff, quickly reading the play, grabbed the receiver underneath his shoulder pads and flung him aside. Just as the receiver got airborne, limbs flying like a life-size Raggedy Andy doll, Gerome Sapp, on a dead sprint, met the running back helmet to helmet, the sound of fiberglass making a clacking sound, and drove him out of bounds for a one-yard loss. With the receiver on the ground a few feet away from him and the ball carrier at his feet, never having made it out of the backfield, Willingham allowed himself a wicked little smile. It was the kind of ruthless statement for which he'd been yearning all season. On the final drive, they had finally delivered.

12

FLORIDA STATE

O N MONDAY NIGHT in Seattle that October 14, 49ers receiver Terrell Owens made a statement about the black athlete's place in the hip-hop era of sports. It was a time when more and more athletes took any opportunity they could to celebrate their accomplishments on the field of play. And they usually did so with no shame. Terrell Owens was a player whose behavior was emblematic of the times.

In the second quarter of the 49ers-Seahawks game, Owens glided past Seattle cornerback Shawn Springs for a touchdown. Upon making it to the end zone, Owens reached down into his sock and produced a Sharpie marker — the kind autograph hounds offer professional athletes when they seek their signatures on photos, T-shirts, and footballs. Standing in the end zone, Owens scribbled his signature on the ball, then tossed it to a friend in the front row. The man was a financial advisor and a mutual friend to both Owens and Springs.

In the following weeks, the incident caused the kind of stir that had come to define Owens's young career. He had already raised the ire of sports fans in a 2000 game against Dallas, when, after scoring a touchdown, he had sprinted to the middle of the field, stood on the famed blue-carpeted star, tilted his head back, raised his arms, and posed as if God Himself had asked him to. In so doing, Owens had become the divining rod for all that was wrong with the modern athlete. Though consistently productive and cleverly creative, he lost many older fans, both black and white, for whom his self-aggrandizing acts represented a generation of athletes who seemed more obsessed with celebrating themselves and their accomplishments than their team's.

But it wasn't the actions themselves that made Owens the center of controversy; it was his defense for his actions. Hypersensitive and thoughtful, Owens responded to the specific incident in general terms. "You have a white-guy announcer and a white sportscaster," he said. "Me, I'm black. We're just more expressive than the white guys."

It was fitting that while Terrell Owens was shaking up the sports world, Notre Dame was preparing to play Florida State. Florida State was, of course, the alma mater of Deion Sanders. More than any other black athlete of the previous two decades, Sanders had made the self-congratulatory post-touchdown dance not merely a main staple of football but the definitive statement for the young black athlete. Florida State's home field, Doak Campbell Stadium, was, in many ways, the house that Deion built. And the Florida State players were known for dancing, trash-talking, and excessive celebration after big plays. But one Notre Dame player's view of Owens — and of Sanders for that matter — suggested that this behavior wasn't necessarily a cultural thing, or specifically a black thing, but a generational thing.

Gary Godsey, a senior tight end from Tampa, Florida, had spent the off-season training with Terrell Owens and some other college and NFL players in Atlanta. Before becoming a tight end, Godsey had come to Notre Dame as a quarterback. After Arnaz Battle broke his wrist and missed the 2000 season, it was Godsey who took the snaps. His first start was a 23–21 win over eventual Big Ten champion Purdue. But right then, Godsey was enjoying playing tight end during the Tyrone Willingham era. "He's great, isn't he?" said Godsey of his coach. He imitated Willingham, reciting one of the coach's most oft-repeated expressions: "*Now, men.* What we must do to win . . ."

When asked about the then infamous "Sharpie incident," Godsey shook his head and offered an easy smile. He knew it was one of those topics that Willingham probably considered off-limits. "I don't see what the big deal is," said Godsey, who is white. "I thought it was pretty cool, actually. That's just him. I probably wouldn't do something like that because I'd look stupid, and everyone at home would laugh at me. But I don't think it's a black-and-white thing." From his goatee to the way he said hello by casually tilting his head up rather than nodding it down, it was obvious that Godsey had logged some meaningful hours around the brothers — enough to know that cultural differences are only what you make of them.

In this debate, Willingham represented the generation of older black folks who, while pleased the younger generation had more freedom than they did, in some ways fretted about the social ramifications that accompanied such freedom. In some ways, Willingham couldn't distance himself from the patriarchal stance that most older blacks took on such matters of self-expression. Of course, as was the case with any issue, Willingham had a practical view of the Sharpie incident.

"We have to look at Terrell's behavior and say, 'When did I do that?'" said Willingham. "There's a time in each of our lives when we can say, 'Okay, I did something to that effect.' It probably wasn't on TV with thousands of people in the stands, but it was probably something with poor judgment along those lines. If he wanted to give his buddy the ball, he could do it after the game. But there was a larger issue there. What he says to me is, 'Everything I do is done to grab the spotlight.'

"Now there are more productive ways to get the spotlight. Who's knocking on his door right now to offer him commercials? I don't know. There could be a lot. But because of his behavior, he may have been cut out of that market. For a guy who loves the spotlight, wouldn't that be a great way to get it? One of the best receivers in the league? Having all those advertisers, wouldn't that be good?"

Actually, advertisers did capitalize on Owens's gesture. On December 24, Owens appeared in a full-page print advertisement in *USA Today*. In the ad, a metallic silver marker is sticking out of Owens's sock, and the caption reads: "Mr. Owens, have we got a stocking stuffer for you." Owens got some exposure, but he didn't get paid. Instead, Sharpie donated $25,000 to the Alzheimer's Association in his name.

But getting the attention of advertisers wasn't the only point Willingham had made in discussing Owens. Willingham was talking about performance. He thought that while on the football field, a player's athletic deeds, not his self-expression, should get him the exposure he deserves. For Willingham, it was simple — he just wanted to win at everything he did. But Owens was a different person, from a different generation, who took a different approach.

"That's the age we live in," said Willingham. Shaking his head and laughing to himself, he said, "But you can autograph a ball *after* the game."

One of Willingham's favorite expressions that season was "It's a shame when many are judged by one." He usually made it in reference to his place as college football's most highly visible black coach, but that statement also applied to black people in general. And by disagreeing with Owens's stance that his actions were "black," Willingham offered proof that black folks, in thought, feeling, and practice, were not a monolithic people. In his view, the only thing black folks shared across the board was the color of their skin. And not even *that* was totally uniform.

"There are so many beautiful shades of black in this world," he said. "There's black, there's blue, there's brown, there's chocolate, there's midnight black, and *pe-can* tan. With that many shades of black people, how can we fit under one hat? But most of this stuff crosses all kinds of social lines. If it was truly cultural, then all African-Americans could dance, couldn't they? But all African-Americans can't dance. Some are just *terrible*. So some things aren't cultural."

At Tuesday's press conference, with the Terrell Owens issue still the hot topic of discussion, Tim Prister was eager to dive headfirst into it. He broached the topic midway through the conference. "It has been suggested by some athletes who choose to celebrate their successes on the football field that the criticism from the media is a cultural misunderstanding on the media's part. Do you concur with that assessment?"

Willingham, genuinely humored by Prister's foray into the cultural world, something Willingham would never approach with the local media, dropped his head and laughed. Willingham had established himself as *the* artful dodger of South Bend, and Prister's straightforward question on such a no-no topic really tickled him. Even if he weren't the football coach at a conservative university like Notre Dame, he wouldn't have touched the subject. The issue of race was one he rarely discussed in public, simply because race was such a potentially volatile issue and open to so many interpretations. Besides that, he was just a private person.

"No, I'm not even going near that one," said Willingham.

"I thought it was a pretty good question," said Prister.

"It was," replied a game Willingham. "And I really love the way you worded it. But you should have known I wouldn't touch that one."

It was a good moment, a fun, lighthearted moment when the season-long tension between Willingham and the local media succumbed to actual humor. During the preceding three weeks, these men had settled comfortably into their roles, and the press conferences had become informative comic relief.

On Thursday afternoon, October 24, it was a chilly 40 degrees in South Bend, but to simulate Saturday's game conditions in Florida, where it was averaging about 80 degrees, Willingham conducted Thursday's practice inside the Loftus Center. After stretching and warm-ups, the managers turned on the PA system. Immediately, the air was saturated with the Seminoles war chant. It was captivating at first, even cool and intimidating, but after a few minutes, the redundant eight-beat chant got downright sickening. "Oooh-oh-o-o-ooooh, oooh-oh-o-ao-o-oooh . . ." Always one to turn a negative into a positive, Willingham didn't use this just to get his players accustomed to it; he wanted them to feed off it. "I want them to get fired up when they hear that," he said delightedly. "Just like I suppose the other team does."

By the next day, though, the players didn't seem to notice it. They drowned it out and had one of the better Friday practices they'd had all season. In fact, it had been one of their best weeks of practice all year. Especially for Nick Setta. In the game against Air Force, Setta was 0–2 on field goal attempts, so early in the week, Willingham was asked to defend Setta's "slump." In typical Willingham fashion, he refused to engage in someone else's negative language. "I don't use that term," he said.

As he did at every Friday practice, Willingham frequently interrupted the team period to practice field goals. Now that Setta was struggling, that tactic was especially important. He leaned forward and blew his whistle. "Field goal!" he shouted. The field goal unit assembled at various distances. And Setta, with the Seminoles war chant blaring from all directions, calmly hit each one. After he hit a 58-yarder, he was done for the day, having hit nine in a row.

After practice, Setta strolled into the media room and spoke to a couple reporters. His confidence was obvious. He was about 5′11″ and just shy of 180 pounds, with dark hair and a muscular build for a kicker. He stood up straight, maintained eye contact, and spoke in a loud voice, heavy on bass. He was ready to prove that nothing had changed, that he was the same guy he had been all season long. He was the same guy who had kicked five field goals against Maryland and provided all the offense in the early part of the season. His attitude came as no surprise to Willingham, who had commented, "I think Nick Setta is one of the most confident players I've ever been around."

With the biggest game of Willingham's Notre Dame career falling in October, the date provided a reminder of another significant moment in black football history. In October 1963, Darryl Hill became the first black player in ACC history. When he and his Maryland teammates took the field at Bowman Gray Stadium in Winston-Salem, North Carolina, racial slurs rained down on Hill like hailstones. But when Hill, who was captain that day, walked to midfield, Wake Forest running back Brian Piccolo put his arm around him and apologized for the fans' behavior. The stadium fell silent. Of course, this was the same Brian Piccolo whose friendship with black teammate Gale Sayers spawned the all-time tearjerker in football movie history, *Brian's Song*.

When Willingham took the field at Doak Campbell Stadium, he met Bobby Bowden at midfield. It wasn't exactly the sentimental maelstrom *Brian's Song* was, but it did merit a certain poignance. Willingham was college football's hottest story, and with Nebraska's Tom Osborne now serving in the U.S. Congress, Bowden, along with Penn State's Joe Paterno, was among college football's last "legendary coaches." This wasn't lost on Willingham. Earlier in the season, two days after the Michigan game, Willingham already had an eye on Bowden and Florida State. "Bobby is coaching on regular old fuel right now," said Willingham at the time. "But by the time we get to them, he'll be on that supersonic jet fuel."

That may have been true, but Bowden's team had already suffered two losses, one to Louisville in overtime and one to Miami. The Seminoles were 5–2 and ranked 11th by the AP, but they were still favored by 10 points over No. 6 Notre Dame. As he had against Air Force, Willingham loved having that kind of thing to motivate his team. He thrived on finding ways to pour his competitive fire into his teams. Four days before the game, seated in his office, Willingham had been calm and focused when he said, "The best team doesn't always win. The team that *plays* best wins."

Perhaps it was his way of conceding that Bobby Bowden, at least in total number of athletes, had a deeper team than he did. And Florida State had more speed at key positions like receiver. In Anquan Boldin and Robert Morgan, Shane Walton and Vontez Duff were up against the most explosive receivers they'd seen all season. And the defensive line was facing the best runner they'd seen all year in Greg Jones.

Of course, the game's other plotline came from the last time these teams had played each other in a truly big game. In October 1993, Florida State, then the consensus number one, lost to then number two Notre Dame, 31–24. The subplot that day had been two black quarterbacks. In that game, Florida State was led by Charlie Ward, and Notre Dame by Kevin McDougal. Following that season, Charlie Ward, the first black quarterback in Florida State history, also became the second black quarterback to win the Heisman Trophy. Afterward, Bowden proclaimed in his renowned, self-effacing folksy humor: "We finally figured out they could throw the ball."

It was a fitting presage to the current game because although his team was 7–0, Carlyle Holiday was still under intense scrutiny as he mastered the complexities of the offense. More than halfway through the season, he was still regarded by most college football fans as the option quarterback who couldn't throw the ball. He'd shown some flashes of his ability, most notably against Michigan. And even while struggling against Pitt, he had still maintained a steely poise; he just needed to do it consistently. In Tallahassee, he was going to see more speed, more raw athleticism, and more open hostility from the defense. But prior to the game, in making all of the right reads and throwing the ball with zip and touch, Holiday had had his best week of practice all year.

Kickoff on Saturday, October 26, 2002, was at high noon, when the temperature was 70 degrees. Many of the 84,106 screaming fans had spent the morning tailgating outside Doak Campbell Stadium, and though it was early, the crowd was already pretty well liquored up. Notre Dame won the toss and, as usual, deferred to the second half. After a quick three and out, Florida State punted. Willingham walked quickly downfield, from one 30-yard line to the other, covering the distance in about the time it would take most men his age to sprint it. When he settled at the 30 and crossed his arms, it was obvious he was waiting for someone on the field to join him at that spot.

On the offense's opening play, the Irish not only removed the Florida State crowd from the game in one fell swoop but also drained the life from Doak Campbell Stadium and sucked the rest of the country wholeheartedly into Willingham–Notre Dame mania. They took the field and, without using a huddle, lined up ready to go. Holiday, on a half rollout, drifted to his right and lobbed the ball downfield. Arnaz Battle bolted from his stance and ran a "go route," a deep route that took him down the Notre Dame sideline. Within three seconds, Battle had the cornerback beaten by a full three yards. When Battle reached the spot almost directly in front of Willingham, Holiday's throw settled into Battle's hands, and he burned a trail through the middle of the field, outrunning the safety to the corner of the end zone for 65 yards. Battle stood on a patch of burgundy grass and mimicked Florida State's signature gesture, the tomahawk chop. With his right hand, he made the chopping motion, and then, with the same hand, he gestured as if he were violently slicing his own throat. Though understated, it was certainly Terrell Owensesque.

He earned a 15-yard penalty and, even worse, a reservation for Sunday morning running with Willingham. But for the moment, that was meaningless. All Willingham cared about was that his team was finally getting off to a quick start. He and Diedrick had preached that all year, and for the first time, they had executed it. He pumped his fist and walked to the other end of the sideline. *"Yes!"*

For most of the first quarter, that play served as a muzzle for the Seminoles and their fans. On the next drive, Florida State did manage to kick a field goal. But Nick Setta, after an 11-play drive, offered further proof that he was *that* Nick Setta, the one who had provided all the offense in the first two weeks of the season. After he kicked a 39-yarder, it was 10–3, and Notre Dame had control of the game. But then, Florida State mounted a 20-play, 93-yard drive that took up most of the second quarter. It was one of those give-and-take drives in which the offense would give an indication it was ready to take control of the game only to have the defense reassert itself as the real deal.

The key play was on second-and-10. Florida State quarterback Chris Rix wanted to hit receiver Anquan Boldin on a slant, but Boldin was wise enough to know that Glenn Earl was lurking in the middle of the field. After seven games, Earl had garnered the most coveted reputation for any defensive player — the hitman. As Boldin slowed down and let the ball sail wide, the ball hit Earl in his arm loud enough to make a smacking sound heard on the sideline. Having a missile lock on Boldin, Earl was already intent on drilling Boldin's skull and never saw the ball coming. That kept the drive alive. On the next play, Rix hit Boldin on a slant, and he took it 39 yards to the two-yard line.

On third-and-goal, Baer and Mattison knew Florida State

liked the naked bootleg, in which Rix faked to Jones, hid the ball, and casually ran in the opposite direction. Baer and Mattison screamed in hoarse voices, trying to warn the defense. "Watch the boot! Watch the boot!" Problem was, they didn't run a boot. Seminoles fullback Torrance Washington took the ball, found a crease in between Darrell Campbell and Kyle Budinscak, squeezed through it, and tied the score at 10.

With exactly 7:30 left in the third quarter, Notre Dame found its killer instinct. After the teams traded punts, Florida State had a first-and-10 on its own 34-yard line. Chris Rix was trying to attack the middle of the field, and he wanted Boldin on a crossing route. But Courtney Watson, dropping to his zone, jumped to Boldin's left, plucked the ball off his shoulder, used the vision he had as a running back to cut back across the field, and returned the ball to the 23-yard line.

The offense, still committed to developing a power running game, had Ryan Grant run three straight times before losing two yards on third down, and Notre Dame settled for a 35-yard field goal, which Setta easily made.

On the ensuing kickoff, with Notre Dame leading 13–10, reserve linebacker Carlos Pierre-Antoine decided he wasn't going to be blocked anymore that day. The third man from the left on the kickoff team, Pierre-Antoine blazed past his man and laid his helmet on freshman running back Leon Washington. It was a precursor to the rest of the afternoon.

After a loss of three yards on a running play, Rix, who was obviously frustrated that his team was losing, tried to win it himself. A good runner who had the balls to attack opposing linebackers and safeties, Rix took off downfield. At the 17-yard line he met up with Glenn Earl. Seeing Earl before him, and knowing Earl's reputation, Rix didn't even pretend to *think* about sliding headfirst. But Rix had been trying the defense all day, daring someone to hit him. As Rix lowered his shoulder, Earl sliced into him, his helmet landing squarely on the ball, sending it squirting out behind Rix. Earl hit him with such force that the ball rolled all the way to the two-yard line, where Vontez Duff finally chased it down and cradled it.

On the next play, Ryan Grant took a pitch, ran a few steps to his right, and cut back, stepping into the end zone with an authority he hadn't displayed all season. Notre Dame 20, Florida State 10.

On the next kickoff, still intoxicated by the fumes he had ingested the previous kickoff, Carlos Pierre-Antoine sprinted by his man and once again put it to the returner. But this time, Pierre-Antoine knocked the ball loose on the 17-yard line, where Brandon Hoyte quickly fell on it.

Willingham was standing, arms folded, on the 20-yard line at the moment of impact. The second the ball appeared, he instinctively leaped into the air, raising his arm in the process. When he came down, he tightly pumped his fist in the direction of the pile forming around the ball. Behind him, Justin Tuck screamed, "We smell blood! We smell blood!"

They did smell blood, and for the first time, it wasn't just the defense drawing it. From the opening play, the offense, defense, and special teams had begun to compete with the kind of lusty vengeance for which their coach thirsted.

Three plays later, Carlyle Holiday dropped back, set his feet, and lobbed a beautifully arced fade to Omar Jenkins in the corner of the end zone to make the score 27–10. As senior offensive guard Sean Mahan hoisted Holiday into the air, Willingham pointed at Holiday the same way basketball players point to one another after an assist. Holiday grinned and pointed back, wearing a toothy grin that said "Yeah, I told you I was a passer!"

The play was just the way they had practiced it and just the way they had planned to execute it, and for those few seconds, things were absolutely perfect. Well, almost perfect. On the ensuing Florida State drive, nose tackle Cedric Hilliard partially tore some ligaments in his knee and would be out for about a month. But at the time, not even losing their best defensive lineman could stop their momentum. They were starting to believe in themselves.

With just over eight minutes to go in the game, receivers Maurice Stovall, Carlos Campbell, and Rhema McKnight huddled at the end of the bench. There was about 10 feet separating them

athletes, if not the best team, they had faced all year, his team had done something they hadn't done before. They had jumped on an opponent's back and stayed there until it was over.

Well, *almost* over. The final five minutes were a disaster and represented the complete antithesis of what Willingham preached and the competitive spirit upon which he stood. And Willingham didn't hide his disgust. Fifteen minutes after the game had ended, he still had *the look*. "When you have a chance to bury an opponent, you should do so," he told his players.

But an hour later, Willingham's mood changed as he made good on a promise. He had told his team that if they won, he would dance. As the bus rolled toward the Tallahassee Airport, the bus driver pumped up the radio as Al Green came on. While his team urged him on, Willingham stood up in the aisle and slowly grooved to the old-school beat. No one knew right then that this was as good as it would get for them all season.

13

BOSTON COLLEGE

O VER THE COURSE of ten weeks, Notre Dame had become the biggest story in college football, and Willingham, with his infamous poker-faced sideline demeanor, was a legend in the making. He had come to Notre Dame and done nothing but win, beating teams other first-year Irish coaches couldn't beat. Not even Lou Holtz had won against Michigan his first season, and no other Notre Dame coach had beaten two ranked opponents on the road in successive weeks. But in the quest for a ninth straight victory, over Boston College, Notre Dame faced a rival whose hunger to beat them topped all others'.

The Boston College rivalry was a little different from the other rivalries. It transcended football tradition and settled on a question of identity. Like Notre Dame, Boston College was a Catholic school, and the game on November 2 was the latest installment of a contest known to some as the "Catholic Super Bowl." But it was more a rivalry for Boston College than it was for Notre Dame. Notre Dame didn't pay too much attention to their neighbors in Boston. Some Irish students thought you only went to Boston College after failing to get accepted at Notre Dame. And Boston College didn't share Notre Dame's stringent view of separate but equal when it came to the Big East. Notre Dame had joined the conference in 1995 for all sports except football.

There was also the question of Notre Dame team's identity

that week. By beating Florida State, they had clearly established themselves as a team worthy of recognition. Ranked No. 5 by the AP, they were a natural favorite to go to a BCS bowl game. But some around the college football world still questioned them. Early in the week, ESPN analyst Kirk Herbstreit said Notre Dame had beaten an overrated Air Force team and a Florida State team that was average at best.

But that wasn't the discussion around South Bend that week. Since Notre Dame was a place where history seemed to repeat itself, the topic of the week was the 1993 Boston College game.

On November 20, 1993, after having beaten then top-ranked Florida State 31–24, Notre Dame was No. 1 in the nation and hosting Boston College in the last home game of the season. From the start, Boston College had one of those days that defies description. Everything they did worked. At halftime, they led 24–14 and eventually pushed their lead to 38–17. But in the second half Notre Dame, led by quarterback Kevin McDougal, scored 22 unanswered points to go ahead 39–38. Then, with just over a minute left and with Boston College starting on its own 25-yard line, the Eagles drove downfield and into field goal range. Boston College kicker David Gordon kicked a 41-yard field goal as time expired, and the Irish fell from No. 1. A month later, Notre Dame beat Texas A&M in the Cotton Bowl to finish 11–1. Although Florida State also finished with an identical 11–1 record and the Irish had beaten the Seminoles, Bobby Bowden's team was awarded the national championship.

On Tuesday morning, knowing the comparisons were coming and quick to launch a preemptive strike on the topic, Willingham fired the first shot as he brought up the 1993 game in his weekly press conference. "When you don't know history, you run the risk of repeating it," he told a crowd of reporters. The least superstitious person on the planet, Willingham didn't believe that what had happened in 1993 had any bearing on what could happen nine years later. But this wasn't just about him. It was about his team. And he knew what they were up against in terms of public perception.

Ever resourceful when looking for a motivational tool, Willingham found this one quite convenient. "It could go either way," he said. "For some people it gets them sharper and more focused on what they have to do."

Willingham pored over the Boston College scouting report in his office one night. "This young man [Derrick Knight] is running the ball extremely well. Of course, they had another young man [William Green, who had been a first-round pick of the Cleveland Browns in April] who ran the ball well against us at Stanford last year."

While Willingham's eyes looked more tired than usual, he was fired up and ready to play the game. "We have momentum now," he said. "And you gotta ride the big 'mo' while you have it! It's not like a light switch. You can't turn it on and off."

Through a yawn, he said the biggest concern for the team that week would be the distractions that come from postseason expectations. He leaned back in his swivel chair and exhaled. "Aw, man, these guys will have family calling them and asking them where they should make reservations for January. They have the students getting in their ears and telling them, 'Oh, you don't have to worry about *that* game.' And, of course, they'll have all the girls approaching them, trying to become the 'new' girlfriend." He leaned back and smiled. "People are jumping on the bandwagon now. And that's okay. Just as long as the wagon is still moving downhill."

He narrowed his eyes while he spoke. Although the stakes were higher and the pressure was mounting, he was determined to stick to his plan and to allow nothing to influence his daily preparation. "I remember something [former NFL running back] Terry Allen once said to me: 'If you put enough internal pressure on anything, it will eventually burst.' The key is not getting too uptight. When you enjoy your job, it's that much better."

He leaned forward and held up a tight fist. "If you have your butts too tight, then you can't play." He tilted his head back and pondered that thought. He knew it applied to him as much as it did to his team.

As the team stretched for Wednesday's practice, Willingham walked with a bouncy step, up and down the rows of players.

Over the past few weeks, the team had become more vocal in terms of its goals. As they warmed up at practice, random players would shout that week's goal. First it had been "Six and oh," then "Seven and oh," and that week the objective was one that would have been met with laughter had it been uttered by fans in August — "Nine and oh!"

On that cold afternoon, Willingham waited until it was abnormally quiet before he got into the act himself. Feeling a little rakish, Willingham conjured up some Johnnie Cochran rhyming skills when he let loose with, "If you're not trying to get nine, then you're wasting time!" It hit the mark as the team, which up to that point had been lethargic, cracked up, then woke up and had a great practice.

After practice, when a small group of reporters gathered around him and the rivalry topic arose, Willingham got annoyed. Someone asked if he was aware of how big the Notre Dame–Boston College rivalry was. Willingham spoke in his normally even tone, but for a second, his voice grew cold as he stared the man down. "I've been coaching for twenty-some-odd years, and I understand the nature of this rivalry and other rivalries like it."

He knew what the Boston College rivalry meant, and he knew what had happened in 1993, but he was more concerned with the specific game itself and how each win raised the stakes for him and his team. At 8–0, they were not only in the hunt for the national championship but also, with USC as the only remaining threat on their schedule, carrying the biggest gun. "With each win it gets bigger," he said. "If we win this one, the Navy game becomes huge." The thought tickled him because Navy wasn't a good team, and using something like a shot at the national championship as motivation made him smile.

At Friday night's pep rally, the fans in attendance got to learn a little about Notre Dame's reticent coach. They were addressed by a man who at the time was probably the second most popular black coach in America.

A little after 7:30, as Willingham led his team into the gym, he was followed by then San Francisco Giants manager Dusty

Baker. Just five days earlier, Baker's Giants had lost Game Seven of the World Series to the Anaheim Angels, so Baker had come to South Bend to visit his friend. Willingham and Baker weren't close friends, but they had a mutual respect, and Baker had been invited to speak to one of Willingham's Stanford teams as well.

As a kid in Southern California, Baker had grown up listening to Notre Dame games on the radio. Later, when Baker became a USC fan, the Irish-Trojans rivalry got him even more acquainted with the Notre Dame tradition. But this particular visit had little to do with football. It had something to do with Tyrone Willingham's impact on the sports landscape and everything to do with Baker's feelings for Willingham as a man. Baker also insisted that he wasn't there to visit the Chicago Cubs, who at the time were aggressively seeking his services as a manager. He was there because he had always watched Notre Dame on television, and now that he had a friend and respected colleague sitting in the big chair, in the big office, it was the ideal time to drop in for a visit.

After taking the mike, Dusty Baker painted a warm, open portrait of Willingham. The crowd giggled because like the rest of the college football world, they yearned for small glimpses of Willingham with his guard down. And Baker happily obliged.

"Last year at about this time, while Tyrone was wrestling with the decision to leave Stanford for Notre Dame, he came and visited me in the hospital while I had prostate cancer," said Baker. "I was touched that he came to see me that day. The next time I saw him was on TV, getting off the plane, wearing his hat and long coat, looking all cool."

Baker told the audience how much that gesture meant to him and that he hoped when his 3-year-old son, Darren, was old enough to go to college, he would choose Notre Dame. Turning around to look at Willingham, Baker said, "But that would be thirteen years from now, right, Coach?" Baker, like everyone else, knew that because of Notre Dame's incredible season, NFL general managers would surely come sniffing around South Bend as they had while he was at Stanford.

For the moment, Willingham was more concerned with the fans before him than with any NFL admirers. Before introducing

Baker, he had already done some quick crowd management. Many Irish students and fans felt Boston College desperately wanted to *be* Notre Dame. And when a group of BC fans showed up at the Notre Dame pep rally, there was proof of that theory. Dressed in their maroon and gold, waving spirit sticks, they sat in the rafters and shouted at all the inappropriate times. Of course, the most inappropriate of these times was when Willingham was at the mike. As was his custom, Willingham took some rather lengthy pauses, and during one of those pauses, a BC fan shouted, "Let's go, Eagles!"

Maintaining eye contact with his audience, Willingham deadpanned, "I saw a commercial the other day in which a person says, 'This is *our* house. They can go home.'" At each of these rallies, the crowd was quick to applaud anything Willingham said, but that terse little admonition to some unwelcome visitors got the Irish fans positively geeked, and they erupted into a prolonged cheer.

After making his weekly request that the fans create a sea of green, Willingham dropped a clue that he had something special planned the next day. "I know it will be cold out there tomorrow, and many of you will have to cover up those green shirts with coats," he said.

"No!" the students interrupted him.

Willingham, tickled by the response, relented. "Okay, maybe you won't have to cover them up." But it was his way of telling them "It's okay, you've done your job. You've done what I've asked you to in terms of supporting this team by wearing the green shirts. But tomorrow we'll do *our* part to maintain the sea of green."

The next day, during pregame warm-ups, Willingham had the equipment managers hang green jerseys in each player's locker. No one, not the other coaches, not even the captains that day, had any clue that Willingham had chosen this game to incorporate one of Notre Dame's more colorful traditions. In doing so, Willingham had taken a cue from the late Dan Devine. In 1977, before Notre Dame played USC, the Irish had gone through warm-ups in their traditional blue jerseys. But before kickoff, when they came spilling from the tunnel, they wore green. The stadium went wild, and the Irish crushed USC 49–19.

Twenty-five years later, a similar scene unfolded. But the goal wasn't just to get a rise from the fans; Willingham wanted to connect with them. When Courtney Watson, Preston Jackson, Glenn Earl, and Gerome Sapp came bursting from the tunnel, clad in the metallic broccoli-colored shirts, a record crowd of 80,935 erupted, and Willingham sensed the school had achieved a singularity of spirit.

Their first drive was among their best all season. They went 10 plays — eight runs and two passes — getting to the 20-yard line. And on fourth-and-one, Willingham went for it without hesitation. But after Eagles defensive end Mathi Kiwanuka got underneath the 300-pound senior guard Sean Milligan and stopped Ryan Grant in his tracks, everything changed. The game was different, and the season was different.

Before that play, the season had been about as close to perfect as it could possibly be for any team and its first-year coach. Oh, they weren't perfect in execution, not by any stretch of the imagination. They were never a great team, and at times, they weren't even a sound team. They were a team that believed they were better than they actually were. And when that kind of team is pushed hard and plays hard, that kind of belief is a good thing. It makes them, for lack of a better word, a "blessed" team. Seven minutes into the game, after the momentum ceased on that drive, they were still blessed. But for the rest of the day and the rest of the season, they were also painfully mortal.

Notre Dame's second drive consisted of one play in which Ryan Grant and Holiday fumbled the exchange. Boston College recovered, and a few minutes later Derrick Knight scored on a three-yard run to make it 6–0. When the Irish got the ball back, Notre Dame again easily went downfield. Two minutes before the second quarter, they still looked as though they possessed the magic that had defined their season. But once inside the red zone, the ensuing chain of events would culminate in disaster.

On second-and-four from the 11-yard line, Holiday and running back Marcus Wilson couldn't execute the handoff, and the ball ended up on the ground again. Holiday recovered it, but they'd lost seven yards in the process.

Then, on third-and-11 from the 18, Carlyle Holiday sprinted to his right and lobbed a ball to Omar Jenkins. Running a short crossing route, Jenkins had the corner beaten, and as he put his right foot down in the end zone and pulled the ball to his chest, he appeared to have possession. But it was ruled an incompletion.

Making matters worse, on that play, Holiday had taken a helmet-to-helmet shot from a Boston College defender and was knocked woozy. Holiday staggered to the sideline, where an equipment manager placed a jacket around his shoulders. He would have to leave the game until the second half. Things got even worse when Nick Setta came out to try a field goal. After holder David Miller bobbled the snap, Setta couldn't even attempt the kick. They ended the drive with nothing to show for it.

Four series later, Pat Dillingham, in relief of Holiday, did something any ambitious backup tries to do when his team is struggling. He tried to make something happen. For the third time that half, Notre Dame had driven into the red zone, to the 14-yard line to be exact. But on third-and-six, Boston College sent cornerback Trevor White on a blitz. White came off the edge untouched, and when he got his arms around Dillingham, the quarterback remembered what he'd been told by Bill Diedrick: "Never take a sack in the red zone." It was better to just throw the ball away than to lose precious field position in that area. So with White on his back, Dillingham tried to throw the ball, underhand, to the nearest receiver. But the ball was intercepted by Eagles linebacker Josh Ott, who returned it 71 yards for a touchdown. After a two-point conversion, two things happened: Boston College led 14–0, and Notre Dame ceased to be a "blessed" team.

But you couldn't have convinced the Notre Dame players of that at halftime. They didn't actually believe they would lose to Boston College. Willingham finally had them believing they could beat anyone. He just told his offense to take care of the football. Carlyle Holiday had been cleared to play the second half. As they returned to the field, they were confident. They had beaten Florida State, and they knew they would beat *this* team.

In the second half, there was one play in the midst of Notre Dame's woefully human performance that was aesthetically beautiful, and in its timing and execution, it was nothing less than superhuman. Eight minutes and 42 seconds into the third quarter, Notre Dame still trailed Boston College 14–0 when, on first down, Gerome Sapp, who in recent weeks had relieved Shane Walton as the defensive playmaker, intercepted a pass. Sapp's timing couldn't have been better because just one minute before that pick, Marcus Wilson had laid the ball on the ground to give the Irish its fifth fumble of the day. And less than one minute after that pick, Ryan Grant, who for some reason had lost the ability to put his arms together to form a pocket to receive the handoff, had the sixth fumble of the day.

But in between, Gerome Sapp made a remarkable play. Boston College quarterback Brian St. Pierre rolled out to his right waiting for Sean Ryan, his tight end, to drift across the formation on a crossing route. Sapp trailed Ryan, hovering on his upfield shoulder, watching St. Pierre's eyes, waiting for him to throw. Ryan was chugging toward the Notre Dame sideline, and the second St. Pierre began his throwing motion, Sapp made a decision. There's a universal rule in man-to-man coverage that states: "Don't ever cut in front of your man unless you're absolutely sure you can get your hands on the ball. If not, just stay in position to knock the ball down or make the tackle."

Sapp cut in front of Ryan and went after the ball with the kind of conviction that ensures not just a great play but a memorable one. As he neared the Notre Dame sideline, Sapp dived into the air and, for lack of a better word, "sailed" for about five yards. As he descended, he caught the tip of the ball, pulled it to his chest, and landed a few inches from the sideline.

His teammates erupted. It was the first big play anyone had made that afternoon, and for a split second, even though they trailed by two touchdowns, it seemed as though they had taken control of the game. That's the way it had been all season. Whenever they needed someone to make a play, someone always did.

But a second later, with new life on the 22-yard line, the unthinkable happened again.

At just over eight minutes left in the third quarter, as he charged the line of scrimmage, Ryan Grant's arms weren't wide enough for Pat Dillingham to slide in the ball, and the ball hit Grant's hip and tumbled to the ground. BC recovered. As Grant came to the sideline, Buzz Preston walked with him to the bench. Grant looked shell-shocked. He would finish with another 100-yard game, but the last fumble defied logic. It wasn't the result of contact; he had just failed to execute the basics.

Starting with the first day of training camp, Preston had put the backs through a nonturnover drill. It was a simple drill, both fun and practical. Simulating the quarterback, Preston would bark a cadence and hand a dark-blue weighted football to the back, who would run through the rope ladder. As each back ran through, knees high, two student managers, each wielding a big foam-rubber shield, would flog him as he passed, trying to simulate defenders swiping at the ball. But by midseason, he figured they all knew how to take a handoff. So Preston stopped playing quarterback, and during the drill, he usually grabbed a bag and joined in the pounding.

As Grant sat on the bench, his eye black smudged and looking much younger than his 20 years, Preston squatted in front of him, his face a mask of surprise and shock. "What's going on?" Preston asked. Grant didn't have an answer because there wasn't one. He was a driven guy, and all of his coaches knew how hard he was on himself. Plagued by nightmarish mistakes almost the whole game, he now looked only stunned.

Upstairs in the coaches' box, Bill Diedrick was just as stunned. At that point, he didn't know which running play to call. Each one ended up on the ground. It just didn't make sense.

The Irish didn't score their first points until the fourth quarter. With 2:25 to go, after a scrambling Holiday found Maurice Stovall in the back of the end zone for a 20-yard touchdown pass, the BC lead was only seven.

Willingham put his faith in the defense. Rather than trying an onside kick, he had Setta kick the ball deep. Eagles returner Will Blackmon received the ball at the BC three-yard line, and special teams ace Carlos Pierre-Antoine, still playing at the top of his game, made the tackle at the 28-yard line. The Eagles had successfully run the ball against Notre Dame all afternoon, so they just kept doing it. After the two-minute mark, Derrick Knight carried four times, and Brian St. Pierre carried once as the Eagles ran the clock down to 22 seconds before punting.

Vontez Duff returned the punt for four yards, and Notre Dame took over at their own 24-yard line. But then it was too late and too cold, and they were too far away to create another miracle. With 12 seconds left, Holiday heaved the ball to Omar Jenkins at midfield, where it fell incomplete. A holding penalty moved them back to their own 14-yard line. As the clock ran out, Holiday's pass to a cluster of Notre Dame receivers at the Boston College 38-yard line fell onto the turf.

After almost four hours, in which Notre Dame had not only played its worst game of the season but also made the kind of fundamental errors seldom seen above the Pee Wee level, it didn't matter what the team and its fans had gained in terms of unity that season. All that mattered was that they'd lost their chance for the national championship.

When it was over, the Boston College players danced around the field. One ran down the Notre Dame sideline, frantically waving at the team, rubbing in the fact that their title hopes had vanished. And, just as they'd done in 1993, reminding the Irish that this game was a turf war, some Boston College players dug up pieces of the field and hurled them at the Notre Dame sideline. As chunks of sod floated toward the Notre Dame bench, a Boston College defensive back screamed into the lens of the TV camera at the top of his lungs, "Over-rated! Over-rated!" Once inside the confines of the stadium, the Eagles took it a step further and completely trashed the visitors locker room. Boston College acted like a team that had just won a Super Bowl — that it was only the Catholic Super Bowl didn't seem to matter.

Stunned, the Notre Dame players began to solemnly leave the field. As they walked off, Darrell Campbell put his arm around Mike Goolsby and led him to the tunnel. Campbell knew his hotheaded teammate wouldn't react too graciously to all that turf-throwing.

After the game, for the first time that season, the Notre Dame players walked into the losing team's locker room. They had endured adversity and doubt throughout the season. They had endured two weeks of absolute futility on offense; they had endured all the negative energy from doubters saying they weren't as good as their record or their ranking. But now they were in unfamiliar territory — they hadn't simply lost, they had lost to the worst team on their schedule thus far.

Shane Walton, who each week had skipped through the tunnel after a victory, slowly exited the field with a somber disbelieving expression. Vontez Duff walked next to him, his face wiped clean of emotion. Duff, who along with Jeff Faine, Darrell Campbell, and Jordan Black had been a captain for the game, was silent, perhaps thinking of what to say to his teammates. Once inside, Duff and Faine immediately assumed damage control for what they feared to be a room full of bruised psyches. "Take it like a man," they told their teammates. "Take it like a man."

A few minutes later, Tyrone Willingham addressed the media's wave of questions about Notre Dame's inability to hold the ball. His demeanor in victory was just as it was in defeat. His response was forthright. "We do not need to change our focus," he said. "We work on not turning the ball over every day, and we work on creating turnovers every day. I think the plan we have in place has served us well this year. Now, we just have to get back to executing it the way we know we can."

An hour later, Shane Walton went to dinner with some friends who were visiting from San Diego. By the time he made it home to the apartment at Candlewood, it was late. His postgame ritual normally consisted of turning on ESPN and watching highlights from the other games. But it was good that he had gotten home too late that evening, because he wasn't feeling football. He called his mom, Shari, and told her that going to dinner was a good thing because it had taken his mind off the game for a while. Then he just lay on his bed and thought about what had transpired. He had chances to make plays, but he couldn't hold on to the ball that day.

In the first quarter, he nearly had his seventh pick. On third-

and-14, just like in the Maryland game, Walton, while playing zone, timed the throw perfectly and broke on the ball. But this time, the ball slipped through his hands for a 16-yard gain. And in that dreadful third quarter, he had returned a punt for 30 yards, all the way to the BC 45-yard line. But it was nullified by a holding call.

Normally unflappable, Walton wasn't going to get over the loss anytime soon. It wasn't just that they'd lost, it was that they'd lost to a group as sorry as that one. True, Boston College had done enough to win the game, but there was no denying that they were not a very good team. *Man, I wouldn't take one guy from their team and put him on ours,* he thought. *Not one.*

While Walton replayed the game in his head, a salty quartet of Notre Dame fans sat at the bar at the local Chili's. With the place teeming with Boston College fans, the two couples stayed at the bar, the men swigging from 16-ounce glasses of Sam Adams. Both men stood about six feet tall, with salt-and-pepper hair, and wore the traditional Notre Dame alum uniform — khakis and Notre Dame sweatshirts. Their wives sat in the stools in front of them. One had short frosted hair, and the other had a long black ponytail. The women sat facing each other, sipping Kendall-Jackson Chardonnay, oblivious to the conversation taking place behind them.

The two men articulated the absolute worst fears of those Notre Dame fans who had any reservations about a black coach taking over their beloved program six months earlier. Oh, it wasn't that Tyrone Willingham might fail. Bob Davie had failed, as had Gerry Faust, so they knew that to be a realistic possibility. But when those men failed and got fired because of it, there was no threat of social backlash. If this guy failed, and they wanted to fire him because of it, outside forces might not allow them to do so.

"They're playing just like they did under Davie," said one of the guys.

"Yeah, I told you a black coach would never make it here," said the other.

"Yeah, but you know Jesse Jackson and the NAACP will get involved, and we'll never be able to get rid of him."

*   *   *

On Sunday morning, Trent Walters sat in his office grading game tape. From the stereo next to his laptop came the voice of Myra Clark, singing a song called "Peace! Be Still."

"Master, the tempest is raging . . ."

Walters was still friendly, but certainly more subdued than usual. On the bright side, he had been standing a few feet away when Vontez Duff told his teammates to "take it like a man," and Walters had been pleased with that reaction. It gave the coach enough of a boost to declare his guys fit for the next obstacle. His unit was the glue to the defense, and he was encouraged that its psyche was still intact. He was also lifted by Gerome Sapp's interception in the third quarter. He ran it back several times, watching Sapp flying toward the sideline in a prone position.

"Did he catch it?" he asked through a big grin.

A few minutes later, right after he was done watching the tape, Trent Miles walked into Walters's office. "That was one of the most depressing things I've ever seen," he said. "We weren't sure if we could throw the ball on them. But in that first half, we were chucking it. And that catch that Omar made. There was no doubt about that one." After Miles left, Greg Mattison, having just watched the tape, walked in, shaking his head in disbelief. "Man, all they did was bootlegs because they couldn't protect the quarterback."

He was right. Boston College's game plan had been to run the ball because they knew there was no way St. Pierre would have time to set his feet and throw against the Notre Dame defense. The offensive line couldn't pass protect to save their own lives, let alone their quarterback's. But they were more than capable run blockers, and that's what their focus was. They had succeeded; tailback Derrick Knight had rushed for 129 yards, the most yards any back had gained against Notre Dame all year.

Down the hall, Buzz Preston returned to his office. He had to meet with a recruit that morning, so he had come in at 7:00 A.M. to grade the offensive tape. The game had been so ugly that it was probably a good thing he had to alter his normal routine. Seated in his office, watching the kickoff team, Preston was even-toned but still clearly hurt. "We broke away from what we normally do," he said. Perhaps the most expressive member of the staff, and one who took all mistakes to heart, Preston's depression was clearly etched into his face that morning. "We got outside our normal routine," he said. "The green jerseys? I don't know . . . We just . . . lost focus."

The truth was, when a *distraction,* like changing uniforms, is thrown into the mix, it lasts only as long as the first few minutes of a game. And with the Notre Dame defense holding BC to 19 yards on its first drive and the Notre Dame offense driving 54 yards on 13 plays on its first drive, the game started out well for the Irish. The jerseys weren't the issue. They couldn't be blamed for Godsey's dropped pass on the first series of the fourth quarter. They couldn't be blamed for Ryan Grant's third-quarter fumble, and they couldn't be blamed for a mishandled snap on a field goal attempt. These were all fundamental errors that not only supported superstition but also defied simple logic. But nothing, not superstition, not logic, not any kind of rational explanation about anything related to football could have reached Bill Diedrick for a few minutes that morning.

Next door to Diedrick's office, Preston was relieved to finish the offensive tape and move on to the special teams. While Preston watched the punt return team, Trent Miles, while walking back to his office, casually remarked, "Bill's locked himself in his office. I fear he's committed suicide."

Diedrick had come in at his normal time, about nine. Looking calm and dressed in jeans and a gray sweater, he seemed fairly composed, as he did every Sunday morning. But this wasn't any Sunday morning. This was the Sunday morning after his offense, the one that had steadily grown over nine incredible weeks, suddenly crumbled into several unfamiliar pieces. They had fumbled *six* times. And none had been the result of vicious contact. Were there words to describe such a thing? Probably not. And if there were, Diedrick couldn't find them that morning. Behind the closed door, the silence was broken by a sharp, crisp *"FUCK!"*

In the next office, Preston kept moving forward. Like Diedrick and the other coaches, he knew that if this team was to rebound from this, if they were to regain their focus, then they had to pull it together and immediately set the tone for next week. "Hey, I'm a *ball coach*," said Preston. "I'll just keep pushing on."

Folks around South Bend wanted to know if Tyrone Willingham would be able to keep pushing on. Two days after his first loss as the coach of Notre Dame, Willingham sat on the sofa in his office. It was about 6:15 on a Monday night, and he was signing a football. From the speaker behind his desk, Stevie Wonder crooned "I Wish," a song about his childhood. Willingham lightly bobbed his head, tapped his foot, and quietly sang along. If the loss to Boston College had unnerved Willingham, he certainly didn't show it.

While unfailingly polite, Willingham hadn't gone overboard to ingratiate himself to the media as Gerry Faust or even Lou Holtz had. Through those first nine weeks, Willingham hadn't been rude, but he'd established a comfortable distance from those seeking knowledge of him. Each Tuesday morning, when the mission had been to find chinks in the armor, he had given them nothing. But things would surely be different now. Sure, in victory Willingham had been his even-tempered self, flashing his dry wit while remaining consistently enigmatic. But after such a shameful loss to a bitter rival and inferior team, perhaps the local media would finally get the chance to see a flash of anger.

Surely the green jerseys would be considered a gross miscalculation by a person who was known for his precision. Surely the decision to change, from a man who was sworn to being amazingly consistent, could lead to his undoing — at least temporarily. Surely Willingham, after coming out of the chute with such confident force, after enduring such humiliation, would let it out in one profanity-laced tirade.

Willingham knew what they were thinking, but he wasn't about to let them force a negative attitude on him. That night, as he sat in his office amid 15 boxes of footballs, T-shirts, helmets, and assorted Irish paraphernalia, he simply said, "I bet I can get all of this stuff signed in less than an hour." The critics could wait until morning. In the meantime, he was already resetting his competitive compass by challenging himself to perform the most mundane of tasks with impeccable speed and accuracy.

"Okay, what time is it?" he said, taking the cap from a marker. "It's six-fifteen now. I bet I can get all these done before seven o'clock." Willingham knew that the primary issue of concern from the local media would be his decision to wear the green jerseys. Though he was prepared for it, he was dismayed that such a thing would even be an issue. He had used the jerseys as part of his plan to unify the Notre Dame family. Throughout the year, the students had created a connection with the team by wearing the green shirts, and Willingham wanted the players to solidify that connection through their uniforms. Of course, he knew his players would get an emotional boost from them as well. But Willingham thought the emotional effect from the jerseys was just like that of a fiery pregame speech — it lasts only as long as the first few minutes. After that initial excitement, you still have to play the game. Willingham shook his head and laughed. "You would think people who have been around it as long as they have would have an understanding of it."

While Willingham signed footballs, he was preparing for the storm, knowing that all eyes would be squarely on him the next morning, waiting for some kind of reaction. He was human, and now, after a defeat, the college football world would try to unearth his "real" identity. But he was prepared for the worst.

Willingham tried to be aware of just about everything that happened around him and even of some things beyond his horizon. He had heard about what went down at Arkansas that spring, and he had taken mental notes on it. While Willingham was signing Notre Dame paraphernalia, another black coach was pondering a lawsuit against his former employer.

Like Tyrone Willingham, Nolan Richardson had once been the lone black head coach at his school. Arkansas University fielded 17 varsity sports, but only the men's basketball team was coached by a black man. A driven man, Richardson's personal expectations easily matched those of his employers. Even his team's nickname, Razorbacks, was a testament to his intensity. Because of the relentless full-court pressure his teams applied to opponents, a Razorbacks game was termed "40 minutes of hell." But after 17 years as coach, during which time he led them to three Final Fours *and* the national championship, Richardson had a very public and costly meltdown.

In February 2002, his team was 13–13, barely clinging to a shot at the NIT, and Richardson felt the walls of great expectation closing in on him. Before a small media gathering after practice, unable to keep his emotions in check, Richardson vented like a human being who had clearly grown weary of being examined by other human beings who he felt just didn't "get him." The only problem was, in speaking his mind, he momentarily forgot that his white employers had more in common with his white audience than they ever would with him.

"When I look at all of you people in this room, I see no one who looks like me, talks like me, or acts like me," he said. "Now, why don't you recruit? Why don't the editors recruit like I'm recruiting?" As Richardson continued to speak, the expectation of what he still needed to achieve that season collided with resentments he had built up in seasons past. He had clearly thought of it before. But he had never said it. Not until then.

"My great-great-grandfather came over on the ship, not Nolan Richardson," he said. "I didn't come over on that ship, so I expect to be treated a little bit different. Because I know for a fact that I do not play on the same level as the other coaches around this school play on. I know that. You know it. And people of my color know that. And that angers me."

He concluded by saying he would step aside if the university — Frank Broyles, the athletic director, in particular — would buy out his contract, which amounted to $500,000 per year over six years. Given such an ultimatum, it came as no surprise that Arkansas chancellor John White made good on Richardson's offer and fired him on March 1.

Richardson was as outspoken as Tyrone Willingham was guarded. Richardson was an imposing physical figure and Willingham a slight one. So Willingham knew of Richardson, but he didn't really know him. But Willingham *did* know Herman Edwards. He knew him because, like him, Edwards, as head coach for the New York Jets, was part of the black coach "movement." Edwards, along with Tony Dungy, was one of two black head coaches in the NFL. Everything Edwards did that season counted for something. And if there were going to be more black coaches after the 2002 season, what he did counted for everything.

Like Willingham, Edwards was preternaturally positive and deeply spiritual. But in the throes of adversity, he too had just about lost it. A week earlier, at his weekly press conference, Edwards, whose team had fallen to 2–5 after a 24–21 loss at home to the Cleveland Browns, had been asked if his team had quit on him. Edwards left the podium and took two steps forward. His arms waving angrily, he stared down the reporter and chastised him, his voice rising. The year before, in his first season, the Jets had made the playoffs. But at the time, they had no real offensive identity, and the defensive players had begun taking public shots at one another. With all of that spurring him on, Edwards took another step from the podium. He knew he didn't have any quitters on his team, and he made sure this reporter understood as much. "Hello, you play to win the game!" yelled Edwards.

Willingham lightly chuckled when asked about the outburst. "I saw the end of it," he said. "Did he go off?" Willingham asked rhetorically. Looking up from the little white football that awaited his signature, he answered his own question. "Yes, he went off." Then he shook his head sadly, as if this was the kind of damage from which Edwards, or any other black public figure, would have a difficult time recovering. Willingham knew a raised eyebrow, the slightest voice inflection, or even sustained eye contact could lead to his being perceived as "angry." And he'd been in this business too long not to know that he didn't have the luxury of losing his cool. "You can't ever do that," he said. It was just the way it was, and even though he had clearly accepted it, the reality of it annoyed him. He said the words slowly, *"You . . . can . . . never . . . lose . . . control."*

Willingham's expertise in the art of public self-control was the model for all black coaches. For better or worse, the most prominent black men in this country are affiliated with sports. And although the public perception is that the sports world is a self-contained society, for the black coach and athlete it isn't.

Sports is simply the most visible stage for double standards that apply to society as a whole. Bobby Knight had made a living at being a tyrant and never had to apologize for it. His reputation as a tyrant and, more important, as an asshole, was permanently etched into sports lore after he once tossed a chair onto the court. Spike Lee spoke for many black sports fans when he said that that type of behavior would never be tolerated from a black coach. "If John Thompson had done that, he would have been lynched," said Lee at the time.

He was right. Lee's reference to Thompson was especially poignant because Thompson, at 6′10″, was a physically imposing man. His size and the possibility of what he might do when seriously provoked breathed life into the double standard. But in most settings, any black man, even one who stands just 5′7″, cannot express his emotion without the perceived threat of physical violence. That's why Willingham knew it was critical that he maintain impeccable decorum at all times.

Later that season, Knight's black successor at Indiana, Mike Davis, would be suspended for a game after running onto the court to protest a call. Before settling on a one-game suspension, Big Ten officials flirted with the idea of suspending him for six games, a number supported by the local media. When Bobby Knight was caught on tape strangling Neil Reed, he had kept his job at Indiana. Yet after Mike Davis's outburst, one local pundit had even described the scene as "frightening." Uncalled for? Certainly. Out of character? For sure. But *frightening*?

After the loss to Boston College, Willingham knew he could not give the slightest impression of anger in his reaction. But therein lay the irony. Willingham wasn't angered by the loss; he was hurt by it. He said as much immediately after the game, but it was doubtful if anyone really heard him. Hurt is a term that describes the pain that comes from a sense of loss or sorrow. Hurt is a term used by human beings during times of great disappointment. A football coach couldn't be hurt, could he? Surely it would make sense for him to be pensive. And Willingham was pensive. "The older you get, the fewer chances you have to do things over," he said. "At my age, there aren't too many redos left." He looked up from a helmet he was signing. "Wouldn't it be a shame if that game cost us the national championship?"

It was obvious he was pained by the loss. He knew his guys had played hard, but they'd made mistakes. He'd been coaching college football for 22 years, and he often said the thing he enjoyed most about it was its imperfection. The NFL game was played by men whose bank accounts, mortgages, and marriages were directly affected by what they did on Sunday afternoon. But the college game was played by kids. And kids made *mistakes.*

Despite the hurt, it was painfully obvious that Willingham would do everything in his power to bounce back. And he would do so in his normally composed, upbeat manner. His team had done more than anyone had expected of them, so it would make no sense for him to lose his cool now. As he placed the last ball into a box, Willingham sat behind his desk, preparing to watch film of Navy. "Oh, let's see," he said, looking at his watch. "What time is it? Seven? See, I did it," he said while opening his laptop. "If you're gonna compete, you should compete."

On Tuesday morning, the minute he strolled into the WNDU studio, Willingham set the tone for his first press conference after a loss with composed, stylish flair. When he briskly stepped to the podium, his customary business shirt and power tie had been replaced by a camel blazer over a black mock-turtleneck sweater. More often than not, perception is reality, and Willingham was determined to show that the first loss of his Notre Dame career would not turn him into a surly tyrant. His public image was already one of aloofness, so to counter that perception, he altered his style. Willingham's dress was casual and, for the most part, so was his mood.

As expected, Tim Prister was the first to the mike, and his question, though very cleverly worded, was predictably a question about Willingham's decision to wear the green jerseys.

"Lou Holtz used to say there are two or three games in every football season where it's difficult to get your team up emotionally. Would you agree with that? What does a coach try to do other than changing the color of the jerseys?"

Willingham leaned slightly forward and spoke even more

softly than normal. "First of all," said Willingham, "we'll get a lot of questions about the color of jerseys, so we might as well speak on that right now. The color of the jersey had nothing to do with us not winning the football game or holding on to the football or any of those other things. The color of the jersey was not to get our football team up. We recognized that Boston College was an important team on our schedule, and with the things we wanted to accomplish, we needed to beat them. We just failed in some areas to execute our game plan, and therefore did not allow ourselves the opportunity to beat them."

"Will you continue to wear green?" asked Prister.

Willingham was cool. "That will be a decision made when I feel it's appropriate."

But for many Notre Dame fans, those who needed to have one specific reason for their team's meltdown against an inferior team, Willingham's decision to outfit the Irish in green jerseys had been an inappropriate one. When it came to picking up on the school's traditions, this was a tough crowd to please.

14

NAVY

O N MONDAY AFTERNOON, at about 4:00 P.M., Shane Walton, Gary Godsey, and Justin Tuck went to the Boys and Girls Club on Eddy Street, located about four miles from campus. The club had a recreation room with four pool tables and a couple of billiards tables. There was a reading room, a computer center, a day-care room, and a gym. Walton, Tuck, and Godsey strolled in, dressed in sweats and Notre Dame football shirts, and the 30 or so kids, predominantly black but a few white and Hispanic, instantly came to life and converged on them. Walton immediately went to work at a pool table, where several boys were waiting to challenge him, while Tuck went to a table at the far end of the room to take on an especially hyperactive boy. Godsey opted to play a confident little cat in billiards.

Walton was clearly the fan favorite in these parts, especially to the girls. He was excited that day, more enthusiastic than he would be on Saturday. He still stung from the loss to Boston College and never got too excited about playing Navy. Many people thought he didn't like Navy games because they reminded him of his absentee father, who was a naval officer. But they were wrong.

"I don't like playing Navy because they're sorry," he'd said. "It's like playing against a high school team." It was that attitude that the coaches were worried about — especially coming off a big loss to an inferior team. Willingham had to get his troops up to play a 1–7 team that Notre Dame had beaten 38 consecutive times, and he knew he had his work cut out for him.

While Walton played eight ball that afternoon, a pack of four girls, armed with a disposable camera, approached the table. The leader of the group was a tall 13-year-old white girl with long black hair who was clearly in a hurry to be much older than she was. She motioned for the other three to gather around Shane. He dropped his cue for a second, and the three little girls quickly came forward, craftily jockeying for position. While he smiled, the girls clung to him, each one absolutely beaming. After the picture, Walton was about to return to the game when another little girl, dressed in pink, whose braids were similar to Walton's, asked to take another picture. But one of the staff members quickly interjected. "Okay, you girls leave that boy alone now!" As the counselor ushered her away, the girl in pink pleaded with her. "But we *love* him!"

Walton tried to suppress a smile, but he couldn't. This was his scene. Not because of the unbridled admiration the kids afforded him, but because he knew the lasting significance of his presence. He'd been working with kids since his freshman year and knew from his own experience that this kind of interaction was truly invaluable.

"Oh, this was me back in the day," he said. "See, I never had any siblings when I was growing up, and I just love kids. They're just so impressionable. If they have a positive role model, a positive influence, that's huge for them. And African-American kids just don't have enough of those. They have too many people steering them the wrong way, not the right way." Walton sunk the eight ball into the corner pocket, finishing off his nine-year-old competitor. "Holla," he said.

It was the kind of week all coaches dread. While Notre Dame had dropped only a few spots in the national rankings after the Boston College game — from No. 4 to No. 9 in the AP poll — the staff feared that the loss may have, as Bill Diedrick put it, "cut the heart out of the team." In some ways it had. In the second

half of that game, they hadn't looked anything like the opportunistic team they'd been in September. They didn't look like
the team that never flinched and always expected to make something happen. They looked like the team they had been the previous year. But Willingham insisted it wasn't effort. "All the guys
played hard," he said. "The guys that fumbled the ball all played
really hard too." Willingham wanted desperately to get their
spirit back.

Early in the week, he sat in his office trying to articulate the
feeling of invincibility. He knew he needed a way to inspire his
team. He remembered a game from his college days. "I remember we played Ohio State in '74 or '75, when they were ranked
number one," he said. "We *knew* we were going to win. In fact, we
knew we were going to win that game on the Sunday before the
game."

While at Stanford, he'd started a weekly tradition called
"Champions Thursday." Before Thursday's practice, he'd have a
celebrity guest speaker. Even though his Notre Dame team had a
lot of guest speakers that season, Willingham wasn't going to go
the celebrity speaker route for a while. "I haven't decided when
I'll incorporate Champions Thursday around here," he said.
"Maybe next year, maybe two years from now. But right now, they
don't need a lot of speakers. Right now, they need to hear from
their coach."

At Thursday's practice, the sky was gray, it was about 40 degrees, and the permacloud that would hover over campus until
April had settled into place. Trying to rebound from a demoral-
izing loss, a loss that effectively killed the dream season, was a
tricky line for the coaches to toe. They didn't want to be too hard
on the players because they had worked so hard to reestablish
the pride and confidence that had been lost in the Davie era. But
they didn't want to be too soft and run the risk of allowing them
to lose their edge. The key was to be especially meticulous, paying attention to every detail, so that nothing they had accomplished could be washed away amid the self-pity.

They got back to basics. Buzz Preston assumed his position
as the quarterback during fundamental drills. He handed the

ball to Rashon Powers-Neal, who was due to play his first game since suffering a deep thigh bruise against Pittsburgh in October. Powers-Neal stumbled on the rope ladder. "Come on, dagnabbit!" shouted Preston.

On the other field, Diedrick watched Maurice Stovall drop a ball on a slant. "Go back and do it again," shouted Diedrick. Stovall went back and burst off the ball, but the quarterback, freshman Chris Olsen, underthrew it and the ball landed behind Stovall. Both players were already headed to the next phase of the drill when Diedrick barked, "Do it again! Both of you!" Both Stovall and Olsen sheepishly returned to their spots. With all the other quarterbacks and receivers watching, Stovall ran the route, and Olsen put it right in his stomach.

The Navy game was played in front of a sellout crowd of 70,260 fans at Ravens Stadium in Baltimore, Maryland, on November 9, 2002. Since it was being played there, former Notre Dame defensive end and Baltimore Ravens rookie Tony Weaver was in attendance. About 30 minutes before kickoff, Weaver stood on the sideline watching his boys, the defensive line, warm up. Dressed in a long black leather coat and jeans, a pair of shades wrapped around his bald head, Weaver looked every bit as cool as his reputation. Weaver had been Notre Dame's Most Valuable Player the year before, and the rebirth of this year's team inspired him.

Sure, he was enjoying the spoils of being a pro. He was living in a great city, getting paid long dollars to stop the run, and was only three quarters of the way through the first year of what would surely be a long, productive career. But he had come to the sideline that day to witness something, to feel something, and to identify with something that had more spiritual significance than a professional football career. He had grown up at Notre Dame, learned who he was, learned what he was capable of becoming. Now, with the authority of a new career behind him, he watched his dogs on the D-line. "Darrell is playing well, and so is Kyle," he said. "And I know big Ced will be back in time for the USC game."

In many ways, Weaver was the archetypal Notre Dame football player. The son of a career military man, he was a study in honor, humility, and loyalty. As the embattled Bob Davie exited Notre Dame Stadium for the final time after the Purdue game the year before, Weaver had walked beside him and told him, "You're my coach."

But Weaver took unabashed delight in what was happening to his old team. The loss to Boston College aside, he didn't even have to be on campus to appreciate the change. Of course, Weaver had experienced some of it himself, had got a glance of Willingham in action.

In February, while Weaver worked out for pro scouts, Willingham watched him. Knowing that the scouts love to push a prospect to exhaustion, Willingham offered him some advice. "Work at your own pace," he told Weaver. Taken aback by advice from someone who had nothing staked in his future, Weaver thanked Willingham, finished his workout, and became a second-round pick in April's draft. Now, with a chance to see how Willingham's energy had manifested itself on the program as a whole, Weaver shook his head and smiled. "Totally different atmosphere, man. Totally different atmosphere."

From the very start of the Navy game, Willingham exuded more sideline energy than he had all season. As he had said, this certainly was a time when they needed to hear from their coach, when they really needed to feel his presence. Even in the midst of mounting an eight-game win streak and, in the process, vaulting into the Top 5, his team had needed constant prodding. Now, Willingham pushed them even harder.

The opening play combined the optimistic spark they had against Florida State with the absolute futility that enveloped the Boston College game. After a sweet little play fake to Grant, Holiday set his feet and threw a perfectly arced ball to Omar Jenkins. Sixty-two yards downfield, after Jenkins had beaten the corner by a yard and the ball had settled softly in his hands, it looked as though things just might return to normal. As usual, Willingham was standing right at the spot where Jenkins made the catch. But before Willingham could put his hands together to celebrate, the safety closed on Jenkins, batting the ball from his hands. And the cornerback immediately fell on it. Willingham turned on his heels, seething, and stalked to the other end of the sideline.

On the following Irish drive, determined to regain the offensive flow that marked the first two months of the season, Diedrick had Holiday go downtown again. But Rhema McKnight, open at the goal line with a chance to score his first touchdown, lacked urgency. It was a perfect throw, laid just over the corner's head. But rather than reaching up and aggressively snatching the rock, McKnight waited for the ball to come down. As it settled into his hands, the corner hacked his wrist, and the ball bounced into the end zone. As McKnight came to the sideline, Willingham met him, thrusting his hands in the air. "Come on now! You gotta go up and get that!"

In those first few minutes, Willingham was urging his team to make plays, willing them to reacquire the energy they had back in September. Thus far, they had squandered two wonderful opportunities. But as Joey Hildbold placed a punt into the right corner, directly on the five-yard line, Willingham pumped his fist the way Tiger Woods does after sinking a putt. Hildbold had remained one of the most consistent performers on the team. He was on his way to placing 30 of 78 punts inside the 20-yard line that season. Buzz Preston said earlier in the week, "Man, I'm gonna miss that kid. Without him, I may have to really coach next year."

As it had in the early part of the season when the offense was struggling, the Notre Dame defense put them on the scoreboard. At 10:38 in the first quarter, after Navy failed to make a first down, punter John Skaggs lined up on the 34-yard line. But a bad snap sent the ball careening past him. Skaggs sprinted to the end zone behind him, retrieved the ball, then wisely stepped out of the end zone for a safety.

But on their next possession, the Navy offense, its wishbone attack led by backup quarterback Aaron Polanco, acted nothing like Shane Walton's description of them as "sorry." The Notre Dame defense had battled teams all season long, but right then, a week after their first loss and in the midst of a long, sustained drive by the Navy offense, they looked exhausted. And the first place exhaustion manifests itself is in the fundamentals.

During that drive, they didn't tackle worth shit. Running an option attack, which was just as quick as Air Force's but not nearly as efficient, the Midshipmen gashed the D-line for a 38-yard run. Willingham darted to the other end of the sideline, excitedly motioning to any defensive players within earshot. "We have to wrap up! Come on. Wrap up!" On option plays, Glenn Earl was responsible for the quarterback. But as he closed on Polanco, Earl ducked his head, hitting absolutely nothing, and Polanco slipped into the end zone. The Midshipmen went 95 yards in 12 plays, and after Polanco scored on that 12-yard touchdown run, Navy led 7–2.

The Irish quickly answered with their own 13-play drive, which culminated in fullback Tom Lopienski scoring from the one-yard line to give Notre Dame a 9–7 lead. But 10 minutes into the second quarter, Ryan Grant's late-season nightmare continued. On second-and-seven, Navy linebacker Eddie Carthan roared through the guard-tackle gap, meeting Grant in the hole. Before Grant could lower his shoulder, Carthan put his helmet directly on the ball, and it squirted from Grant's arms and landed behind him. Carthan immediately pounced on it.

As Grant sat on the bench afterward, Buzz Preston calmly spoke to him. He knew the kid was tired, knew he was both mentally and physically worn out. Willingham knew that too. Willingham started walking toward the bench, planning to say something to Grant. But he froze in his tracks. He trusted his coaches, and he knew that Preston had control of things. Thinking better of it, he slowly turned back toward the field.

On their next drive several minutes later, after Carlyle Holiday left the pocket and took a hard shot from Carthan, things briefly spiraled out of control. As Holiday lay on the ground with trainer Jim Russ kneeling over him, Willingham, needing to do something, needing to get directly *involved*, helped Pat Dillingham warm up. Willingham stood next to his backup quarterback. Dillingham threw the ball to tight end Billy Palmer, and Palmer fired it back to Willingham, who handed it to Dillingham. They had completed several reps when Holiday, feeling fine, came to the sideline. Holiday regained control of his senses, and the Irish put together an eight-play drive, making it all the way to the Navy 35-yard line. But after Nicholas Setta's 53-yard field goal attempt was blocked, the Notre Dame team, which had looked almost invincible against perennial power Florida State, limped into the locker room, clinging to a 9–7 lead over lowly Navy.

When the Notre Dame defense took the field again in the third quarter, it looked as though Navy's long drive in the first quarter had drained some life from the Irish. At 12:08 in the third quarter, the Midshipmen put together a six-play drive, scoring easily on an Aaron Polanco run. By then, cornerback Vontez Duff had seen enough. As Navy kicker Eric Rolfs followed through on the extra point, Duff came flying from the edge, launching himself into the air in an attempt to block the kick. But the kick was good. That made it 14–9, Navy.

Although he missed blocking that kick, or *because* he missed blocking that kick, Duff came to the sideline fired up. He briefly huddled with the kickoff return team, and when he returned to the field, he lined up on the goal line and eagerly awaited the kick. When Rolfs's kick settled into his hands, Duff took several steps forward, found a crease in the middle of the field, and exploded for a 92-yard touchdown. "No one was having any fun at that point," said Duff later. "I *had* to make a play."

But the fun and the momentum would end almost immediately. The Irish tried a two-point conversion. After Carlyle Holiday's pass to Omar Jenkins fell incomplete, Notre Dame led 15–14, and Navy took over. The Midshipmen sustained a 12-play, 80-yard drive, during which the Irish defense struggled in a way they hadn't all season. On several plays, they missed tackles. And after Navy running back Eric Roberts scored a 10-yard touchdown, Navy had taken the lead 20–15, and Notre Dame appeared to have lost its fight.

That's when Willingham finally regained control of things. Actually, his preferred style of offense gained control and kept the Irish from sinking into an even deeper abyss. Whereas Diedrick loved the thrill of the passing game, Willingham loved to pound it out on the ground. At the time, Notre Dame's running game needed some concentrated violence. With 13 minutes left and his team now trailing 23–15, Willingham and the offense huddled before taking the field. Preston, Miles, and Denbrock addressed the team while Willingham stood on the outer edge of the circle.

He knew that the defense, as great as it had been all year, couldn't do much more than it had done, and he knew the offense would have to take another step toward maturity. So he let the others talk while he stood with arms folded, listening to his coaches tell the offensive line they needed more from them. As the offense took the field, Ryan Grant stood next to Buzz Preston on the sideline. In the third quarter, Grant had taken another wicked shot and lost yet another ball, so Diedrick, knowing he would need Grant at his best for the USC game in two weeks, had taken him out. Willingham watched contentedly as the next two drives unfolded just the way he wanted them to.

He loved the kind of drive sustained by a vicious surge up front and decisive runs by the backs. On an off tackle run, following a block by Jordan Black, Rashon Powers-Neal, playing for the first time in four weeks, got 14 yards. Then he got three more, and Holiday scrambled for nine. They punted after the series, but on the drive, it looked as if they had finally found a way to maintain their fire.

After three more carries by Powers-Neal, it was time for Omar Jenkins to run his signature route. The team's most technically sound route runner, Jenkins had mastered the skill of selling one thing and doing another. On second-and-eight, he fired off the ball, running hard, furiously pumping his arms, driving the corner backward toward the middle of the field. The very instant the defender stopped backpedaling and turned to run for his life, Jenkins broke to his right. As Jenkins drifted to the sideline, Holiday hit him for 29 yards at the two-yard line. Then it was back to the power game, and with two more hard carries, Powers-Neal broke into the end zone from one yard out. On the sideline, Willingham pumped his fist, then signaled for two. After Holiday hit Arnaz Battle in the back of the end zone, the score was tied at 23.

After giving up nine yards on four plays, the defense forced Navy to punt. The next series was one and done as Willingham, taking another opportunity to make his team find its opponent's jugular, immediately went downtown. Starting from their own

33-yard line, Jenkins ran the corner route, and once again, Holiday put it softly in his hands for a 67-yard touchdown.

Notre Dame led 30–23, but the defense had to make two more stands. With just over two minutes left, Navy got the ball back, but the four-play drive ended with a Glenn Earl interception. With 1:32 to go, the offense was supposed to run out the clock. But after a Navy timeout, the Irish were forced to punt when Rashon Powers-Neal failed to gain a yard and Holiday's pass to Arnaz Batte fell incomplete.

That meant the defense had to take the field one last time. Possessing an offense completely devoid of a passing game, Navy didn't have much chance of moving the ball. They threw two incompletions before Courtney Watson stepped in front of a pass with 31 seconds left for his third pick of the season. The game was over, and the Notre Dame players began to make their way to the locker room.

But defensive-line coach Greg Mattison needed to speak to his guys. While Justin Tuck, Darrell Campbell, and Kyle Budinscak sat on the bench, Mattison kneeled in front of them and lectured. "You aren't supposed to finish a game like that," he told them. "You guys are supposed to dominate fronts. You're supposed to have the mentality of the best defensive line in football."

It was true. They hadn't resembled the defensive line that had dominated Air Force's offense a month earlier. But at least they'd won. With equal parts patience and force, the offense had come from behind to win a game. True, it was against a much weaker opponent, but for a team groping in the dark for lost confidence, the win over Navy was a welcome source of light.

There wasn't anything unusual about Willingham's post-game press conference that day, save that one of the 48 people in the tiny press room at Ravens Stadium just happened to be the national security advisor. A day after the United Nations voted 13–0 to disarm Iraq, Condoleezza Rice took in the Notre Dame game. While Willingham calmly told his audience that what Ryan Grant was experiencing — four fumbles in two weeks — was something every athlete goes through at some time in his career, he wore a cheerful little smile. That's because he knew someone special was in attendance.

Rice stood in back, her head cocked to one side, listening to her friend, obviously immensely proud of what he had accomplished. Dressed in a blue-and-green plaid blazer, black slacks, and loafers, Rice stood with her legs crossed, absorbing Willingham's words. Her friendship with Notre Dame's football coach notwithstanding, Rice had always had a passion for football. And of course, having received a master's degree from Notre Dame in 1975, she had an interest in Notre Dame football. But this wasn't about football. She and Willingham were buddies. And she knew better than anyone that after the previous week, he could probably use a friend.

When Willingham finished speaking, he beamed at Rice, no doubt proud to have her there and genuinely warmed by the gesture. They had so much in common. It was no coincidence that Willingham's oldest daughter was attending the University of Denver, the same school from which Rice graduated cum laude and Phi Beta Kappa in 1974 and earned her Ph.D. in international studies in 1981. And it was no coincidence that when pressed in interviews, Willingham, like Rice, was firm without being rude, never breaking his code of politeness. It was no coincidence that the screen saver on Willingham's computer contained a quote from Rice's boss, George W. Bush: "We have never backed down, and we never will."

When he was done fielding questions, he walked over to her, and they hugged. Just then, Omar Jenkins and Carlyle Holiday stepped to the podium and began to answer questions. Out of respect to the young men, Willingham and Rice hurried outside. After a brief update and congratulations, there was only time for another quick hug. "Well, I have to get back to DC," said Rice. Willingham smiled. "Thanks for coming, friend."

15

RUTGERS

BY THE ELEVENTH WEEK of the season, Shane Walton was no longer the obscure soccer player turned cornerback. His was no longer a tale of scrappy comeuppance told with the cute but condescending "Little Engine that Could" kind of tone. After ten games, six picks, and a slew of big plays, he had earned national credibility. He had been named to the Walter Camp All-America team, one of the oldest and most prestigious honors in college football. In addition to that, he had been named a finalist for the Bronko Nagurski Trophy, given to college football's Defensive Player of the Year. Along with E. J. Henderson of Maryland, Terence Newman of Kansas State, Terrell Suggs of Arizona State, and David Pollack of Georgia, Walton had been invited to attend the black-tie dinner in Charlotte, North Carolina, in December.

But with all the accolades and attention Walton was getting, Willingham wanted more for him. So did Trent Walters. As they prepared for the final two games of the season, they wanted to do all they could to push Walton a little more. Still trying to instill a sense of hunger in his team, Willingham wanted Walton to keep pushing for accomplishments, to never be satisfied with what he already had. On Monday night, at a little after six, Walton strolled into Walters's office to pick up that week's scouting report. Before he left, Walters went to the grease board and drew up a play. "We put in a new punt block this week just for you," said Walters.

Walton, normally one of the guys who blocked the free releasers on the punt return team, was supposed to shoot through the gap between the guard and tackle. "If you just shoot through this gap, you might be unblocked, and you can get one," said Walters. "It's the Shane Walton Block."

While Walton nodded his silent approval, Walters leaned forward, lowering his voice as his eyes bored into Walton's. It was a look he had undoubtedly given his son Troy a million times. Having just clinched the Walter Camp honor, Walton had proved that he was one of the best cornerbacks in the nation, and Walters wanted him to know that he could make other All-America teams as well. Besides that, the upcoming game against Rutgers would be his final home game, and knowing Walton was one of the most popular Irish players, Walters wanted to send him out in style. "Okay, big push this week," said Walters. "Big push."

As they prepared for Rutgers, a 10-win season in sight, Shane Walton wasn't the only one whose success had gone from the realm of "scrappy little underdog" to the bright lights of the mainstream. The same scenario applied to Willingham. A victory against the 1–9 Scarlet Knights of Rutgers would make him the all-time winningest first-year coach in the history of Notre Dame. It would move him past the 9–1 marks of Ara Parseghian in 1964 and Terry Brennan in 1954. In 1986, Lou Holtz, like Willingham, had taken over a 5–6 team to play a similar schedule to the 2002 season, including home games against Michigan and Pitt and a road game at Michigan State. But in 1986, Holtz had lost all three, and the Irish finished 5–6.

It was fitting that the new James Bond film, *Die Another Day*, was set to open in theaters later that week. Willingham wasn't so much a James Bond fan as someone who identified with what Bond stood for. "Oh, you know I love Bond," he said excitedly. "I like that Bond is a winner. See, he's like Superman in that sense. He always overcomes the odds to become successful. I like all movies where the good guy wins. And Bond *always* wins." A year from his fiftieth birthday, Willingham even entertained the thought of buying himself a sports car, no doubt the influence of the unflappable British spy.

There was an added element to the latest Bond flick that Willingham appreciated — Halle Berry played the role of the latest "Bond girl." "I once heard someone say she's so fine she could stop the hands on a clock," Willingham said. He nodded his head and with pursed lips and a playful smile said, "You know, that's probably about right."

In March, Berry had become the first black woman to ever win the Oscar for best actress. That same night, Denzel Washington won the Oscar for best actor, and the Academy also honored Sidney Poitier — the original modern black actor whose foray into the mainstream made him *the* elegant, smooth-talking, dark-as-midnight pioneer for all future generations of black actors. Perhaps it was the Academy's way of silencing all those folks who screamed for years that the only parts available to black women were as hookers and hoes, maids and jigaboos. Perhaps in bestowing on both Washington and Berry its most prestigious honor, the Academy had declared the black man and woman officially worthy of race-neutral roles. Or perhaps parading three prominent black actors across the stage in its most hallowed event was Hollywood's way of trying to forever silence its most outspoken critic, Spike Lee.

Whatever the reason, on that "historic" night, toting her first Oscar, Berry had no doubt gained access to Hollywood's mainstream society. There was nothing more mainstream than playing a sexy, gun-toting, wisecracking Bond girl. Berry's character, Jinx, makes her entrance in a scene borrowed from *Dr. No*, the original Bond flick. In the 1962 film, a bikini-clad Ursula Andress emerges from the Caribbean, packing a knife while searching for conch. Forty years later, Berry, also accessorizing her two-piece with a blade, makes the same entrance. She's a Bond girl, all right. She just *happens to be black.*

Willingham's debut season at Notre Dame had coincided with a year of cultural firsts. That season, *Essence* magazine did its first story on a Notre Dame football coach, and Black Entertainment Television (BET), the largest and most powerful black-owned and -produced medium of black communications, also made its maiden voyage to campus. In December, Robert John-son, the billionaire founder of BET, would be awarded the NBA franchise in Charlotte, making him the first African-American to own a majority of a major league team.

While on campus, BET had interviewed Willingham and taped Vontez Duff and Shane Walton for a promotional spot. While Walton acknowledged it was the first time BET had ever been to the Notre Dame campus, he felt that it was only logical that they eventually show up — Willingham's presence aside. "Yeah, Notre Dame is blowing up this year, so we're showing up everywhere," said Walton. "But the TV in the locker room is always tuned to that channel anyway. All we watch is videos, so it only makes sense that we support BET and they support us."

The Rutgers game followed a bye week in which Willingham had given his team four days off. With rival USC still on the horizon, as well as the possibility of a bowl berth, he knew they needed the rest. But so did he. Unfortunately, he never got it. On Monday night, November 18, nine days after the Navy win and five days before the home game against Rutgers, Willingham's eyes were tired, and he lacked his normal ebullience as he spoke about how, for the second consecutive year, politics controlled his team's postseason.

"It's no different from last year," he said. The previous November, almost exactly a year to the day of the Boston College game, Willingham had led Stanford, then 5–1 and ranked No. 10, into Husky Stadium. Early in the fourth quarter, the score was tied at 28, and Stanford had been right in the middle of the BCS hunt. But after two costly turnovers, Washington pulled away to win 42–28.

"Now if Stanford had just taken care of business against Washington that day, politics wouldn't have played a role," said Willingham. "If we win that game, we don't have to worry about hoping other teams do this or that. If we win that game, we go to a big-time bowl. But since we didn't take care of business on the field, we had to settle for a bowl [the Seattle Bowl] that really didn't even want us there."

Still, the BCS standings were as absorbing to Willingham as to anyone on the college football scene. "People are complaining about the BCS, saying they don't get it and it doesn't work, but it keeps people *interested* in college football, and it makes them watch every week. I know I call in every week to cast my vote."

On Saturday afternoon, Willingham had caught the last few minutes of the Illinois–Ohio State game, which the Buckeyes barely won. He rolled his eyes. "They almost had it, didn't they?" he said, referring to the Illinis' near upset. Five days later, on Thursday night, top-ranked Miami would play Pittsburgh in a nationally televised game, and Willingham was excited. "Now if Miami loses to Pittsburgh, the entire world will be thrown into chaos," he said. "And you know that is a very exciting thing."

But Willingham seemed bothered that he couldn't focus all of his attention on the BCS puzzle. "I didn't get to watch as much football this weekend as I would have liked," he said. Notre Dame had a shoe contract with Adidas, and one of the football coach's responsibilities involved speaking to people from that particular organization. Over the weekend, Willingham had flown to Phoenix to speak to 400 Adidas reps. "I didn't get back until about four A.M. So I didn't get much rest," he said. He folded his arms, leaned back, and smiled. "You don't get to rest until it's over . . . but it's never over."

That statement marked the first time all season that Willingham had allowed himself to admit that being the Notre Dame coach was indeed a stressful position. And the next morning, in a cryptically humorous way, he even admitted it to the media. At his Tuesday press conference, the telephone moderator mistakenly introduced the Notre Dame football coach as John Heisler. That got a laugh from both Willingham and Heisler, who was the associate athletic director.

"Hey, I've been promoted," joked Heisler.

From the podium, Willingham laughed. "I'm not so sure that's a promotion, John."

By Friday afternoon, the BCS standings were the hottest topic in South Bend. The night before, on November 21, Miami had beaten Pittsburgh 28–21 in a vicious contest. With that victory, Miami had passed the last true obstacle to reaching the Fiesta Bowl. The only mystery was which team the Hurricanes would play for the national championship. All of this had Willingham pumped.

Willingham said that while the BCS may have been difficult to understand at times, there was no denying that it created some genuine excitement. Notre Dame's place in the BCS was something that, in the wake of the Boston College game, could have been a sore topic for him. But Willingham put a positive spin on that as well. "You get emotional watching these games now," he said. "And you find yourself rooting for teams that you never, *ever,* thought you would root for." That was an obvious reference to rival Michigan, who was set to play Ohio State the next afternoon. If Michigan beat the Buckeyes, who were ranked No. 2 at the time, then Notre Dame, ranked No. 8, could possibly be right back in the BCS mix.

Each Friday afternoon before a home game there was a luncheon for Notre Dame alumni, fans, and local boosters at the Joyce Center. This week, after Willingham was introduced, there was unqualified proof that he had been embraced by the Notre Dame community. As he approached the stage, he received a standing ovation. Maybe it was because of the great season, maybe it was because of his perseverance in the face of what he had endured that year and in his career, or maybe it was because it was the final luncheon of the year. Most likely, it was because Tyrone Willingham had brought back to the program a level of excitement that transcended the BCS standings. He had reminded Notre Dame what it felt like to have a football team that captured the attention of the nation.

When Dave Peloquin, one of the senior student managers, came to the stage to share his thoughts on the season, he essentially shared a new vision for the future. He was a polite, handsome brown-haired kid with a major in marketing. He said he had no concrete plans for life after graduation, and he only half-joked about having his résumé on him just in case someone there wanted to see it. But after the emcee, Bob Nagle, asked him how he had enjoyed that season, his answer revealed that he saw Tyrone Willingham as more than a football coach. He saw him as the model for professional success. He may have been a student manager talking about a football coach, but he represented a generation of white students who would carry with them into the corporate world a lasting impression of a dignified authority figure who just happened to be black.

"It's been a fantastic season to work for the team," said Peloquin. "I've learned so much from Coach Willingham on organization and how to be a professional and a leader. I'll take this experience with me for the rest of my life."

A few hours later, the last pep rally of the year brought things full circle and, in some ways, made Willingham and his team the ultimate example of mainstream success. It was Senior Night, when all the fourth-year players and their parents are introduced to the Notre Dame students and fans. But before that took place, something unusual happened. A little after 6:00 P.M., about 20 minutes before the team was scheduled to arrive, Chuck Lennon, donning his customary letter sweater, proudly announced a special guest performer, "Please welcome South Bend's own Darryl B!"

Four months and nine wins removed from his spirited performance at Simeris, the dreadlocked Darryl B once again prepared to offer his humble contribution to the Notre Dame tradition. But this time it wasn't on an outdoor stage in the comfort of summer before fellow subway alums; it was in the dead of winter in the middle of the Joyce Center, the heart of Notre Dame nation. Soaking up the hyperkinetic energy of rabid college kids, he grabbed the microphone. The bass line began to boom over the PA. "Go-Go-Go-Go-Go — Go Irish! Go-Go-Go-Go-Go — Go Irish! What's the name? — Notre Dame!"

The crowd immediately began to clap with him, seduced not only by the beat but also by the *idea* behind it. Darryl didn't attend Notre Dame, but he loved the school and wanted to be accepted there. With the crowd behind him, he rocked energetically, his confidence growing even as his voice weakened, becoming a hoarse cry. They clapped and swayed along with him, telling him that they enjoyed his music, but he couldn't tell if they really *felt* him. But shortly after he reached *the* line of the song, he had his answer.

"It's 2002, and *Willingham's the man!*"

In midbeat, the crowd briefly erupted, and if they hadn't

cared about anything Darryl B had said prior to then, there wasn't any denying that with that line he connected with them. Everyone agreed that Willingham was indeed "the man." He was the man, and he was the man worthy of being the Notre Dame head football coach.

About 30 minutes later, after the senior players and their parents had been introduced, it was clear that the Notre Dame players were more than just physical tokens of the university's tradition. The guys Willingham had coached back into national prominence, the ones who hit people, talked shit, and won all those games, were also young men worthy of the Notre Dame student-athlete tradition.

Courtney Watson's parents weren't able to attend the rally, and when his name was called, he came forward unescorted to have his picture taken. But as he stood in the center of the gym, sporting that tight-lipped smile, his boys in Zahm Hall cheered. As he headed back to his seat, one of them flung a red T-shirt at his feet. As Watson spun to pick it up, Willingham acknowledged their sincere affection: "That's a heck of a family you got there, Courtney," the coach said.

Bob Davie, who had been Notre Dame's archvillain before George O'Leary's brief reign of embarrassment, had accused the Irish faithful of "living in the past." Perhaps he thought the time when academically sound kids could go to class, stay out of jail, *and* win big-time, big-money ball games had passed. There was at least some truth to that. It was ridiculous to think Notre Dame could win the national championship every year simply because it was *freakin' Notre Dame.* What Miami was doing that season, staking claim to a second consecutive championship, was extraordinary by modern standards. In the previous four years, the title had been won by Oklahoma, Florida State, Tennessee, and shared by Michigan and Nebraska.

But it wasn't farfetched to believe that when Notre Dame was in the hunt for the gold, they could win with bright, articulate young men. Willingham certainly thought so. On many occasions that season, he'd said there were quite a few guys on his team who had great talent and passion for the game but who valued more than just football.

For this last pep rally, one of those players, safety Gerome

225

Sapp, was the speaker. One of the more popular players, Sapp was well received by a raucous ovation. He greeted his dorm mates in St. Edwards Hall with "What's up, St. Ed's!" They returned the love with their applause. Sapp then told the story of the moment he and his teammates were convinced that Willingham was "the man."

"We were doing winter conditioning at six-thirty in the morning," said Sapp. "It was a time when other people were coming home from partying the night before. At the end of each session, he would make us do this sit-up and push-up station." He then told them how he'd looked over at Courtney Watson and said, "Who is this man, and why is he doing this to us?" He recounted how Willingham had told them to "stop whining."

The crowd responded with a laugh. It was a delightful anecdote, a perfect blend of Willingham's stern yet loving authority and the overall buoyancy of the season. But right after Sapp said, very accurately, "That moment was a microcosm of our season," the little pep rally briefly lost its charm.

The word *microcosm* sent a murmur through the gym, and some in the crowd snickered. "Oooh, *big word*," said a small, frail waif of a girl standing in the aisle. Sapp, hearing the undercurrent but unaware of its origin, finished speaking. For a brief second, it was as though some of Sapp's classmates were unaware that, like them, he had chosen Notre Dame because of the professional opportunities it afforded him. Perhaps they were unaware that he, too, thought about his future, and that even though he was, for the moment, a Notre Dame football player, he would at some point be thrust back into the mainstream. Perhaps they didn't know that in the summer, Sapp had been an intern at Merrill Lynch in Houston, Texas, and that even now, when he dressed to go to class, he did so with a stylish corporate flair.

In the not-so-distant past, and because of ugly events from the past, the image of the Notre Dame football player had changed. Clean-cut players like Sapp were thought to be the exception. But maybe that image was in the process of changing again. Perhaps hugely talented clean-cut players could once again be the rule.

A few rows behind Sapp, Courtney Watson sat and listened.

He knew how it felt to be misperceived. A few weeks later, Watson was talking to some friends about a book on Harry S. Truman when a young woman, overhearing the conversation, said, "Oh, you're smart for a football player." Watson, taken aback but not shocked, laughed and gently explained that he was smart for a tennis player or golfer or any other kind of player. "In fact," he said, "I think I'm smart even if I weren't any kind of player." The girl was drunk, so the point was lost on her, but both Watson and Sapp were living, breathing examples of Notre Dame players who challenged people to see beyond their talents as athletes and to embrace them as total persons.

On Saturday, November 23, 2002, the game against Rutgers turned out to be more an act of "confirmation" than an actual football game. Arnaz Battle validated himself as a receiver, scoring two touchdowns in one game for the first time in his career. The second one was a 63-yard play in which he ran by his man, adjusted to an underthrown ball, and caught it while staying in bounds, displaying all the skills coveted by NFL scouts.

In the second quarter, Shane Walton confirmed his All-America status with his seventh pick of the season — the most by an Irish defender since Todd Lyght had eight in 1989 — which was also Walton's second touchdown. He returned Rutgers QB Ryan Hart's pass 45 yards for a score and gave the opportunistic Irish its eighth nonoffensive touchdown of the season.

On offense, Ryan Grant confirmed that he was as resilient as any player in college football. After suffering through two horrific weeks of turnovers, Grant looked confident and rested. In the third quarter, the offense ran 45 Escort. Grant took a handoff and started left, wrapping the ball tight with both arms. But as he turned upfield and prepared to take on an unblocked linebacker, he quickly and carefully switched the ball to his left hand. Just as he did, the backer came up and weakly dove at Grant's waist, and Grant lowered his right shoulder, churned his legs, and kept going. As he sailed down the sideline for a 28-yard touchdown, Buzz Preston watched, expelling a satisfied breath of relief. "That's exactly what he needed."

Grant finished the game with 68 yards to give him 1,001 for

the season, making him the seventh player in Notre Dame history to rush for more than 1,000 yards in a single season — something not even Jerome Bettis or Ricky Watters accomplished while playing for the Irish.

For Willingham, the game confirmed his belief that his team could respond even when they were heavily favored. Not even he had the energy to wage an "us against the world campaign" every week of the season.

"I don't want to go through every game as an underdog," he'd said earlier in the week. "I want this team to go out and win, and to have an easy game now and then." He shrugged when he said it because he knew they still lacked that fire that would put them over the hump. "But you know, I still want them to develop a killer instinct."

That's why at halftime, with a 14–0 lead, he calmly told his team it was time to "cut their opponent's hearts out and put them away for good," and that's exactly what they did. In the third quarter, they scored 28 points, the most points any Notre Dame team has ever scored in the third quarter of a game.

After the game was well decided, the little-used players took the field. It's customary for any team that in the last home game of the season, the guys who haven't played much, particularly the seniors, finally take the field. One of those seniors was Tim O'Neill, a 5'6", 170-pound tailback who was among the most popular players on the team because of his relentless intensity. He had originally been a walk-on, but prior to the Maryland game, Willingham brought O'Neill into the office to sign some scholarship papers to reward him for his service and dedication.

With the score 42–0, O'Neill took a handoff, exploded off the left tackle, found the sideline, and accelerated. Willingham watched him scamper by, applauding his effort but silently hoping he wouldn't make it to the end zone. The last thing he wanted to do was run up the score.

But Buzz Preston, who was standing next to Willingham, was thrilled. Preston took off and sprinted down the sideline, almost catching O'Neill as he urged him on. He said it was one of those moments a coach lives for, to see a kid like that finally get his. O'Neill wasn't the only one. Trent Miles gave Bernard Akatu one final chance at an official reception for the books.

Split to the left side of the formation in front of the Notre Dame sideline, Akatu ran an eight-yard out and waited for the ball. The corner was playing deep, and as Akatu made his break, he ended up right in front of Miles. Dillingham, who took over for Holiday in the fourth quarter, sprinted toward Akatu and lofted a nice soft ball his way. Akatu raised his hands, but a second before the ball arrived, a second before he would be rewarded for his four years of scout-team service, he jumped. The ball had been thrown perfectly — chest high and true — but when he jumped, it went through his hands and fell softly to the ground. On the sideline behind him, Miles threw his head back and shut his eyes. He had noticed how nervous Bernard had been as he ran in there. The coach was pleased to have given him an opportunity, since he had never been given that before. But a catch would have been so much sweeter.

Standing on the sideline was an offensive lineman from Cretin Derham-Hall High School in St. Paul, Minnesota, named Ryan Harris. The Rutgers game was the final recruiting weekend of the season, and at 6'4", 267 pounds, Harris was one of the top offensive linemen in the country. In his top 250 prospects, recruiting guru Tom Lemming listed Harris at No. 30. In addition to Notre Dame, Harris had narrowed his final choices to Miami, USC, Michigan, and Stanford. Harris liked Notre Dame, but he had some concerns. A Muslim, he was concerned about the lack of diversity on the Notre Dame campus. He was interested, but he still wasn't sure if Notre Dame was the place for a young black man who wasn't Catholic.

But the postgame atmosphere that day did provide unmitigated proof that this was indeed the place for Tyrone Willingham. Moments after Willingham ran into the tunnel pumping his fist, the band launched into the *1812* Overture, and the fans euphorically gave the Willingham salute. A woman seated in the lower right-hand corner of the stadium held up a sign that read ANNIE LOVES TY. Just three weeks after the loss to Boston College, a loss that one fan said "would have led to Bob Davie being hung in effigy," the Notre Dame faithful had not only forgiven the first-year coach but also welcomed him as one of their own.

16

USC

O N SUNDAY MORNING, November 24, Trent Walters had already graded the punt return film from the Rutgers game when Willingham walked into his office. Walters looked up from his computer screen, bewildered by what he'd seen. Willingham said, "I already know what you're gonna say."

In the middle of the second quarter, they had run the Shane Walton Block. Walton had come upfield completely untouched. But when he reached the block point, about two yards in front of the punter, rather than laying out and diving, he only casually extended his arms, not going after the ball as though he really *wanted* it. By Willingham's humble estimation, his failure to block that punt meant that Walton was done working, that he was done *achieving* things. The failure to compete, the unwillingness of anyone to accumulate as much as he possibly could, was a concept that baffled him. "If you want to make more than just one All-America team, go ahead and block that punt," he said. "Maybe you score on that too. Be a consensus All-America."

Walters, just as incredulous, agreed. Walton, who wasn't challenged that day, hadn't played with his normal intensity, and it was evident all over the tape. "Yeah, I told him, 'Don't relax,'" said Walters. "'You're up for the Bronko Nagurski Award.' Shoot, go ahead and cover those guys up!"

It was the same message Willingham had given to every

member of his team. He just didn't understand complacency. Neither did Courtney Watson. That's why Watson didn't need very much prompting from anyone, including Willingham. He was a self-starter in every sense of the word. When Watson had learned before the Rutgers game that he'd achieved one of his goals — making the list of finalists for the Butkus Award — he celebrated the announcement with Christina. He and Christina sat at Coach's watching the TV screen and waiting for the names to scroll across the bottom. During a *SportsCenter* telecast, Watson saw it: "Butkus Award finalists . . . E. J. Henderson — Maryland . . . Teddy Lehman — Oklahoma . . . Courtney Watson — Notre Dame."

"There it is!" he said to Christina. He leaned over and lightly kissed her cheek. Watson was pleased to be two thirds of the way through his journey. He led the team in tackles, and now he was a Butkus Award finalist. While he was pleased to be almost there, at season's end he faced another dilemma. He had one more year of eligibility left, but he wasn't sure if he wanted to stay for a fifth year. He would graduate in June with a business degree, and he was still flirting with the idea of making himself available for the draft. A consummate thinker and observer, he was an expert on the NFL draft, and because of that he was well prepared for the most likely scenario. He'd watched and studied the draft since he was a kid, and Watson had a pretty good idea of when he might get picked.

As with Walton and Battle, the agents had already begun hounding him, so he had the calls forwarded to his parents. "This one guy called my dad and said, 'Oh, Courtney is a definite first-rounder.'" A bottom-line kind of guy, Watson was offended to hear such a bold-faced lie. "Man, I'm an undersized backer. They never pick guys like me in the first round," he said.

The big 250-pound run-stuffing linebacker who haunts the tackle box but can't do much else is usually the type to get picked in the first round. But guys like Watson, the quick 225-pounders who can run with anyone and cover the tight end or the running back, who don't come out on passing downs, usually stay on the draft board until the middle rounds.

With that in mind, Watson had already decided the agent in

question was some charlatan who was trying to get into his good graces by telling him things he wanted to hear. He shook his head disgustedly. "I told my dad to never speak to that guy again."

On Monday of USC week, Willingham took the night off to see Nathaniel's basketball team play at the Discovery School. "He plays forward, but he's not a forward," said Willingham, laughing. "He's not a guard or a center either. He's playing *basketball*."

In some ways, watching 12-year-olds play wasn't too far removed from watching his own team's practice habits. Fourteen weeks into the season, he was still trying to get his players to practice well on a regular basis, and he could barely disguise his disappointment with their poor practice that week, leading up to the biggest game of the season.

There was a lot at stake. If Notre Dame won, they were guaranteed a spot in a BCS bowl game. At the time, both the Orange and Rose Bowl committees had expressed interest in the Irish. But if Notre Dame lost, they would most likely be headed to the Gator Bowl, repeating the scenario of 1998. That year, after a 10–0 loss to USC at the Coliseum, Notre Dame lost a BCS bid and went to Jacksonville for the Gator Bowl.

On Wednesday, right after the team had finished stretching and begun warm-ups, Willingham didn't like what he saw. The players were quiet and seemed to be going through the motions. He stalked around behind them and loudly revealed that his disgust had reached the third-person level. "Coach Willingham does not like how this practice is going so far," he said. "I'll start this practice over from the beginning. I'll start it over a hundred times if I have to!" The team knew he was pissed because he condensed the words *one hundred* into a hurried *ahunid*.

In his view, poor practice habits began early and were the result of a lack of focus. "Kids don't really like to play sports anymore," he said. "They go to practice and play the game, but kids just don't *play* like they used to." For a moment, he reflected on his childhood in North Carolina. "The wall outside my house was completely dirty from me throwing this little rubber ball up against it," he said. "I would be out there all hours of the night throwing it, catching it. I'd pretend I was catching ground-ers in baseball. I would do it until the neighbors or someone else would tell me to stop." But he lamented that such passion was rare for the current generation of athletes. "These kids have these video games and don't want to go out and really play. But you know, there's always that one kid who has all the video games but chooses to go out and do it because he has a *passion* for playing."

Willingham was about to shower and watch film when Lisa Mushett, an assistant for the Sports Information Department, told him that Shane Walton was not a Jim Thorpe Award finalist. Troy Polamalu, the All-America safety from USC, Terence Newman from Kansas State, and Mike Doss of Ohio State were finalists for the award given annually to the top college defensive back in the nation. The field of three was selected from a group of 14 semifinalists, a group that included Walton.

Willingham cocked his head to the side. The news clearly annoyed him. Not only did he think Walton should be a finalist, but he thought he deserved to win it. But rather than dwell on his disappointment, he would use the bad news to his advantage and get Walton to work harder.

Walton and Duff had faced a half-dozen of the best receivers in the nation, but in freshman sensation Mike Williams and crew, USC had easily the best group of wideouts they'd seen all year. Williams, at 6'5", 210 pounds, was almost an exact replica of former Trojan wideout Keyshawn Johnson. With astounding body control for an 18-year old, Williams could easily dominate a game. And with junior Keary Colbert and senior Kareem Kelly in the mix, the heart of the USC offense was its receiving core. In addition, there was quarterback Carson Palmer, who was playing the best ball of his collegiate career.

Willingham knew that everything Walton and the rest of the secondary had done that year would have to be intensified tenfold for this game, and he was eager to use any means he could to motivate them, including the news of the Thorpe finalists. "Hmm, that's good information to pass on," said Willingham slowly. "See, that's motivation for Shane to have a better game than the other guy."

By Thursday afternoon, both Walton and Duff were short-tempered and edgy. That was fairly evident as Walton tried to do a phone interview. Willingham kept track of those players who missed interviews with local media throughout the season, and those guilty of the crime were punished with Sunday morning running. That in mind, Walton, who was always reticent to speak to the media, snapped into the receiver. *"Hello! Hello!"* Irritated, Walton finally took the cell phone and stormed outside, where it was about 40 degrees. But it was more than the cold that had him pissed off. And it was more than not being invited to the Thorpe Award dinner. For the USC game, Walton and his teammates had returned to underdog status. They were ranked No. 7 and USC No. 6, and the 9–2 Trojans were favored by 11 points.

All week, practice took place in the Loftus Center. With 14 heaters overhead and little circulation, the Center captured the conditions of the Los Angeles Coliseum. On Thanksgiving weekend, it was 75 degrees and sunny in Southern California. And to prepare for the noise, Willingham borrowed a page from the Florida State game plan. A tape of two songs ran continuously. There was the USC fight song, followed by their victory march, during which Trojan fans held up two fingers to form a V, which they incessantly waved at their opponents. For most of the afternoon, the field house was saturated with the annoying cacophony. And Willingham had on his game face.

In USC he was not only taking on a former Pac-10 rival but also facing Pete Carroll, one of the few coaches whose youthful energy and competitive fire matched his own. Just as he'd done before the Stanford game, Willingham gave his team a message to take to the West Coast. Even though his Stanford teams had beaten USC three times in a row, and despite the fact that his current team was 10–1 and had enjoyed a truly fantastic season, Willingham wanted Carroll and everyone else to know that he was still hungry.

Wearing a pair of khakis, Willingham lined up with the receivers and released upfield. It was clear that he wanted USC, and Pete Carroll in particular, to know that the BCS, the national rankings, and all the extracurricular crap took a backseat to beating the Trojans. The schools had met 73 times, with Notre Dame leading the series 42–26–5. But this rivalry transcended football. USC and Notre Dame had similar images. Notre Dame was a pri-

234

vate school that stood in the middle of rural blue-collar South Bend, Indiana, and USC was a private school whose affluent gated community stood right in the heart of urban Watts, Los Angeles. When opulent alumni from the two schools annually met, it was a contest to determine not only who had the better football team or the bigger tradition but also who had the heaviest wallet.

It was fitting that the path from the Notre Dame locker room to the L.A. Coliseum's field crossed a faded, burnt-orange running track because the Notre Dame season had been much like a 400-meter race, one of the most grueling events in all of sports. That race, one lap around the track, is equal parts sprint and middle distance, combining the best and worst elements of speed and endurance. Treat it like a middle-distance race and you'll surely lose because you didn't have the balls to push hard; treat it like a sprint, and you take the risk of running out of gas at the end. Of course, Tyrone Willingham, fueled by competitive fire, chose the latter. In treating his maiden voyage like a sprint, he had pushed his guys — hard. And they had responded in kind.

In August they had exploded from the chute, legs churning with heart-pumping intensity. They had treated the first four games like the first 100 meters of the race — getting off to a quick start, full of hope and optimism. By 200 meters, they hadn't slowed down, maintaining a strong, defiant pace. Then came the loss to Boston College, the first visible sign of fatigue as they came off the curve and approached the straightaway. But on the Saturday night after Thanksgiving, November 30, 2002, as they gathered at the edge of the Coliseum's tunnel fully prepared to hurl themselves down the track for the last, most critical part of the race, their legs were suddenly incapable of nothing more than lethargic transport. That night, 91,432 people saw the Irish put up as much fight as they had for as long as they could.

The Irish secondary had clearly been the team's strength all season, but that night, it wouldn't matter. From the beginning, USC went right at them. In most games, if a team averages 50 plays on offense, if they throw enough times, they're gonna complete some balls. But that night, USC ran an unthinkable *84* plays, throwing the ball 46 times. On the first play of the game, USC quarterback Carson Palmer zipped an out to Alex Holmes for 12 yards. Two plays later, he threw a slant to Keary Colbert for eight yards, followed by another deep out route to Mike Williams for 17 yards.

Late in his senior year, Carson Palmer had emerged as a legitimate Heisman Trophy candidate. He was enjoying a breakout season similar to that of former Notre Dame quarterback Rick Mirer, who had played for the Irish back in 1992. More than a few coaches who played Notre Dame during that 1992 season said that Mirer was easily the most improved player on the Notre Dame team. As a result, Mirer was the second overall player selected in the 1993 NFL draft. It looked as though Carson Palmer was headed down the same path.

Palmer was a huge kid, about 6'5" and 225 pounds, and he threw the rock with serious heat and accuracy. But most important, he got rid of the ball in a hurry. Most times, Palmer didn't even set his feet before he threw. That made it damn near impossible for the defensive line to get their hands on him. Palmer took the snap, reared back, and discharged, moving his offense with precise and astonishing ease. And while Notre Dame had two excellent corners in Walton and Duff, USC, with receivers Williams, Kelly, and Colbert and running backs Sultan McCullough and Justin Fargas, had them outnumbered. Notre Dame couldn't match up man for man against USC, so they were forced to play mostly zone coverage.

Sometimes it was "cover two," with safeties Gerome Sapp and Glenn Earl lined up at 15 yards, taking away the deep ball. Other times it was "quarter-quarter," in which both the safeties and cornerbacks lined up deep and denied the USC receivers access to the seam routes. But that didn't matter to Palmer. He just went to work on the short game, throwing to receivers in the middle, in the flat, and on the sideline. The strength of the Notre Dame defense was quickness. But the USC backs and receivers were even quicker. By the time the first half ended, Palmer had already thrown for 242 yards and two scores.

When USC wasn't throwing the ball, they moved the line of scrimmage with a punishing run game. In Justin Fargas, USC had a runner who was wicked after contact. Pete Carroll called him the most competitive player he had ever coached. Coming out of high school, Fargas had chosen Michigan. But after a severely broken leg, which resulted in two surgeries, the first two years of his college career had been lost. He transferred to USC, and after playing behind incumbent Sultan McCullough, he finally got a shot. In this season, his final one, Fargas had found his rhythm, and the USC staff gave him the opportunity to feel it.

Prior to that season, he was best known for being the son of actor Antonio Fargas, one of the regulars on the 70s cop show *Starsky and Hutch.* In 2002, he was either making up for lost time or trying to establish himself as something other than Huggy Bear's kid, but the cat ran hard and low to the ground, never allowing tacklers to get underneath him. It was a style reminiscent of former USC tailback and Heisman winner Charles White, who navigated the field like a pinball, bouncing off bumpers and flippers. Fargas ran the same way, often accelerating after the first hit, as if he really dug getting hit by people. That night, Fargas gashed Notre Dame for 120 yards.

But this was more than a game to decide some BCS ranking. It was more than a rivalry. It was a fight, and it was personal. A lot of traditional Irish rivals — Michigan, Boston College, and, in recent years, Florida State — satisfied a serious hate jones when it came to Notre Dame. But that night, it was more than just hate; it was concentrated fury, both in the stands and on the field. Some USC fans may have been angry because Notre Dame's rise had overshadowed USC's own return to glory that season, or because most of the nation had come to identify Tyrone Willingham as college football's most popular coach instead of their own Pete Carroll. Or maybe some people at the Coliseum that night couldn't have cared less about Notre Dame but were still sickened by the fact that Al Davis had taken the Raiders away from them. Perhaps all they had left to cheer for was a college team.

Whatever the reasons, midway through the second quarter a collective loathing floated down from the stands and onto the Notre Dame sideline. Willingham may have been the media darling of college football all season, but that night at least one man had seen enough of the Notre Dame coach. He was a middle-aged guy wearing a red polo shirt and looking as though he had just strolled off the eighteenth green. With veins bulging from his neck, he yelled for a good minute: "Willingham, you suck! You suck, Willingham! You suck!"

A few minutes later, there was more sideline drama. A slight man wearing a silver NASA-looking windbreaker, a beatnik beret, and wire-rimmed glasses must have done something to annoy the Notre Dame security guard, because the guard rushed him. "Get your ass out of here!" the guard shouted as he grabbed him by the coat and tried to roll him off the field.

Almost directly above that little fracas, two USC fans intensely heckled Irish nickelback Preston Jackson. In the first quarter, with Jackson in coverage, Palmer completed a five-yard out route to Kareem Kelly. The two fans immediately began screaming, "You got burned, Jackson. You got burned!" Jackson broke the most fundamental rule in terms of players and hecklers when he acknowledged them with a little smile. After that, it was on, and for the remainder of the evening they patiently waited for Jackson to come within earshot. When he did, they hung over the railing, turning beet red, damn near ripping their vocal cords as they greeted him with a maniacally incessant chatter. "We got you, Jackson! We got you! We burned you! We burned you! We burned you!"

And another fan sitting a few rows behind the depraved magpies held a much more peaceful and calculated demonstration. He solemnly held up a maroon T-shirt with raised gold letters that read: "The Glory Stops Here — 11/30/02."

That fury spilled onto the field as Shane Walton refused to die easily. He had been arguing, fussing, and fighting with Trojan receivers all night. Part of his angst was directed at Kent Baer's defensive game plan, which was heavy on zone coverage. Walton, who wasn't intimidated by Baer, pleaded with his coach to play man coverage. Walton thrived on playing one-on-one ball, especially against big-time receivers like Mike Williams. His ability to shackle that kind of receiver is how he had become an All-America in the first place. But Baer knew better than to abandon his scheme. USC was moving the ball, but they had managed only one score. Of course, that would change.

If Notre Dame's last regular season game was the end of a 400-meter race, then the last three and a half minutes of the game's first half were the Irish's final, desperate push to the tape. Right after USC made a 22-yard field goal to make the lead 10–6, Holiday, trying to kickstart a drive, forced a ball to Omar Jenkins, but it was picked by USC corner Darrell Rideaux. It was Holiday's first pick in 127 attempts.

On the very next play, from the 11-yard line, it was time for Mike Goolsby to break another streak. He read a pass on Palmer's face and dropped into a seam in between two receivers, and when Palmer threw to Keary Colbert, Goolsby stepped in front of the ball, caught it at the Irish goal line, and returned it to the 18-yard line. It was not only Goolsby's first career interception but also Palmer's first interception in 147 pass attempts.

Then, Holiday, again trying to throw downfield to Jenkins, was picked once more — this time by Trojan safety DeShaun Hill. After the third consecutive pick, the Irish defense rose one final time, and on three plays they kept the Trojans from gaining a single yard. On fourth down, Carlos Pierre-Antoine rushed the guard-center gap, blocked and recovered the punt, and scored to give Notre Dame a brief 13–10 lead.

For several minutes, it looked as though the Notre Dame team from October had resurfaced. They were overmatched, but they were fighting and clawing to make plays. After they blocked the punt, it seemed as if Notre Dame could actually beat the Trojans. But after USC took only seven plays to go 80 yards, with Mike Williams scoring his second touchdown with five seconds left in the half, USC took a 17–13 lead, and the Irish faded.

After the touchdown there were only a few seconds left in the half, but Carroll wanted more. The Trojans tried an onside kick, which they recovered. Then Palmer immediately threw to Williams again in the back of the end zone. The pass fell incomplete, but Shane Walton, whose frustration had been mounting, lost it. Walton and Williams were behind the goalpost when Williams more or less questioned his credentials as an All-America. Walton smacked Williams in the face mask, and Williams swung back.

USC led only 17–13 at halftime, but Notre Dame was running on fumes. They had scored their final points of the game.

At the start of the second half, Pete Carroll, addressing the

ABC field reporter, flashed a wicked smile and said, "This is going to be fun." It was a smile that suggested he knew something. He knew that if his team won, they would be awarded a BCS game. He also knew that if his team won and Washington State lost the following week against UCLA, they had a shot at the Rose Bowl. And maybe Carroll also knew that if his team not only beat Notre Dame but also posted some criminal numbers in the process, Carson Palmer would win the Heisman Trophy.

As Arnaz Battle and Vontez Duff waited to receive the second-half kickoff, the LAPD helicopter, better known as the Ghetto Bird, circled over the Coliseum. It was fitting because several hundred feet below, the Trojans began to beat the Irish as if they'd stolen something.

The kick sailed over Battle's head and out of the end zone. Battle hadn't touched the ball much that game, and even when he did, he couldn't hold on. On one play, Battle lost his man and ran a deep crossing route. Holiday put the ball right above Battle's heart. But as he began to wrap his hands around the ball, Battle slightly turned his head to get upfield, and the ball fell to the ground. With just two catches for a paltry six yards, Battle had been anything but a playmaker that night. From both a technical and emotional standpoint, Battle's rise that season had been nothing short of phenomenal. As a person and a player he was light-years removed from that afternoon in 1998 when he'd been a nervous freshman thrown into the fire. But if he had been hoping for some redemption in the Coliseum on this day, he was sorely disappointed.

After three plays, Notre Dame punted. It took the Trojans less than two minutes to travel 55 yards and make the score 24–13. After that, USC started playing fast-break football, scoring 20 more unanswered points in the second half. Of their eight offensive possessions in the second half, USC scored either a touchdown or field goal on five of them.

Like its offense, the USC defense was also predicated on speed. In the second half, whether it was a run off-tackle, a quick slant, or a deep ball, by the time an Irish player got to his spot, there were two and sometimes three Trojan defenders waiting for him. Jordan Black put it succinctly, "Whatever we did, they were ready for it."

The Irish would finish the game with just 109 total yards and four first downs — by far their worst showing of the season. But the USC offense had a record performance. They dropped 610 total yards of offense on Notre Dame, the most ever against any Notre Dame team. Carson Palmer completed 32 of 46 passes for 425 yards, four touchdowns, and two interceptions. Two weeks later, Palmer would indeed win the Heisman Trophy, the fifth in USC's history. But USC still wasn't quite done that night.

With less than five minutes left in the game and the score 44–13, things got ugly in a personal way. On second-and-13, Trojans safety Troy Polamalu roared through the guard-center gap untouched and dropped Holiday for a nine-yard sack. On the sideline, Willingham stood, arms folded, motionless and expressionless. USC had not only thrown two passes on their previous series, but with a 31-point lead, they had just sent their best defensive player on a blitz. After the play, Polamalu took himself from the game — an act Pete Carroll called "cute." Willingham stood and watched. He didn't say anything, he didn't yell or scream, he just watched.

Back in September, only days after his first game, Willingham had already had his eye on USC. He knew what that game meant to Notre Dame, knew the depth of the rivalry, and knew win-loss records against bitter rivals are often the benchmark of a coach's career and may determine a coach's success at any school.

After the game, he would shake Pete Carroll's hand and look him in the eye, but he wouldn't say anything to him. And the next morning, Willingham would get up and return to the Coliseum and sit in a director's chair to tape a special segment of *Live with Regis and Kelly*. He would calmly talk about the game, listen to Regis say the Irish played too much zone defense, and laugh at his jokes. But for the moment, Willingham just watched USC and let the image of them celebrating burn into his head. He'd see them again the next October. And he'd remember.

17

SEASON OF CHANGE?

THERE WAS NO DOUBT the Irish had commanded the largest spotlight of any college team throughout the 2002 football season. From the very moment Tyrone Willingham was introduced as coach, Notre Dame had been the biggest story in college football. But it was more than just football that drew attention. Even the most idealistic person who insists that he lives in a color-blind society couldn't deny the significance of Willingham's first season at Notre Dame. Black head coaches in football had become a major issue in sports.

In September, during the week leading up to the game against Michigan State and his showdown with Bobby Williams, Willingham had been featured on the front page of *USA Today*. It was a story about how there were so few minority head coaches in college football and how Willingham's success at such a high-profile university could effect change. But perhaps even more significant was the change being effected at Notre Dame itself. By season's end, minority student applications were supposedly up 15% from the previous year.

One person who had been watching Notre Dame from the beginning was Bob Minnix. As both the president of the Black Coaches Association (BCA) since 2000 and a Notre Dame graduate, Minnix was doubly interested in the Irish. When Minnix arrived as a freshman running back on the Notre Dame campus in the fall of 1968, things were happening. From 1968 to 1972, Minnix's time in South Bend coincided with some of the most turbulent moments in American history. While at Notre Dame, Minnix had seen students murdered at Kent State, he'd protested the Vietnam War, and he'd seen Strom Thurmond, the creaking symbol of racist ignorance, get invited to speak on the Notre Dame campus. Minnix, Clarence Ellis, Tom Gatewood, Ernie Jackson, and Herman Hooten made up the largest black freshman class ever at Notre Dame. But it wasn't until 34 years later — the day Tyrone Willingham became coach — that Minnix once again witnessed history at Notre Dame.

During the course of the 2002 season, Minnix watched Notre Dame from afar. An associate athletic director at Florida State, Minnix saw Willingham guide the Irish to a 10–2 record. Of course, Minnix had met Willingham before, at Black Coaches Association clinics and programs. "I knew him when he was just the coach at Stanford and not someone as famous as the Notre Dame coach," said Minnix. "I've always appreciated his efforts and professionalism. And he hasn't changed a bit. In fact, you wouldn't even know he was the coach at Notre Dame."

Although he never saw Willingham during his daily interactions with the team, Minnix did see some similarities between Willingham and his old coach, Ara Parseghian. "I do know that having talked to him and observed him from afar, he's very confident, much like Ara was," said Minnix. "He also has an excellent ability to identify outstanding assistants. I can tell you [that] regardless of your position, the head man is only as good as his assistants. I've had the opportunity to meet all the assistants. They're all outstanding coaches and human beings. He's also very well organized, like Ara was."

For Minnix, Willingham's prosperity in 2002 had both professional and personal significance. Minnix called Willingham's hiring a "coup" on Notre Dame's part. "If you recall, he was not the first choice, and Notre Dame was fortunate that he was still there when the situation developed with the other coach," said Minnix. "And give Kevin White some credit for having the insight to go back and hire him. That's overlooked a lot because the lesser person would have moved on to the next white coach, basically. That took some heart, for lack of a better word, to move forward and say, 'This is the guy I want to hire.'"

Still identifying with his alma mater, Minnix continued. "That's an embarrassment as an alumnus that we've gone this long and never hired any minority, forget a black person, in the position of head coach. Not in any of our sports, be it minor or major. Now you can't claim that you're a leader in athletics in this country when diversity is not one of your top priorities. That hire has done more in a year to bring the issue to the forefront — of the need for minority coaches and the abilities of the minority coaches — than I could do in three years as president of the BCA."

But there didn't appear to be many folks who shared Minnix's view. The season began with 16 head coaching vacancies in college football, and by Christmas only one had been filled by a black coach, UCLA's Karl Dorrell. Dorrell played receiver for the Bruins from 1982 to 1986, and before serving as the receivers coach for the Denver Broncos, he'd been the offensive coordinator for both Colorado and Washington.

UCLA athletic director Dan Guerrero took some heat for choosing the 39-year-old Dorrell over some more experienced coaches like Greg Robinson, the defensive coordinator for the Kansas City Chiefs, and Mike Riley, a former head coach at Oregon State and with the San Diego Chargers.

Heading into the twelfth hour of his coaching search, Guerrero said Dorrell distanced himself from Riley and Robinson through his interview. It turned out that Dorrell had a strong historical perspective regarding some other black men in UCLA history. Dorrell told the *L.A. Times,* "UCLA is the school of [African-American Nobel Peace Prize winner] Ralph Bunche, Arthur Ashe, Jackie Robinson, and Rafer Johnson. And this is one more step in that succession. We should be a school that steps out and gives opportunities to African-Americans, and I'm excited about that."

Many said Guerrero took a risk hiring Karl Dorrell, a man with no head coaching experience. Sure he took a risk. But was that risk any more daring than the one Colorado took when they hired Rick Neuheisel, a 33-year-old with no head coaching experience? So many schools, Notre Dame included, look for a coach who understands "their way" of doing things. Dorrell, a reserved, clean-shaven brother known to all as a "straight arrow," could not have been a better fit for the "football is important, but it ain't everything to us" folks in Westwood. When it comes to hiring in college football, the rule is pretty basic. It's "Get in where you fit in."

It was a concept Tyrone Willingham had mastered. One day in his office, in his typically straightforward and economical way, Willingham broke down that rule. "See, when I was growing up, it was made pretty clear," he said. "Oh, no, you don't belong here. No, no, no, *you* go over there. When people reach about their mid-30s, they start to realize there's a double standard. Oh, it's always been there, you just haven't seen it because it's been cloaked. But your reputation is all you have. As African-American men, we have to maintain a good reputation. Whatever you do, you need someone to verify that you're good enough. People can look at the level of your work and say, 'Oh, this is pretty good.' But most often, your reputation has already preceded you. That's why I'm here."

Willingham also outlined the basic necessities that both current and past generations of blacks would have to possess if they were to ascend to great professional heights. "If you're any kind of minority, you have to be just like the majority," he said. "You need to match his mannerisms, match his habits, if you want to advance."

In 2002, Washington Redskins defensive coordinator Marvin Lewis had replaced Tyrone Willingham as the "black candidate" when MSU started wooing him. In November, after Michigan State fired Bobby Williams, Lewis became the leading candidate. But having little to gain from a college job, Lewis turned it down.

Actually, Lewis's saga had begun two years earlier. In 2000, while defensive coordinator for the Baltimore Ravens, Lewis directed a defense that set the NFL record for fewest points allowed in a 16-game season, with 165. Over a three-year span, for nearly 40 weeks, the Ravens didn't allow a 100-yard rusher in a game. But after Baltimore's victory over the New York Giants in

Super Bowl XXXV, Lewis was bypassed for head coaching jobs throughout the league. He interviewed in Cleveland and Buffalo and was thought to have a shot at both. But neither panned out, and Lewis settled on a lateral move, agreeing to become the defensive coordinator for the Redskins.

But on January 14, 2003, Marvin Lewis found a home as the head coach of the Cincinnati Bengals. The Bengals had just completed their twelfth consecutive losing season, and their 2–14 record in 2002 was an all-time franchise low. Since taking over the team for his father, Paul Brown, in 1990, Bengals owner Mike Brown had led the team to a stunningly awful 55–137 record. With those less-than-sterling credentials, the Bengals couldn't possibly go wrong by choosing Lewis. It was the ultimate Queen City public relations bonanza.

This was the same city where, in the 1990s, Cincinnati Reds owner Marge Schott had publicly made an ass of herself on a regular basis. The chain-smoking Schott had once referred to homosexuals as "fruits" and to black player Eric Davis as one of her "million dollar niggers." Conducting business in her smoky shadow, the Bengals were by mere proximity guilty of greater sins than losing. Cincinnati had also seen racial unrest in 2001 when several unarmed black men were shot and killed by police.

When the Bengals hired Marvin Lewis, they took a step to both build a winning team and save their floundering image. It was a blueprint familiar to those around South Bend.

Just a few days after the Bengals hired Lewis, an interesting statement came from Jacksonville Jaguars owner Wayne Weaver. After firing Tom Coughlin, Weaver hadn't been interested in Lewis. Weaver did, however, interview former Vikings coach Denny Green. But Green told Weaver he also wanted the general manager title, so Weaver went instead to the college ranks, hoping to hire Oklahoma's Bob Stoops or Iowa's Kirk Ferentz. After Stoops and Ferentz withdrew their names, Weaver chose Carolina Panthers defensive coordinator Jack Del Rio. In selecting Del Rio, Weaver once again exercised that one basic rule of corporate hiring: qualifications be damned; you gotta go with the guy with whom you're most comfortable.

"I just looked at him and knew there was chemistry there,"

said Weaver of Del Rio. So what if Del Rio, at 39, had but one year under his belt as a defensive coordinator and only six total years experience as an NFL assistant. Weaver's rationale spoke volumes about the hiring process. It didn't matter that Marvin Lewis had been a coach for 11 years and was one of the most successful coordinators ever. That was irrelevant. For Weaver, "chemistry" made Del Rio the right guy. In the aftermath of Del Rio's appointment, Marvin Lewis made the appropriate statement.

"I've always stated [that] the owner of an NFL team has the opportunity to hire a coach he feels best fits his direction and his needs," Lewis said. "And you can't tell somebody who to hire." It was the perfect statement because those individuals for whom race is never an issue don't want to hear that the color of a man's skin ever plays a factor in personnel decisions. Those who never deal with race want to be assured that all is exactly as it should be in the world. And the key, for an ambitious black coach, is to make those people feel comfortable. To ensure his chances of achieving "chemistry" with an employer, a coach must do all he can to avoid being seen as *black* and commence being seen as, you know, *normal.* Like Willingham said, the minority must match the habits and mannerisms of the majority. Especially when that majority just happens to own professional football teams, preside over universities, and command major corporations.

In October, HBO's *Real Sports* aired a special about the number of black head coaches in the NFL. It was noted that only six of the 400 men who had ever coached in the league's 83-year history had been black. And of 231 Division I-A and I-AA schools, there were only four black head coaches. For this particular episode of *Real Sports,* the field reporter was Bryant Gumbel himself. The story was so big that Gumbel left the studio to personally interview New York Jets coach Herman Edwards, Chicago Bears defensive coordinator Greg Blache, and Atlanta Falcons executive vice president Ray Anderson.

Dark, smooth, and good-looking, Anderson had once been Tyrone Willingham's agent, but a year earlier he had left his career in sports representation to assume a front-office position with the Falcons. He was the least known of those interviewed, but the message he delivered carried the most weight. A Stanford alum and Harvard Law School graduate, Anderson didn't mince words. He smiled at Gumbel and said, "As an African-American you have to be the absolute best at what you do in order to advance. That's just the reality of it."

Of course, the reality wielded by Johnnie Cochran and his partner Cyrus Mehri was one grounded in controversy. Inspired by the subtle racial issues that arose during Marvin Lewis's two-year journey to head coach, celebrity / civil rights and social activist attorney Cochran sounded off on NFL hiring practices. Cochran teamed up with Mehri to write a manifesto called "Black Coaches in the National Football League: Superior Performance, Inferior Opportunities." In their report, they proposed "mandatory diverse candidate slates for top coaching positions to foster fair competition." For those teams that didn't at least interview a minority candidate, Mehri and Cochran suggested penalties in the form of forfeited draft picks. In the beginning, some folks around the league weren't exactly thrilled by Johnnie Cochran invading their turf. Said one owner, "He'll have O. J. Simpson coaching my team."

Assured that wasn't a possibility, league representatives took the matter seriously. Joe Browne, the NFL's executive vice president, said that while they would discuss the idea of sanctions, those sanctions wouldn't involve draft choices. Said Browne on December 23, "The owners strongly agreed on the principle that they would interview one or more minority coaches before they made a final decision."

In other words, there was no way in hell anyone was going to be punished for not trying to hire a nonwhite coach. The NFL would continue to operate the same way it always had. The main thrust of Mehri and Cochran's plan was simple. It was designed to put pressure on NFL executives to at least make an effort to interview black candidates when vacancies arose. Unfortunately, there was no way to actually legislate a general manager's motives. Sure, you could put pressure on him to *call* a black candidate, but how could you account for his sincerity when he did?

In essence, Cochran and Mehri were encouraging what was already taking place — the token interview for the token candidate. It was just too easy to pick up the phone and chat with a guy to make it appear as if you were interested in him. That's pretty much what had taken place initially with Tyrone Willingham and Notre Dame the previous year. And it would surely continue to happen.

In February 2003, San Francisco filled its head coaching vacancy with a brand of sound and fury that was meant to suggest progress but, in reality, signified plain old stagnation. For nearly two weeks, Jets defensive coordinator Ted Cotrell, a black man, was said to be the leading candidate to replace the deposed Steve Mariucci. But when San Francisco named their man, it wasn't Cotrell. It was Oregon State head coach Dennis Erickson, who had never been mentioned as a candidate prior to that day. It begged the question: Had the 49ers really been interested in Cotrell and at the last minute chosen Erickson? Or had they just strung Cotrell along while 49ers owner John York secretly courted his own guy? San Francisco's hiring process was perfectly compatible with the new standards Cochran and Mehri championed, but in the end that didn't change a thing.

When it came to issues of race, Johnnie Cochran's often radical tone was the polar opposite of Willingham's conservative one. But Willingham thought Cochran's involvement was a good thing. "See, you need different tones and voices in this thing," said Willingham. "You need some to work quietly within the system, and you need others to stand outside and shout." When it comes to racial issues, the average white employer will embrace the quiet voice as a sign that everything is okay and disregard the loud voice as that of a disgruntled troublemaker. As a result, nothing changes. But when it came to recognizing black head coaches, Willingham hoped the league would hear both. "Perhaps together, those different voices can solve this problem," said Willingham.

And in truth, there *were* some changes in the sports landscape. "There used to be a belief that blacks couldn't be coordinators," said Minnix. At season's end, among the 117 Division I-A football teams, there were 12 black coordinators, 11 defensive, and one offensive. "It's a slow process," Minnix explained. "They didn't think minorities could be quarterbacks," said Minnix. "And now they're redefining the position."

He was right. Over the last several seasons, the quarterback position had undergone a revolution of sorts. Back in 1994, one year before the Tennessee Titans made Steve McNair their first pick and five years before three black quarterbacks — Cincinnati's Akili Smith, Minnesota's Daunte Culpepper, and Philadelphia's Donovan McNabb — were all selected in the first round, one longtime black assistant coach summed up the old-school owners' view of black quarterbacks: "These owners want to be reminded of Johnny Unitas and Y. A. Tittle," he said at the time. "They don't want to come to the stadium and see Grambling versus Southern."

But by 2002, things had changed. The Eagles' McNabb and the Falcons' Michael Vick had rebuffed, with extreme prejudice if you will, any notion that a brother couldn't lead a team with his head, legs, heart, and soul. And Vick landed the ultimate blow on January 4, 2003. That's when he sauntered onto the sacred frozen tundra of Lambeau Field, where the Green Bay Packers had never lost a home playoff game since the NFL instituted a postseason in 1933, and knocked off Green Bay and Brett Favre. That victory notwithstanding, the black quarterback question had been effectively answered. Minnix saw that as just the beginning. "There's no reason why that couldn't happen with the coaching position," he said. "Look at Edwards with the Jets and how exciting they were."

Also on January 4, when the Jets beat the Colts 41–0, Herman Edwards and Tony Dungy made history as the first black head coaches to ever meet in a playoff game. But something even more significant had already occurred in Baltimore.

On November 25, 2002, Ravens owner Art Modell made Hall of Fame tight end Ozzie Newsome the first black general manager in league history. After Newsome retired as a player from the Cleveland Browns in 1990, Modell made him the Browns' special assignment scout. In 1992, he was promoted to assistant to the head coach / offense–pro personnel. In 1994, Newsome was named the Browns' director of pro personnel, and then Ravens general manager in 2002.

"In the course of becoming discouraged, we have to keep going back to the well and keep pounding away," says Minnix. "As talent, either administratively or athletically, has the chance to define what their abilities are, you'll see you're better off having people of color on your team than not."

By 2003, because it was the starting point in every conversation, story, and reference to the black head coach issue, Notre Dame had become what it always proclaimed itself to be — the leader in collegiate sports. After Willingham doubled the win total from the previous season and in the process brought the Irish back to national prominence and cleansed their image, even the most cynical person would be hard-pressed to doubt that Tyrone Willingham's achievements could and should have led to increased opportunities for other black coaches.

And perhaps that was happening in the NFL. There was one more black head coach than the year before, and because of outside pressure, the league was aware of the problem.

But in college football, despite there being 16 job openings in December 2002, there would be the same number of black head coaches in 2003 that there had been the year before. With Dorrell in at UCLA and Williams gone from Michigan State, there were still only four. In the fall of 2002, the light from the Golden Dome was shining especially bright, but there was still evidence that most of college football was still stumbling around in the dark.

18

VALIDATION

Only days after the crushing loss to USC, the Irish coaching staff hit the road. They would discover their fate in the bowl picture soon enough, but in the meantime, they embarked upon the final two months of intense recruiting. After the loss to USC, Notre Dame dropped from No. 7 to No. 11 in the AP poll. Though their national ranking had fallen, Willingham and crew discovered their national appeal hadn't.

On December 4, Willingham and Greg Mattison took a trip to St. Paul, Minnesota, to see Ryan Harris. Harris, the highly regarded offensive tackle who had come to the Rutgers game, had also attended the USC game. But he had gone to the Coliseum on an official visit for the Trojans. Though Harris watched the 44–13 drubbing from the winner's sideline, when Willingham and Mattison were done with their visit, he had committed to Notre Dame.

"It just seemed like I was destined to go to Notre Dame." Harris told the *South Bend Tribune,* "It's just the right fit for me." In addition to the visit from Willingham, Harris also received some words of encouragement from Tony Scott, a Muslim leader from South Bend. "He assured me that South Bend was a diverse community."

Some Notre Dame detractors, and perhaps some Notre Dame fans, felt that the embarrassing loss to USC could place a blemish on a splendid season. While that game showed Notre

Dame to be "vulnerable," Harris said it didn't cloud the big picture. "What I see in Tyrone Willingham is a man who turned a program around in his first year, going 10–2," said Harris. "That's unbelievable, and I can't wait to be a part of it."

Two weeks before Christmas, more rewards for a 10–2 season started coming Tyrone Willingham's way when he was named *Sporting News* Sportsman of the Year. The publication started giving the award in 1968, with past winners including UCLA basketball coach John Wooden, baseball great Nolan Ryan, basketball legend Larry Bird, and former Notre Dame and 49ers quarterback Joe Montana. But 2002 marked the first time any college football coach had ever garnered such an honor.

As with any time he received an individual honor or award, Willingham was flattered but not really buying it. "This should not be the focus," he said. He was humble and private, and he just preferred that things not be about him. That was perfect because the Notre Dame administration prefers that its success not be about the coach either. It was just one more shred of evidence that Tyrone Willingham and Notre Dame were an ideal match. But Willingham had known this all along. In fact, he knew Notre Dame as well as Notre Dame knew itself.

One day in early December, Sports Information assistant Lisa Mushett asked Willingham to sign some random Notre Dame effects. One of them was a large poster. In the center of the poster was the Golden Dome. Taking the cap off his marker, Willingham carefully signed his name in the upper right-hand corner, as far away from the Dome as he could, saying, "I do not want to upstage the university." Mushett chuckled and said, "But you *are* the university, Coach."

She had a point because, at the time, the name Tyrone Willingham was synonymous with Notre Dame. Willingham, shaking his head, said, "The last person who became the university had to leave the university." It was an obvious reference to Lou Holtz, whose monumental success had hastened his departure in 1996. Willingham was fully aware that the University of Notre Dame must always precede Notre Dame football. He knew that whenever football took center stage, the board of trustees, the president, and all who ran the university would remind everyone that Notre Dame was first and foremost a "scholastic institution." But in 2002, by simply "getting" the Notre Dame tradition, Willingham had done his part, and done it well, in returning the Irish to glory. After he finished signing, Willingham got up to leave. Before he entered the locker room, he shrugged and said, "I still don't know why people want my signature."

Two days later, on Thursday, December 12, Willingham received the ESPN Home Depot National Coach of the Year award. The College Football Awards Show was held at the Disney World Resort in Orlando, Florida. It was the Who's Who of college football. Penn State tailback Larry Johnson won the Maxwell Award as the nation's best all-around player; Iowa's Brad Banks won the Davey O'Brien Award as the nation's premier quarterback; and Michigan State's Charles Rogers won the Biletnikoff Award as college football's best receiver.

In the introduction for the Coach of the Year award, ESPN college football announcer Lee Corso described Willingham's path to Notre Dame in terms of a fantasy. "Tyrone Willingham paid his dues," said Corso. "He interviewed for the job first, and another guy got it. But God wanted him in South Bend, so He sent down a cloud and Tyrone Willingham rode that cloud all the way to Notre Dame." In a way, that description was accurate. It was accurate to describe college football's Coach of the Year in terms of a fantasy because the difference between Willingham and the coach who was honored that night for his lifetime contributions to college football was truly fantastic. The lifetime honoree was a cat named Darrell Royal.

While coach at the University of Texas from 1957 to 1976, Royal had won national championships in 1963, 1969, and 1970. On the way to winning the 1969 championship, Royal's Texas team had beaten Notre Dame 21–17 in the Cotton Bowl. Shortly before that game, Royal was asked why he didn't have any black players on his team. Royal said he had "won without 'em and would continue to win without 'em." Ironically, that Texas team was the last all-white team to win a national championship.

So it was pretty extraordinary that 33 years later, the Coach of the Year just happened to be a black man from Notre Dame whose goal was to take that very thing Darrell Royal once possessed. No, not the spotlight. What Willingham was after, though he only alluded to it in his typically colorful and cryptic way, was a national championship.

After Willingham received his award, a small group of reporters gathered around him, and one noticed the large ring sparkling on his right hand. It was the Pac-10 conference ring he'd won after the 1999 season.

"You think you'll ever take that ring off?" asked the reporter.

"There's only one ring that could replace this one," replied Willingham. Everyone in earshot knew which ring he was talking about.

In the back row of the auditorium, Courtney Watson sat next to Christina. The next evening, Watson, along with Maryland's E. J. Henderson and Oklahoma's Teddy Lehman, would attend a dinner for the Butkus Award. But that night, he and Christina decided to take in the festivities for one of college football's biggest awards shows. Watson sat wedged in between the media section and a group of enthusiastic high school kids. Since the show was hosted by ESPN, the studio audience was encouraged to cheer whenever the opportunity presented itself. Most opportunities arose when the words *Miami Hurricanes* came up.

"How about those Miami Hurricanes?" said Chris Fowler.

"Yeah, let's go, 'Canes," yelled a little chubby kid across the aisle from Watson. Looking a bit annoyed, Watson glanced from the corner of his eye.

But when the Walter Camp All-America team was announced, Watson went from being annoyed to feeling melancholy. Watson had been named a third-team All-America by *Sporting News,* but he was still coming to terms with the fact that he had only achieved two thirds of his goals. Despite missing the opening game, Watson had still managed to lead the team with 90 tackles, and the following night, he would put on his tux and attend a dinner as a Butkus Award finalist. But right then, as a stream of first-team All-Americas sauntered past him, Watson faced forward, looking wistfully at the stage.

Michigan State's Charles Rogers, USC safety Troy Polamalu, and Penn State running back Larry Johnson all marched solemnly to a carpeted staircase, where they would pose for a photo. Shane Walton, too, sauntered by on his way to the staircase.

Walton was having a great time. Walton and Kansas State corner-back Terence Newman, who had won the Thorpe Award as the nation's best defensive back, had formed a bond and talked about how great it would be to play together at the next level.

On seeing his teammate, Walton stopped and smiled. "Hey man, what's up?" Watson shook his hand, congratulated him, and was silent again. Watson was genuinely happy for Walton. They had radically different styles. For Watson, public perception was everything, and talking to opponents like Shane did was something that would never cross his mind. But Watson was pleased to see one of his own get recognized.

After the awards show, the players and their guests walked down the boardwalk for a postshow dinner at ESPN Zone. In a banquet room filled with television sets featuring still images of all their faces, the players gathered for sandwiches and drinks. In the balcony, Shane Walton's mom sat next to him while he played in a video game tournament. Directly below them, Court-ney Watson and Christina quietly ate. The irony was that al-though Watson wasn't a first-team college football All-America, the handsome, clean-cut Notre Dame linebacker and his whole-some, bubbly girlfriend were about as all-American as you could get. And the scene that unfolded while they ate was a truly pre-cious display of Willingham as coach, father figure, and master of the cryptic message.

Willingham, who had been seated a few tables away from them eating a sandwich and talking to John Heisler, walked over to Watson's table. As Watson introduced Willingham to Christina, the waiter arrived with two rum and Cokes, and Christina, quickly lapsing into the role of dutiful girlfriend, swiftly and deftly tried to take both drinks herself. One would have been hard-pressed to fool Mr. Magoo with such an effort. And the hawkeyed Wil-lingham? He saw it all, but as usual he played it cool. While Wil-lingham casually spoke to Christina, saying, "I hope you heard only good things about me," his eyes darted uneasily to the short glasses, the little red straws a dead giveaway to their contents.

"Well, I'm going to head back and get something to eat, and maybe take one more picture," said Willingham. But as he headed back to his table, he glanced over his shoulder at Christina and said with a raised eyebrow, "Oh, you can slide that drink over to the other side of the table now."

Acknowledging that the innocent ruse had failed, Courtney and Christina laughed. "Man, I love that dude," said Watson.

But Willingham wasn't done; he added some more mystery a half-hour later when he got up to leave. He walked over to the table, placed a hand on Watson's shoulder, and said, "Just relax. But I'm going to run the *hell* out of you when we get back."

Watson sat there, his brow furrowed, a confused expression on his face. *What did that mean?* he wondered. Did Willingham mean that he would run Watson personally? Did he mean he would work the team harder because he figured if one of its leaders was drinking that meant the younger, less responsible guys on the team must be doing the same thing?

It was classic Willingham. By leaving Watson wondering what he meant, Willingham had accomplished his goal. Watson was 22 years old and perhaps the most disciplined player Willingham had, and there was no hard-and-fast rule against players drinking. But Willingham relished the opportunity to make his players *think* about everything they did.

That was the case with all of his players and their choices. "It's all about how you present yourself," said Willingham. He had planted the same seed of doubt with punter Joey Hildbold, who had rather provocative tastes when it came to facial hair.

"I have a kicker who looks like the leprechaun," said Willingham.

Hildbold's reddish beard ran from his sideburns and around his chin without the added attraction of a mustache or goatee. "Now, I might look at him, and say, 'He looks okay, I guess. It's not really bothering anyone.' But one day, I might walk by him and say, 'Hey, nice beard.' Now he might say to himself, 'What does that mean? Does that mean he wants me to cut it?'" Willingham shrugged, the thought making him smile. "But the point is this: It may make him go to the mirror and look at *himself.*"

With Maurice Stovall, Ryan Grant, Cedric Hilliard, Carlos Pierre-Antoine, Shane Walton, and several others sporting either braids or cornrows, Willingham applied a similar philosophy to other forms of personal style. "A guy can wear cornrows if it's him," he said. "There were guys who wore them at Stanford. They came in there wearing them. But see, that's the only way I knew them. But there were some other guys who started wearing them later, and I discouraged them from doing so. See, it just wasn't *them*. And I told them that."

The next evening, the Butkus Award ceremony took place in the ballroom of the Renaissance hotel in Orlando. Willingham stood before the small audience and told them what an honor it had been to coach Courtney Watson. Resplendent in a tuxedo, looking like a smaller, blacker version of his alter ego, James Bond, Willingham was in a good mood. He spent the rest of the evening with Watson and his family, making small talk. Watson was happy too. For the moment, he was right where he wanted to be. But he still couldn't make up his mind about what he should do next. He was trying to decide whether or not he should petition for a fifth year at Notre Dame. He had one month left to make himself eligible for the NFL draft, but he wasn't ready to make a decision.

To no one's surprise, E. J. Henderson won the Butkus Award that night. Afterward, Willingham congratulated Henderson and spoke briefly with Henderson's parents before returning to his friends. He was back to the upbeat, energized mood he had when the season began. He practiced his golf swing. "Now it's time to get back to football," he said.

He had scheduled his team's first postseason practice for Saturday afternoon, and he was eager to get back to campus. "We need one more win to make this a successful season. *One . . . more . . . win*." But first he had to go upstairs to the hospitality suite for an appearance. "Maybe next year we can get someone else here and win this thing."

When it was suggested to him that perhaps the same guy could return next year and win the Butkus Award, Willingham perked up. Willingham hadn't conceded that Watson would be leaving, but he was clearly prepared for him to do so. "Hmm," he said, alluding to the specter of Watson staying one more season. He pursed his lips and slightly cocked his head to one side. "That would be nice."

19

THE GATOR BOWL

O N A CHILLY SUNDAY morning in December, Willingham, along with Sean Mahan, Arnaz Battle, and Gerome Sapp, walked into the auditorium inside the football office. The players took seats among a small group of media, and Willingham sat next to Kevin White at the podium in front. Both Willingham and White wore Notre Dame sweater vests, White's blue and Willingham's green. In a way, the interlocked ND on their chests served as visual evidence that White and Willingham were now officially members of the same club.

A second later, Rick Catlett, the Gator Bowl executive director, officially invited the Irish to Jacksonville. Catlett spoke in a heavy Southern drawl, saying, "We're really excited and pleased to be here to extend to you an opportunity to play in the fifty-eighth annual Gator Bowl in Jacksonville, Florida. And please accept because it was a long ride up here!"

After Kevin White accepted on behalf of Notre Dame, an especially upbeat Willingham did the same. A little more than a month earlier, when they were undefeated and ranked in the Top Five, an invitation to a second-tier game like the Gator Bowl would have seemed like a disappointment. But any team that played a bowl game on New Year's Day still had some clout.

That morning, Willingham was genuinely pleased to receive a bid to any bowl game. True, the Gator Bowl would pay Notre

Dame only $1.6 million, which was a far cry from the $13 million a BCS game would bring them. But the reality was that Willingham's team had exceeded a lot of people's expectations, and a bowl game was still a reward for a successful season. "On behalf of our football team, we do accept. We are delighted to accept," said Willingham. He also rather sheepishly confessed to having told his team of the bid a few minutes earlier.

A minute later, Willingham left the podium and joined the small group of reporters in the audience. As Battle, Mahan, and Sapp sat down to answer questions, Willingham looked pleased and proud to finally let his guys have their own voice. Since it was his final game in a well-documented journey, Battle was asked most of the questions. Once again, history was repeating itself. Battle's first bowl game had been the 1998 Gator Bowl against Georgia Tech. And the invitation to play in it had followed another bitter loss to USC at the Coliseum. Battle, dressed in his normal uniform of sweatpants and T-shirt, wore his usual tranquil expression. His easy bayou drawl seemed especially nasally that morning, as he reflected forlornly on that first Gator Bowl, a 35–28 loss.

"I didn't even dress for that one," he said. "But I don't think you could ask for a better situation for this program, just to have this opportunity."

Battle was looking at this game as a way to compartmentalize his experience at Notre Dame. The team's performance against Florida State had been the signature performance of the "Return to Glory" season, and Battle and his teammates always referred to that game as not only the zenith of that season but also the starting point for the program's future. "Notre Dame is supposed to dominate across the board," said Battle. "I think the team understands that Florida State was a great game for us up until the last five minutes. I think we really went out there and dominated. That's what we're supposed to do."

Before leaving for Jacksonville, they had a solid week of practice to prepare for their bowl opponent, North Carolina State. The Wolfpack were ranked 17th and had traveled a similar path as Notre Dame to reach the postseason. The same day Notre Dame lost to Boston College, North Carolina State had seen its own undefeated season come to an end against ACC rival Georgia Tech.

Willingham likened preparing for a bowl game to an extra week of spring practice. Before installing a game plan to stop the Wolfpack, Willingham devoted the first few practice sessions to the basics of football. During that time, Willingham emphasized two ingredients that had been sorely missing in the latter part of the season: conditioning and fundamentals. The team broke into groups, and each group addressed its specific needs. The receivers ran routes, the running backs took handoffs, the offensive linemen fired off the ball, and the defensive backs back-pedaled. But when they did get to some real game preparation, disaster struck.

Two days before they were scheduled to leave for Jacksonville, Courtney Watson was pursuing a running play when one of his teammates rolled into his leg. The result was a partially torn medial collateral ligament on his left knee. Watson accompanied the team to Jacksonville, but he was done for the season. While the team practiced in the sunshine at picturesque North Florida University, he stood and watched, his right leg stiffly encased by a long black array of nylon and Velcro straps. He had good-naturedly teased his friends Cedric Hilliard and Gerome Sapp about their knee injuries and wondered if that had jinxed him. During that week, he spent each night in his room at the Marriott, ordering pizza and calling Christina. After the game, he was heading to Whitefish, Montana, to spend the final days of winter break with her and her family.

Of course, the injury made Watson's decision to return an easy one. It wouldn't make any sense to enter the draft with a bad knee. Besides, he hadn't known what the pro scouts thought of him anyway. Now he'd have a chance to rehab the knee. In the meantime, he'd petition the university for a fifth year of eligibility. Watson actually had a lot to be excited about. He was a vital cog in a program once again on the rise, and he would have one last opportunity to reach his goals. But that was next season. Right then, Watson was depressed because his season would end the same way it had started — on the sideline.

*   *   *

On Sunday afternoon, December 29, Trent Miles was just hoping for things to get back to normal. "I hope we have a good practice today," he said. He and the rest of the team had arrived in Jacksonville 72 hours earlier, fully expecting to finish the season with the same improbable flair they had established back in September. But on their second night in Jacksonville, there had been an "incident."

The team had gone the entire year without any problems. Off the field, the players had been anything but unruly savages. They had not only stayed out of trouble but until that point they hadn't even put themselves in *position* to get into trouble. They had respected themselves, their program, and the Notre Dame tradition, and Willingham wanted to reward them for it. Before they left campus, Willingham said to them: "I'll tell you right now. The first two days you won't have a curfew. But if you do anything to abuse that privilege, I won't hesitate to send your ass home."

A day after landing in Jacksonville, and just six days before he was to play in his last college game, reserve strong safety Chad DeBolt wasn't headed back home, but he wasn't playing in the game either.

On Friday night, the 6'0", 200-pound DeBolt, from Waterloo, New York, had gone to a little spot called the Ocean Club, an upscale establishment a few miles from his hotel. Once there, he proceeded to get drunk, to the point of extreme petulance, ignored an order to leave, and then got arrested because of it. But it would get uglier. After being taken to the station, while changing into his county jumpsuit, he slurred to anyone within earshot, "Nobody laugh, I'm the Fighting Irish."

According to the Jacksonville Police, DeBolt subsequently needed to be put in a restraining chair when he could not control his disruptive behavior. In the mug shot that appeared the next day, DeBolt's eyes were swollen shut and his face was scratched, raising questions about what really happened that night. A month and a half later, the Jacksonville Police Department was cleared of any wrongdoing following an investigation. But DeBolt had already moved on. In fact, he missed his trial date in January because he was studying abroad in London.

tched him,
out that he
ting on the
it since his
way.

ly he main-
impeccably
against the
ter the sea-
uch a short
least a few
is birthday.
Budinscak
er for their
he liked to
ne. Beyond
iperhuman
erson, and
wasn't really
ction to see

dical depar-
y the Com-
Notre Dame
ere assigned
pened to be
a friend of
t happened
haracter for

noan of the
with the big
nderful was
ul of Notre
the people
to say what
nd a few of

New York was guilty of another
otle in nature. Prior to the first
ld he was no longer a walk-on.
was given some papers to sign
final season at Notre Dame as a
ingham had given him a wonder-
l effectively trampled on it.

am some well-deserved freedom.
b well done, and they had done a
some ways, it was also a test. He
o determine just how much he
l failed the test.

Neither Jordan Black nor Bren-
e linemen, had made the trip to
campus under the secret restric-
't known what either had done
because of their actions neither
some members of the team felt
e "right attitude" or hunger nec-
o accomplish as a team.

owl, on a Monday night, a rather
ksonville's Champs Sports Bar.
llingham's forty-ninth birthday,
nds were throwing a little party
a big heavyset brother singing
t. But that was long after Father
minions had vacated the prem-
t crooned the lyrics to the Gap
e last of the front-office people
on to the Commodores' "Brick

tarted. He led his wife, Audrey,
egan to dance. Then Bob and
did Bill Diedrick and his wife.
g, no longer able to resist the
d playing excellent music, Wil-
d he and Kim shook it a little.
yes on him, as always. And as

he danced, he looked into the eyes of those who w
making sure they weren't judging him. If word got
was dancing, people might think he wasn't concentr
game, or that he had, God forbid, lost his focus. B
friends had thrown this party for him, he danced any

Those who watched him that night understood w
tained such a sober public image. They knew his
high standard of behavior was his way of defending
double standard for black men in the public eye. A
son he'd had and the things he'd accomplished in
time, the least of his spoils should have included a
minutes of shaking his ass like a brother celebrating

Some of the players filed in while he danced. Kyl
smiled, as did Tim O'Neill. Was this out of charac
coach? Nah, not really. Truth was, he liked to dance
sing along with music, and he liked to have a good ti
the intensity required to perform his job and the s
intensity required to *keep* his job, he was a happy
happy people find it easy to have a good time. So it
out of character at this particular Notre Dame fun
Tyrone Willingham dance.

There were, however, some things that were a ra
ture from the norm. It was unusual to hear songs
modores and the Gap Band being performed at a
function. And the presence of four white men who w
to the guardianship of a black woman who just hap
the national security advisor, and who happened to
the Notre Dame head football coach, who himself ju
to be a black man — that was all completely out of
Notre Dame.

Amid the soft wail of the saxophone, the low
bass, the clickety beat of the drums, and the brother
booming Gerald LeVert–type voice, something w
taking place. The face and, more important, the
Dame looked different, colorful, and inclusive. An
in that room seemed to be happy about it. It was har
the rest of the administration felt. Malloy, White,

White's people in the Athletic Department had all made brief appearances when the party started, but they were long gone.

Of course, it helped that Rice, because of the company she kept in the White House, was known as conservative, and so was Willingham. It helped because Notre Dame was a conservative place, and since they reflected that, their voices could be heard. If they'd had voices whose pitch or timbre differed from the majority at Notre Dame, they would have had little chance of being received.

The last song of the night was a classic by Maze and Frankie Beverly, and the big cat in the Kangol did it justice. "Joy and pain . . . is like sunshine and rain." Kim took a seat, and Willingham danced with Rice. This scene, with the two of them dancing, could have been a glimpse into a wonderful future. The Notre Dame football coach and the most powerful member of the conservative black intelligentsia dancing together represented great possibilities.

In that room, coolly jamming to the music of Frankie Beverly, was perhaps the future of football's power structure. Rice had made it no secret that she had designs on the NFL commissioner's office one day. With the current commissioner, Paul Tagliabue, talking about retirement, Rice would be in position to at least get an interview, if she so desired. And she had two powerful allies in Dennis Green and Willingham. She had, after all, played a role in getting both men hired at Stanford, and with such successful careers, both had proven her to be of sound judgment on such matters.

It was just a matter of time before Green, who could have probably had the Cincinnati or Jacksonville job that winter, returned to the league. And everyone knew that Willingham's continued success at Notre Dame would make him the hot commodity among NFL general managers. After a 10-win season at Notre Dame, the crucible for football coaches, it was unlikely Willingham would ever be relegated to the role of black candidate. The next time around, he would be, as Darryl B had so aptly put it, "the man."

Two days later, on January 1, 2003, Willingham led his team

out into ALLTEL Stadium and a crowd of 73,491 fans. Four years earlier, they had played in this same stadium and lost 35–28 to Georgia Tech. But this time, in NC State, they faced more than 30,000 Wolfpack fans and their sea of red.

Even so, when they emerged from the tunnel, the Irish wore their home-team blue, and from the start, they acted as though this was their home. The first play began without a huddle. Arnaz Battle jogged out to the area just above the 20-yard marker, and Willingham walked down to the 40-yard line, crossed his arms, and waited. Before settling into his stance, Battle calmly picked up an errant mouthpiece and tossed it to the sideline. Willingham watched him, waiting for Battle to join him just as he had on that opening play against Florida State. And he expected the same results as that day back in October.

As he settled into his stance, Battle was fully prepared to repeat the catch and run. But when he reached the 40-yard line, none of it happened. North Carolina State already knew what was coming. They had just watched the film of Notre Dame's game against Florida State while preparing to play the Seminoles, their opponent in the regular-season finale. They'd already seen Battle go 65 yards on the opening play, so the North Carolina State corner, already playing a deep zone designed to take away the long ball, took a few steps back, and by the time Holiday had lofted the ball deep, long, and outside, the cornerback had blocked Battle's path and cut him off. The ball sailed out of bounds.

Even so, they drove down the field, eventually getting to midfield on that first drive and, on their second drive, getting toward the goal line. But each time, they were turned away as the NC State defense swarmed like a bunch of guys who wanted nothing more than to devour Notre Dame, their tradition, and everyone's fascination with their season.

During the season, Holiday had proved he could throw, and on occasion, he even resembled a real passer, but he was still first and foremost a running quarterback. So on second-and-goal, they ran an option. From the time Holiday received the snap, the play was fraught with disaster. The strong side linebacker, quickly diagnosing the play, rushed lead blocker Chris Yura and met him with such a vengeance that when Yura's body came flying into the backfield, Holiday barely missed tripping over him. Holiday sprinted out to his right, but guard Sean Milligan had fallen to the ground, and as Holiday leaped over him, Wolfpack middle linebacker Dantonio Burnette caught him midair, driving his own head into the spot between Holiday's pectoral and deltoid muscle. By the time Holiday came down, smacking the ground with his back, he had once again separated his shoulder. If there had been any hope of recapturing the spirit of the first two months of the season, it was all sucked out as Holiday lay on the ground.

Of course, they continued to play. They still scrapped and fought as they had all season. A month after the USC game, Shane Walton was still fired up. He would be named a consensus All-America, the first Notre Dame player to earn such honors since cornerback Bobby Taylor did it in the 1993 season. And Willingham's prodding had obviously gotten to him because he played as if he still had more to prove. But Walton's final game was just an ugly continuation of the game at the Coliseum, which made sense because the USC offense and the North Carolina State offense had been born of the same guy.

Prior to joining the staff at USC, offensive coordinator Norm Chow had spent a year at North Carolina State. Though not entirely identical, the North Carolina State offense and the one Notre Dame had seen in L.A. were pretty much the same. Like the USC offense, the strength of the attack lay in the quarterback's quick release. In Philip Rivers, the Irish defense faced a quarterback whose quick sidearm delivery made it difficult for him to be sacked. And also like USC, the receiving corps was deep and talented.

On one play, Walton fired from his stance and jammed Wolfpack receiver Jerricho Cotchery at the line of scrimmage. Cotchery was 6'1", 200 pounds, good against bump-and-run coverage, and had posted a 1,000-yard season. Walton shadowed him upfield, not allowing any separation. After Philip Rivers threw to the other side of the field, Walton escorted Cotchery back to the huddle, pushing his face mask underneath Cotchery's chin, chattering nonstop. But much like the USC game, the receiver had the last word. Cotchery finished the game with 10 catches for 127 yards and a score.

On offense, the Notre Dame coaches wanted to get the ball to the big dog. This was Battle's last game, and they all wanted to send him out with a performance befitting his talent and spirit. They had started the game without Jordan Black and Brennan Curtin. In the first quarter, in addition to losing Holiday, Gary Godsey also left the game with a knee injury. After that, the offense was barely treading water, so they really had no choice but to look for Battle whenever possible.

In the third quarter, trailing 21–3, Pat Dillingham did his best to put the ball in Battle's hands on consecutive drives. On the Wolfpack 24-yard line, on fourth-and-five, Battle drifted to the end zone, where he was bracketed by both safeties and the linebacker. Dillingham, looking at him the whole way, lobbed the ball high, and it floated back down into the hands of NC State free safety Rod Johnson.

In the next series, Battle finally broke free. Getting downfield, he pushed off the corner, getting a yard of separation. The ball was long but not completely out of reach. Battle took another step and dove, but as he stretched out, the ball skimmed off his fingers. Battle jogged to the sideline, sat down in his normal spot, and slowly removed his helmet. He would finish with 10 catches for 84 yards, a good statistical day, but his coaches and teammates knew he wanted so much more than that.

Dillingham came and sat beside him. A second later, Ryan Grant, Trent Miles, and Willingham joined them. "Come on, hang in there, Arnaz," said Miles. They so desperately wanted to win, both for themselves and for him. But by then, they all knew it just wasn't going to happen, and Battle's Notre Dame career would conclude with yet another installment of great expectations followed by a bitter end. Before returning to the sideline, Willingham silently slapped Battle on the knee.

With a few seconds left, the Irish displayed some life when Vontez Duff got into a brief skirmish with one of the Wolfpack receivers, prompting several NC State players to point to the scoreboard. The game ended 28–6.

Notre Dame's sixth consecutive defeat in a bowl game dropped them from 11th to 17th in the AP poll. Their schedule did prove to be as tough as they'd thought; six of the 13 teams they had played finished in the AP Top 25: USC, 4th, Michigan, 9th, NC State, 12th, Maryland, 13th, Pittsburgh, 19th, Florida State, 21st. When it was over, the team, disgusted with themselves, quietly filed off the field and into the locker room. In their haste to vacate the premises, they had forgotten to run down to greet their fans and to sing the alma mater.

But Willingham hadn't forgotten. He sent in Mike Denbrock to get them. A few minutes later, all of them, wearing sheepish expressions, jogged 60 yards to the far end zone. Just as the North Carolina State band began to play with all of its might, an NC State fan, dressed all in red, approached Willingham. He was a heavyset man, probably in his mid-40s with a red, round, stubbly face. All around him, NC State players and their fans hugged one another and celebrated an 11-win season and the biggest victory in their school's history. But this one gentleman knew the significance of Willingham's presence at Notre Dame. And though his reticence to approach Willingham suggested he knew this was a bad time to make a request, he did so anyway. With an uncertain look on his face and a heavy Southern accent, he asked sheepishly, "Can I possibly take a picture with you?"

Willingham never saw him or heard him. He just stood facing forward, still and lifeless, as Chuck Amato ascended the makeshift stage to accept the Gator Bowl trophy. The NC State coach was pumped to have beaten both Florida State in the season finale and Notre Dame in a bowl game. "To have your last two wins against two of the best football programs in America is amazing," said Amato. "I don't know if we will ever be able to re-accomplish something like that because scheduling is involved. That was big."

While Amato was speaking, the Notre Dame players, done with the alma mater, sprinted back to the locker room. When they were all in, Willingham turned and bolted into the tunnel. Once inside, he wasn't hard on his team. Many of the players returning the next season were fairly young, so it didn't make sense to beat them down right then. He had spent the whole season building their confidence, so he stuck with that.

As he had at the last pep rally, Willingham thanked the seniors for their effort. Both Jeff Faine and Arnaz Battle fought back tears. Faine had already met with Willingham to get advice on his future. Though the coach knew he could use the best offensive player on his team, Willingham advised him that it would be a good idea for him to enter the draft. Faine, whom NFL draft guru Mel Kiper had listed as the top prospect at center, would most likely be a first- or second-round pick in the spring.

Even though Battle had come a million miles as a receiver that season, he knew he still had a lot to prove to NFL scouts. And he wasn't about to waste any time getting started. Later that week, he was headed to Atlanta to work out with Chip Smith, a renowned speed coach who would prepare him for the NFL Scouting Combine in February. But first, he spoke to reporters. Outside the locker room, dressed in a black suit, Battle leaned against a wall, already resigned to the next phase of his journey. He was pensive but seemingly content. There was only one way for Battle to sum up his day, his season, and his career. And though his words may have been too simple, or even clichéd, to sum up such a complex five years, he used them anyway. Arnaz Battle shrugged and said, "Sometimes things just don't work out the way you planned."

Though he was disappointed, Willingham maintained a positive vibe because his team had shown him a lot that season. Besides, he didn't have time to dwell on what had already occurred. Like Arnaz Battle, Willingham was also looking ahead to February. The last day a high school senior could sign with a school was February 5. With Battle's departure, one of Willingham's primary concerns was at the receiver position. During the season, he had alluded to the fact that he needed more speed at the position, and by that weekend he would be on a plane in search of it. Of course, the loss of Jeff Faine, the best offensive lineman on the team, would create the biggest hole on offense. And with Shane Walton and Gerome Sapp graduating, the secondary could very easily go from strength to liability.

But in the meantime, Willingham wouldn't accept the excuses that were being offered after two lethargic performances. First and foremost, he wouldn't accept that Holiday's injury had deflated their spirit. "You expect every guy to get the job done," he said. "That's what having backups is all about. If that's not the case, then you should take only twenty-two players. You could just have eleven on offense and eleven on defense. But that's what a team is. When someone steps in, you expect them to perform. And I think we're capable of playing better than we did and being coached better than we were in our last two games, so everybody's at fault."

As usual, he would use any resource he could to make that point. The morning after the game, the cover of *USA Today* featured a picture of Wolfpack quarterback Philip Rivers and the headline: "NC State Crushes Irish." Several weeks later, when the Notre Dame players returned to campus after winter break, each found a laminated version of that photo in his locker. Written underneath was the caption: "What have you done to make us a champion?"

20

RETURN TO GLORY

B Y THE TIME winter had fully descended upon South Bend, the resounding question around campus was, Can Tyrone Willingham do it again? Sure, he had some success with 16 seniors, but could he duplicate that success the next season with a corps of young players?

Willingham said there was no simple, straightforward rule that he applied to recruiting. "It's too complex a society to have one philosophy," he said.

But there was one element essential to football and universal to building a football team. "It's a physical game," said Willingham. "So the first question you have is, Is the young man tough? Unless you're mentally tough, you can't be physically tough. It all starts with that. The last two institutions I've been in were institutions that had great academic traditions. They have high levels of intelligence. The smarter you are, the better decisions you make. You want a person with discipline and awareness."

To sustain the revival of the Notre Dame spirit, Willingham knew what kind of player he wanted. It was the kind of player who could be a ruthless competitor on the field and who kept his wits about him off the field. Of course, many fans and media people had trouble distinguishing one arena from the other. Public perception of a player like, say, Terrell Owens, was that since he did outlandish things on the field, he should be lumped in with those individuals who committed heinous acts of violence off it. But the truth of the matter was, the astute fan and, more important, the astute coach could easily tell the difference between an outspoken competitor and a thug. And Notre Dame had seen outspoken competitors before.

While at Notre Dame, running back Ricky Watters almost single-handedly shouldered the hip-hop swagger of the Lou Holtz years. He was the one player who brazenly stated he should get the ball whenever possible. And Watters's first impression may have been his most lasting. As a high school senior during his recruiting weekend at Notre Dame, Watters told everyone in earshot that if he got the ball, he was going to win two Heisman Trophies.

While with the 49ers, Watters's teammates once poked fun at his overstated style. During his second year, someone had carefully cut out Watters's face from several 49ers programs and pasted it all over the team photo. Underneath the photo were the words "I am the whole team." George Seifert, the 49ers coach at the time, not only nixed the situation but also exonerated Watters for having such a colorful personality. He also dropped a little science in the process. "Regardless of what you think of him," Seifert told the team, "Ricky Watters gives this team its energy."

He was right. Truth was, as much as he talked on the field, Ricky Watters never got into any trouble off the field. In 2003, just like in 1988, Notre Dame needed that type of energy, that type of flavor. Much like the 49ers, Notre Dame is so mired in old-school tradition that it constantly runs the risk of being stale and lifeless in its execution.

"That's why you need some of those 'me guys,'" said Willingham. "You need that energy. You *need* to have some of those guys on a football team." Willingham wasn't suggesting that he was going to fill his roster with a whole fleet of "me guys." But he did make it clear that if he was going to continue to breathe life into the program, he needed some players with a pulse.

"You want people who have a high level of self. No one is successful unless he has drive. And drive is ego. It's the balancing of the ego that's needed. For any coach to tell you 'There's no *I* in team' is great. It's great for the *chalkboard.* But he's lying. There's an *I* in every team. A team is composed of individuals that give up self for team. But it starts with the individual. It's the sacrifice of being humble that makes a great team. But it all starts with the individual. You need someone who always wants the ball," he said.

On January 11, before he hit the recruiting trail, Willingham coached the East team in the East-West Shrine college all-star game in San Francisco. Bill Diedrick and Kent Baer coached the offense and defense, respectively, as the East beat the West 20–17 in San Francisco's Pac Bell Park. Although Jordan Black had been suspended for the last game of his collegiate career, he was allowed to make the trip and participate for the East team. Black played about a half and performed well enough to solidify his status as one of the top offensive tackles in the draft. And Gerome Sapp, by intercepting a pass and leading the East team with eight tackles, raised his status before a multitude of NFL scouts.

A week later, in Mobile, Alabama, Shane Walton and Arnaz Battle were teammates in the Senior Bowl. Battle had a decent game, catching three balls for 27 yards. But it was Walton, again, who shined that day. In the fourth quarter, Walton resurrected his knack for big plays when he stepped in front of a Chris Simms pass on the goal line and went 99 yards for a touchdown. The North beat the South 17–0, and Walton set a record for the longest interception return in Senior Bowl history.

By then, Willingham was in search of his next class of play-makers. He was even more visible than he had been the previous year — sometimes too visible. While on a layover in St. Louis airport, Willingham was at a pay phone, his back purposely turned to the masses. He had his laptop open, and he was watching *The Lord of the Rings* when someone tapped him on the shoulder to congratulate him on his success that season. He was taken aback, as he always is in times of public recognition. But he wasn't put off. "I guess it's a good problem to have," he said. The fans knew who he was, and the recruits knew who he was. But even more important to the men who hired him was that both fans and recruits were beginning to remember who Notre Dame was.

By the last week of January, Notre Dame had enough verbal commitments to garner a Top 10 rating from recruiting guru Tom Lemming. Of course, Willingham was loath to declare such a rating a measure of success until after those young men had actually done something on the field. But it was a nice start to get commitments from several top prospects.

Greg Olsen of Wayne Hills High in New Jersey, who was the younger brother of Irish freshman quarterback Chris Olsen, was rated as the best prep tight end of the past two years by Lemming.

John Sullivan of Greenwich, Connecticut, was said to be the nation's best prep center. That was a pressing need with Jeff Faine's decision to enter the draft.

Linebacker Dwight Stephenson Jr., who was the son of the Miami Dolphins Hall of Fame center, had originally committed to Florida. But a few days before the signing date, he had chosen Notre Dame instead.

Then there was Brady Quinn of Dublin, Ohio. He was said to be the biggest catch of all. He was a 6'4" quarterback, who Lemming said was the perfect guy to run Diedrick's offense.

It was hard to argue that the latest crop of recruits headed to Notre Dame was a starting point, but the real statement of purpose, and statement of fact, was made before Christmas at the postseason awards banquet in the Joyce Center. The previous year, around the same time, Bob Davie had already been fired. Since they had no coach and their season had been such a disaster, the team had voted against having a banquet, and it was canceled. But by the first Friday night of December 2002, everything had changed. In many ways, the banquet provided a panoramic view of not only the football season but also the puzzling and often dramatic calendar year that had passed since Willingham's hiring. It was the first time since January that the entire cast of characters had assembled into one room in an attempt to not only celebrate the season but also make sense of it.

Bob Nagle, who had hosted the weekly luncheons, was the emcee. And as he did every Friday afternoon, Nagle added a certain exuberance that is normally lacking at such events. He pointed out that while they would hand out individual awards, this was a celebration of a team that "blossomed under Coach Willingham's leadership."

Although Willingham had used game captains throughout the season, he had his team vote for the official captains at season's end. Cornerback Shane Walton joined three other seniors, strong safety Gerome Sapp, offensive guard Sean Mahan, and wide receiver Arnaz Battle, as captains of the 2002 Irish squad.

Nagle was right about this being a team effort, but there were a few individual awards that carried special significance. The Student-Athlete of the Year Award went to Arnaz Battle. It was fitting that Battle was presented the award by his coach, Trent Miles. "This young man symbolizes overcoming adversity, and I'm very proud to have coached him," Miles said.

After he handed Battle the little plaque, Miles embraced him. Because of all he had endured and what he had finally enjoyed at Notre Dame, Battle confessed that his connection to this particular team and to the Notre Dame program would be deep and lasting. "We started something great," said Battle. "They say, 'Return to Glory.' This is just the beginning of it."

Jeff Faine won the Nick Pietrosante Award — voted on by the players — as the individual who best exemplifies the courage, loyalty, teamwork, dedication, and pride shown by the late Irish All-America fullback. Pietrosante died of cancer on February 6, 1988.

A few minutes later, when it was announced that Shane Walton's teammates had voted him their Most Valuable Player, the kid from Southern California approached the stage. Wearing the same blue suit and light-blue shirt he'd worn to every pep rally that season, Walton, staring down at the podium, very soft-spokenly shared the moment with his teammates and his coach. He cast a furtive glance at Willingham.

"It's been an honor to play for you, Coach Willingham. And to my teammates, it's been an honor to share blood, sweat, and tears with you guys."

As Walton left the podium and returned to his seat, Bob Nagle, fully aware of what the honor meant to Walton, quietly remarked, "I'm sure Mike Berticelli would be very proud of you tonight."

A competent, if not colorful, speaker, Kevin White summed up the season. "It was exactly 340 days ago when Coach Willingham came to us," he said. "It didn't take him long to renew the spirit and to set high expectations. He said the goal was to win. And he did that. He became the winningest first-year coach in Notre Dame history."

This got an appropriately thunderous applause from the crowd of 1,300 people. White went on to list the statistical accomplishments, like beating four ranked teams in one season. White also mentioned beating nationally ranked Air Force and Florida State in consecutive road games — the first time that had ever been done. In conclusion, he borrowed a phrase that Stanford athletic director Ted Leland had used while Willingham was at Stanford. Said White, "When I go to a lot of functions around the country, people say to me, 'I don't know how you got that guy, but I really like him.'"

But it was what White failed to say, the one thing that none of the Notre Dame brass seemed to go anywhere near, that was most telling. Exactly 340 days prior to that evening, Tyrone Willingham had quietly, humbly, and heroically saved their program. So that night, the night of celebration, it seemed only fitting that at least a healthy chunk of the credit fall on Willingham's side of the yard.

The featured speaker was Mike Golic, a captain on the 1984 Notre Dame team, a tenth-round draft pick who played in the NFL for nine years, and a radio host for ESPN. In the eloquent way only a former Notre Dame player could, Golic captured the essence of all that had taken place on the field. "When Coach Willingham spoke about wanting to make the guys who had worn the uniform proud, I took that to heart," he said. "What I saw as an alum, what I saw as a former player — I can't tell you how proud I am of what you did."

Golic spent the final five minutes speaking directly to the team, in particular the senior class. He acknowledged that whenever a new coach takes over a program, the first people tossed aside are usually the seniors. While some had praised Willingham for taking an interest in the senior class, Golic flipped the script, shining the light on the Notre Dame players. "Coach

Willingham gets a lot of credit, and he should," said Golic. "But congratulations to you guys. You bought into a new system and made it work."

He was absolutely right. Guys like Arnaz Battle, Courtney Watson, and Shane Walton had exhibited extraordinary leadership. They had believed in a new coach and his system. But not just any new coach could have sold his bill of goods to these players. When Bob Davie replaced Lou Holtz, his first order of business was to sell his system to the incumbent Domers. After five years, they had left the store empty-handed, save a new label for Notre Dame — mediocre. But now, after one year, mediocrity was no longer an option.

There was another underlying theme that night, one that deflected one man's vision and influence onto Notre Dame as a whole. And it wasn't confined to Tyrone Willingham and the 2002 Notre Dame team. It was a theme that applied to all sports and, most definitely, to past Irish teams. It was a theme that said "It ain't that hard, right? It ain't that hard to win when you have everything in place." It was the logic that had once been applied to the successes of Dan Devine and, more recently, Lou Holtz. Whereas the consensus around Notre Dame was that the previous five years of misery had been solely the doings of *that freakin' Bob Davie,* the shining success of 2002 was about Notre Dame, not just the Notre Dame coach.

Whenever anyone made reference to the success Notre Dame was enjoying, the word *we* seemed to be the pronoun of choice. But when referring to the past, "he," or "that Davie guy," seemed to flow much more easily from the tongues of those folks who inhabited the Joyce Center. But weren't they the ones who'd hired that Davie guy? And after they fired him, weren't they the same people who tried to replace him with that O'Leary guy?

But now, since Notre Dame had regained some personal and public semblance of its old self in terms of football excellence, it was time to celebrate. It was time to celebrate that Tyrone Willingham, a nonwhite, non-Catholic outsider, did *get* what Notre Dame was about. And it was time for Notre Dame to celebrate that they knew what Tyrone Willingham was all about. In his first year, he had been a successful coach. But he'd coached more

than just his team. He'd coached the fans and the university too.
And he'd applied the same method of instruction to all of them.
He'd asked them what they wanted and where they wanted to go,
and he'd done all he could to guide them there.

But, most important, in so doing, Willingham hadn't com-
promised any of his values, and he didn't expect Notre Dame
to compromise its values either. Chief among those values for
both the coach and the university was the consistent balance
of football dominance and academic excellence. But it didn't
end there.

The sum and substance of Tyrone Willingham the coach and
the man was competition. He still had something to prove. After
one calendar year, 10 victories, and a rekindled Irish spirit both
at home and abroad, Willingham had long since forgiven Notre
Dame for not making him their first choice. But he hadn't necessarily forgotten.

The final speaker of the evening was Father Malloy. After
Malloy was introduced and headed toward the podium, Willingham (obviously not comfortable with having received a standing
ovation when he was introduced) privately stood and applauded
his boss. As Malloy reflected on all that had transpired, he
seemed at ease, not only to have things back to normal but also
to have Tyrone Willingham representing his beloved school. And
he wasn't afraid to say as much.

"Throughout the year, each time we've heard Coach Willingham speaking about different aspects of the Notre Dame tradition, we found ourselves nodding our heads. We found ourselves
saying, 'Yeah, that *is* what we're about.'"

About 15 feet away, to Malloy's right, a chocolate-colored
Southern gentleman sat in the last seat of the dais looking down
at the tablecloth. He had perhaps a touch more gray around his
temples than he did the year before, and he looked happy. With
his glasses perched on the end of his nose, he allowed himself to
smile.

Malloy spoke the truth. Willingham did know what Notre
Dame was about. Hell, he'd *always* known what they were about
because he was about the same thing.

He was about winning.

ACKNOWLEDGMENTS

There are numerous people who were present during this journey. Some I've known my entire life, others I've recently met, but in every case their influence is lasting.

As a kid, my mother would consistently interrupt my complaints of boredom with the statement, "Go read a book." Thanks, Mom. I'm glad you did.

My freshman English teacher at Stanford, Dr. Rebecca Mark, said on my very first day of classes, "Everyone has a voice." At the time I had no idea that simple statement carried such a profound meaning. But you were right, Becky. I'm beginning to understand what you were talking about.

To John Skipper at ESPN, thank you for recognizing what I could do and allowing me to do just that.

During my time in South Bend I met some great people. To the Notre Dame coaches, thank you for your openness and friendship. I'll miss those Sunday mornings.

To the Notre Dame players, thanks for making me a sports fan again.

To my two newest and dearest friends, I'll miss our Thursday night conversations.

To Lisa in the Sports Information Department, thanks for always having time to speak to me.

To all the folks at Main Street Village, thanks for your friendship. I'll never forget you guys.

To the people at Little, Brown, in particular my editor, Liz Nagle, and copy editors, Mari Okuda and Shannon Langone, thanks for your tireless work and amazing attention to detail. I'm truly grateful.

To Greg Dinkin and Frank Scatoni, your passion was key to making this happen.

To Chris Zorich and all those student-athletes, both past and present, who strive to be more than just one-dimensional characters, this is for you.

My dearest Shelly, thanks for always believing in me. You always knew I could do this, even during those moments when I wasn't so sure. All my love.

Finally, I'd like to thank Tyrone Willingham, who was from start to finish of this project, Tyrone Willingham. Your ability to be "amazingly consistent" continues to inspire me.

INDEX

Adidas, 222

Air Force 2002 game: defensive play, 163–64, 165, 166, 168, 170, 216; and game week, 159–64; and Notre Dame football team's identity, 186; offensive play, 165–67, 168, 169, 170; and Willingham, 160, 162–63, 165, 168, 169, 170, 177

Akatu, Bernard, 148–49, 228–29

Allen, Terry, 187

Alumni Association, 54

Amato, Chuck, 269

Ameche, Don, 16

Anderson, Ray, 247–48

Andress, Ursula, 220

Arkansas University, 201–02

Arrington, LaVar, 82

Arute, Jack, 125

Ashe, Arthur, 244

Askew, B. J., 104, 107

Baer, Kent: and Air Force game week, 163; and East-West Shrine college all-star game, 274; and Florida State game, 179–80; and Michigan game, 107; Notre Dame's hiring of, 19, 89–90; and Pittsburgh game, 155; and Purdue game, 89, 90; and Stanford game, 142; and USC game, 238; and Troy Walters, 131

Baggett, Charlie, 112

Baker, Darren, 189

Baker, Dusty, 188–90

Banks, Brad, 254

Banks, James, 24–25

Battle, Arnaz: and Air Force game, 169; awards of, 276; and brother's death, 47–49; college career of, 49–51; and Florida State game, 178–79, 182, 260, 266; and Gator Bowl, 259, 260, 266, 268, 270; and Godsey, 172; and leadership, 146–48, 278; and Maryland game, 72–73; and Michigan game, 3, 4, 103, 105, 106; and Michigan State game, 119, 120, 124–26, 156; and Navy game, 215, 216; and NFL draft, 231, 270; and offensive strategy, 36; and Pittsburgh game, 148, 155–57; and Rutgers game, 227; and Senior Bowl, 274; and training camp, 46–47; and USC game, 240; and visibility of athletes, 94–95, 96, 146–47; and Walton, 70

Battle, Brandon, 47–48, 147, 156

Battle, Sandra, 47–48

Bellamy, Ralph, 16

Berry, Halle, 220

Berticelli, Mike, 70, 71, 276

BET, 220–21

Bettis, Jerome, 228

Big East conference, 157–58, 185

Biletnikoff Award, 254

Bird, Larry, 253

Blache, Greg, 247

Black, Jordan: and Boston College game, 196; and East-West Shrine college all-star game, 274; and Gator Bowl, 263, 268; and Michigan State game, 121; and Navy game, 215; and Purdue game week, 84–85; and tradition, 28; and training camp, 52; and USC game, 240; and Willingham, 159
Black Coaches Association (BCA), 242, 243
Blackmon, Will, 194–95
Bledsoe, Drew, 40
Boiman, Rocky, 63
Boldin, Anquan, 177, 179, 180, 182
Bolen, Lionel, 91
Boston College 1993 game, 186, 188, 195
Boston College 2002 game: defensive plays, 193–95, 198, 199; and game week, 187–91; and green jerseys, 190, 191, 199, 200, 201, 205–06; offensive plays, 191–93, 194, 195, 199; and rivalry, 185–86, 188, 195, 200; and Willingham, 186–88, 192, 194, 200–206, 209, 223
Bowden, Bobby, 177, 178, 182, 186
Bowl Championship Series (BCS): and Michigan's ranking, 98; and Notre Dame's 1998 season, 49; and Notre Dame's 2000 season, 7; and Notre Dame's 2001 season, 6; and Notre Dame's 2002 season, 114, 186, 195, 221–23, 232, 260; and USC, 240
Boyles, Frank, 202
Breakfast Club, 95
Brees, Drew, 89
Brennan, Terry, 219
Brian's Song, 176, 177
Brown, Aaron, 161–62
Brown, Corwin, 98
Brown, James, 160
Brown, Jerry, 113
Brown, Mike, 246
Brown, Paul, 36, 246
Brown, Tim, 28
Browne, Joe, 248
Brown v. Board of Education (1954), 21
Bryant, Bear, 65
Buchanan, Darryl, 56–58, 224–25
Budinscak, Kyle, 90, 91, 164, 180, 210, 216, 264
Bunche, Ralph, 244
Burnette, Dantonio, 267

Bush, George W., 132, 217
Butkus Award, 231, 255, 258
Butler, Tyrece, 105
Byrd, Dominique, 25

Campbell, Carlos, 73, 92, 148, 164, 169, 181, 183
Campbell, Darrell: and Air Force game, 166; and Boston College game, 195, 196; and Florida State game, 180; and Hilliard, 159; and Navy game, 210, 216; and Purdue game, 90, 91
Carr, Lloyd, 98, 103, 105, 109
Carroll, Pete, 133, 234, 236–37, 239–40, 241
Carthan, Eddie, 213
Cassingham, Shari, 69, 196
Catholic Super Bowl, 185, 195
Catlett, Rick, 259
Chambers, Anthony, 92
Chow, Norm, 267
Clark, Jared, 88
Clevenger, Chris, 29
Clinton, Bill, 151
Cochran, Johnnie, 188, 248, 249
Cocker, Joe, 160
Colbert, Keary, 233, 236, 238
College Football Awards Show, 254
College Football Hall of Fame, 29
Coltrane, John, 160
Corso, Lee, 165, 254
Cosby, Bill, 116–17
Cosby Show, The, 116–17
Cotchery, Jerricho, 267–68
Cotrell, Ted, 249
Cotton Bowl, 186, 254
Coughlin, Tom, 16, 246
Craig, Roger, 37
Crouch, Eric, 6
Crowther, John, 81
Culpepper, Daunte, 250
Curry, Derek, 63
Curtin, Brennan, 263, 268

Darryl B, 56–58, 224–25
Daugherty, Duffy, 111
Davey O'Brien Award, 254
Davie, Bob: firing of, 275; and Mattison, 164; as Notre Dame coach, 7, 9, 12, 13, 25, 50, 85, 136, 209, 278; and Notre Dame football fans, 197, 225, 229; and

Notre Dame tradition, 29; and Stanford 2001 game, 5, 6; and Weaver, 211
Davis, Al, 237
Davis, Eric, 246
Davis, Mike, 56, 204
DeBartolo, Eddie, 14
DeBolt, Chad, 262–63
Del Rio, Jack, 246–47
Denbrock, Mike, 19, 37, 142, 168, 215, 269
Denman, Anthony, 82
Devine, Dan, 77–78, 190, 278
Dickey, Gavin, 25
Dickey, Glenn, 138–39
Die Another Day, 219–20
Diedrick, Bill: and Boston College game, 192, 194, 199, 208; and East-West Shrine college all-star game, 274; and Florida State game, 179; and Gator Bowl, 263; and Hannum, 25; and Michigan game, 103; and Michigan State game, 119, 120, 124, 126, 127; and Navy game, 210, 212, 214; Notre Dame's hiring of, 19; and Pittsburgh game, 155; and Purdue game, 88, 92, 103; and recruiting, 275; and Stanford game, 142; and training camp, 40–41, 42, 47, 52; and Troy Walters, 131
Dillingham, Michael, 123
Dillingham, Pat: and Boston College game, 192, 194; and Gator Bowl, 268; and Michigan State game, 121, 122, 123–24; and Navy game, 213; and Rutgers game, 229; and Stanford game, 142, 143; and training camp, 35, 45–46; and Cassidy Willingham, 140
Doll, Kirk, 82
Dorrell, Karl, 244–45, 251
Doss, Mike, 233
Dowis, Dee, 163
Dr. No, 220
Duff, Vontez: and Air Force game, 168, 170; and BET, 221; and Boston College game, 195, 196, 198; and Florida State game, 177, 180; and Gator Bowl, 268; and Maryland game, 66, 74, 76; and Michigan game, 105; and Michigan State game, 122; and Navy game, 214; and Notre Dame tradition, 28; and Purdue game, 93; and Stanford game, 142; and USC game, 233–34, 236, 240

Duke University, 9–11
Dungy, Tony, 56, 129, 203, 250

Earl, Glenn: and Boston College game, 191; and Florida State game, 179, 180; and Michigan State game, 122, 123, 125; and Navy game, 213, 216; and Pittsburgh game, 154, 157; and USC game, 236
East-West Shrine college all-star game, 274
Eddie Robinson Classic, 64
Edwards, Braylon, 105, 107
Edwards, Herman, 39, 202–03, 247, 250
Ellis, Clarence, 243
Elway, Jack, 132
Elway, John, 89
Erickson, Dennis, 249
ESPN Home Depot National Coach of the Year award, 254

Faine, Jeff, 168, 196, 270, 275, 276
Fargas, Antonio, 237
Fargas, Justin, 236–37
Fasani, Randy, 5
Faust, Gerry, 8, 197, 200
Favre, Brett, 250
Ferentz, Kirk, 246
Fiesta Bowl, 7, 8, 183
Fisher, Tony, 37
Florida State 1993 game, 186
Florida State 2002 game: defensive play, 179–80, 181; and game week, 172–76; and Notre Dame football team's identity, 186, 193; offensive play, 178, 179, 180, 181; as signature performance, 260; and Willingham, 175–79, 181–84
Fouts, Dan, 135
Fowler, Chris, 255
Foxx, Redd, 116
Francisco, D'Juan, 54–55
Friedgen, Ralph, 66

Gatewood, Tom, 243
Gator Bowl: defensive plays, 267; and Notre Dame's 1998 season, 232, 260; and Notre Dame's 2002 season, 232, 259; offensive plays, 266–67, 268; and Willingham, 259–61, 262, 263, 265–66, 268–71

Geiger, Andy, 132–34
Giles, Zachary, 41–42
Godsey, Gary: and Boston College game, 199; and Florida State game, 183; and Gator Bowl, 268; and Maryland game, 88; and Michigan State game, 124; and Owens, 172–73; and Purdue game, 88, 92; and visibility of athletes, 207; and Willingham, 172
Golden Dome, 28, 77, 253
Golic, Mike, 277–78
Goolsby, Mike, 62, 108, 144, 195, 239
Gordon, David, 186
Grant, Ryan: and Air Force game, 167, 168, 169; and Boston College game, 191, 193, 194, 199; and Florida State game, 180, 181, 182; and Gator Bowl, 268; and Maryland game, 72, 73; and Michigan game, 104, 106; and Michigan State game, 120, 126; and Navy game, 211, 213, 215, 216–17; and personal style, 257; and Pittsburgh game, 157; and Purdue game, 88, 91–92; and Rutgers game, 227–28; and Stanford game, 144–45; and training camp, 35, 37–38, 52–53; and Willingham, 27
Gray, Karla, 150
Green, Al, 184
Green, Denny, 11, 42, 89, 113–14, 133–34, 137, 246, 265
Green, William, 187
Gruden, Jon, 13–14, 16, 86
Guerrero, Dan, 244
Gumbel, Bryant, 247

Hannum, Josh, 25
Hanratty, Terry, 111
Harmon, Jason, 121
Harper, Jesse, 146
Harridge, Chance, 163, 165, 168, 170
Harris, Joey, 90
Harris, Kwame, 135, 145
Harris, Ryan, 229, 252
Hart, Ryan, 227
Haslip, Ken, 49
Hayes, Gerald, 155
Heisler, John, 79, 116, 222, 256
Henderson, E. J., 66, 88, 218, 231, 255, 258
Henry, Cedrick, 120

Herbstreit, Kirk, 165, 186
Hesburgh, Theodore, 16
Hildbold, Joey, 212, 257
Hill, Darryl, 176
Hill, DeShaun, 239
Hill, Fitz, 64
Hilliard, Cedric: and Air Force game, 165; and Air Force game week, 164; and Campbell, 159; and Florida State game, 181; and Gator Bowl, 261; and Michigan game, 104, 107; and personal style, 257; and Purdue game, 90, 91; and training camp, 53
Hockaday, Sidney, 55
Holiday, Carlyle: and academics, 95; and Air Force game, 166, 168; and Battle, 50; and Boston College game, 191–93, 194, 195; and Florida State game, 178–79, 181; and Gator Bowl, 266–67, 268, 271; and Maryland game, 72, 73, 74, 75; and Michigan game, 103, 104, 106, 107, 108, 121, 178; and Michigan State game, 118, 119, 120, 121–22, 126, 127; and Navy game, 211, 212, 213, 214, 215, 216, 217; and Notre Dame football fans, 33; and Pittsburgh game, 155, 156, 178; and Purdue game, 88, 92, 93, 121; and Rutgers game, 229; and Stanford game, 142; and training camp, 35, 38–41, 45, 52; and USC game, 239, 240, 241
Holmes, Alex, 236
Holtz, Lou: Davie as replacement for, 278; and Ismail, 30; and media, 200, 205; and Michigan, 185; and NCAA rules, 17; as Notre Dame coach, 8–9, 97, 219; and Notre Dame tradition, 29; and Rice, 8, 66; and relationship with University of Notre Dame, 9, 253; and Watters, 273
Hooten, Herman, 243
Hornung, Paul, 28
Hoyte, Brandon, 83, 152, 181

Indiana, 55–56
Irons, Grant, 90
Ismail, Raghib "Rocket," 29–31, 98, 99–100

Jackson, Ernie, 243
Jackson, Jarious, 49

Jackson, Jesse, 197

Jackson, Keith, 135

Jackson, Marlin, 104, 105

Jackson, Preston, 107, 121, 143, 191, 238

James, Edgerrin, 129

Jenkins, Carol Marie, 56

Jenkins, Julian, 25

Jenkins, Omar: and Boston College game, 192, 195, 198; and Florida State game, 181; and Ismail, 31, 100; and Maryland game, 72; and Michigan game, 104, 106; and Michigan State game, 120–21; and Navy game, 211, 214, 215, 216, 217; and offensive strategy, 36, 37; and Pittsburgh game, 148, 155; and Purdue game, 88; and training camp, 45; and USC game, 239

Johnson, Keyshawn, 233

Johnson, Larry, 254, 255

Johnson, Lewis, 108, 145

Johnson, Rafer, 244

Johnson, Robert, 221

Johnson, Rod, 268

Johnson, Teyo, 143, 144, 145

John Thompson Foundation Challenge Football Classic, 65

Jones, Greg, 177, 180

Jones, Julius, 27, 37

Joppru, Bennie, 107

June, Cato, 106

Kelly, Kareem, 233, 238

Kickoff Classic, 64–65, 66, 73–75, 82

King, Martin Luther, Jr., 117

Kiper, Mel, 270

Kirkley, Raymond, 154

Kiwanuka, Mathi, 191

Knight, Bobby, 204

Knight, Derrick, 187, 191, 195, 198

Knight Riders, 56

Knott, Eric, 125

Knute Rockne, All American, 16, 63, 77

Ku Klux Klan, 55, 56

Laws, Trevor, 162

leadership: and Battle, 146–48, 278; and Holiday, 40; and Peloquin, 224; and Walton, 146, 278; and Watson, 82, 146, 157, 278; and Willingham, 28, 82, 276

Leahy, Frank, 28, 75, 146

Lee, Spike, 204, 220

Lehman, Teddy, 231, 255

Leland, Ted, 13, 16, 134, 138, 141, 277

Lemming, Tom, 25, 229, 275

Lennon, Chuck, 85, 87, 224

Leonard, Matt, 143

Leprechaun Mike, 85–86, 167

Lewis, Chris, 135, 143, 144, 145

Lewis, Marvin, 245–46, 247, 248

Lombardi, Vince, 53

Lopienski, Tom, 167, 169, 213

Lott, Ronnie, 144

Lott, Trent, 152

Lowe, Montrell, 91

Loy, Raillon, 56

Loy, Richard, 56

Lyght, Todd, 227

Mahan, Sean, 54, 181, 259, 260, 276

Malloy, Edward A., 16–18, 141, 263, 264–65, 279

Marie DeBartolo Complex, 14

Mariucci, Steve, 13, 14, 16, 249

Marolt, Bill, 60

Marotti, Mickey, 34, 35

Marquess, Mark, 133

Maryland 2002 game: and Bowl Championship Series, 114; defensive plays, 68, 72, 75; and game week, 59–60, 62–64; offensive plays, 72–74, 75; and Willingham, 66–67, 72, 73, 74–76

Matter, Kyle, 135

Mattison, Greg, 162, 164, 179–80, 183, 198, 216, 252

Mattison, Lisa, 164

Maxwell Award, 254

McBrien, Scott, 68

McCartney, Bill, 60

McCullough, Sultan, 236, 237

McDonell, John, 19, 41–42, 127, 142

McDougal, Kevin, 57, 177, 186

McGrew, Mario, 55

McKnight, Rhema, 25–26, 52, 120, 149, 181, 212

McNabb, Donovan, 250

McNair, Mike, 167

McNair, Steve, 250

McPherson, Adrian, 182, 183

Media: and Boston College game, 188, 196, 200, 205; and Edwards, 203;

Media (*cont.*)
and Gator Bowl invitation, 259–60; and Maryland game, 64; and Michigan game, 98; and Michigan State game, 116, 118, 125–26, 242; and Navy game, 216–17; and Notre Dame football team, 242; and race relations, 64, 247; and Richardson, 202; and Setta, 176; and USC game, 240; and Walton, 233–34; and Willingham, 78–81, 93, 117, 118, 125–26, 138–39, 174–75, 188, 196, 200–206, 216–17, 222, 237

Mehri, Cyrus, 248, 249

Michigan 1989 game, 98

Michigan 2002 game: defensive plays, 104–05, 106, 107; and game week, 97–102; and last-minute win, 146; offensive plays, 103–04, 106; and Willingham, 3–4, 97–103, 106, 108, 109, 118

Michigan State 1964 game, 111

Michigan State 2002 game: defensive plays, 122–23, 125; and game week, 114–18; and last-minute win, 146; offensive plays, 119–22, 123, 124; and Willingham, 115–19, 123, 125, 128, 143

Miles, Trent: and Battle, 47, 276; and Boston College game, 198, 199; and Florida State game, 183; and Gator Bowl, 262, 268; and McKnight, 26; and Michigan State game, 120, 126; and Navy game, 215; Notre Dame's hiring of, 19; and Pittsburgh game week, 148, 149; and Purdue game week, 81; and Rutgers game, 228, 229; and Stanford game, 142; and training camp, 36–37

Miller, David, 192

Miller, Ken, 24

Milligan, Sean, 191, 267

Minnesota Vikings, 114

Minnix, Bob, 242–44, 249–50, 251

Minority Alumni Network, 54–55

Minority Coaching Fellowship, 113

Mirer, Rick, 28, 236

Modell, Art, 250

Monk, Thelonius, 160

Montana, Joe, 49, 124, 253

Moore, Casey, 5, 136

Morgan, Robert, 177

Moss, Dawan, 125

Moss, Randy, 9, 122

Most Valuable Player, 276

Mushett, Lisa, 233, 253

NAACP, 197

Nagle, Bob, 223, 275–76

Native Americans, 132

Navarre, John, 105, 107

Navy 2002 game: defensive plays, 212, 214, 215, 216; and game week, 207–10; offensive plays, 211–12, 213–15, 216; and Willingham, 188, 208, 209, 211, 212, 213, 214–15

NCAA rules, 8, 17, 65–66

Nesfield, Kevin, 93

Neuheisel, Rick, 17–18, 60, 244–45

Newberry, Jared, 143

Newman, Terence, 218, 233, 256

Newsome, Ozzie, 250–51

Nick Pietrosante Award, 276

North Carolina State University, 112, 113, 260–69

Notre Dame football fans: and Boston College game, 188–91, 197, 201, 206; and Devine, 78; expectations of, 35, 41; and Fan Appreciation Day, 32–34; and Gator Bowl, 269; and green T-shirts, 4, 101, 103, 108, 137, 190, 201; and Maryland 2002 game, 68, 72, 73, 75, 76; and media, 80; and Michigan game, 4, 103–04, 108–09; and Michigan State game, 123, 125; and Nebraska 2000 game, 6–7; and offensive strategy, 35–36, 67, 103–04; and pep rallies, 84–87, 102, 137, 149–52, 188–90, 224–26; and Rutgers game, 223, 224–26; and Stanford game, 145; and training camp, 43; and USC game, 252; and Willingham, 85–87, 101, 103, 106, 145, 188–91, 197, 223, 224–25, 229, 274, 279

Notre Dame football team: and academic standards, 7–10, 12, 152, 226–27; awards banquet of, 275–79; decline in spirit of, 6; identity of, 143–44, 158, 165, 186; independent status of, 158, 185; ranking of, 93, 127, 146, 159, 177, 186, 195, 196, 208, 211, 223, 234, 252, 259, 269; and recruiting, 25–26, 162, 229, 252, 272–75; and red zone, 73, 93,

191, 192; and special teams, 92, 142, 181, 182, 195, 199; tradition of, 28–30, 46, 63–64, 85, 86, 99, 100–101, 138, 206, 224–25, 254, 262, 266, 273, 279; and West Coast offense, 36–37, 39–40, 47, 67–68, 100. *See also* specific players and games

Notre Dame Glee Club, 140

O'Brien, Coley, 111
O'Leary, George, 14–15, 19, 26, 225, 278
Olsen, Chris, 35, 121, 210, 275
Olsen, Greg, 275
O'Neill, Tim, 228, 264
Orange Bowl, 232
Orton, Kyle, 88–89, 90, 91, 93
Osborne, Tom, 177
Ott, Josh, 192
Owens, Terrell, 171–74, 179, 272–73

Palmer, Billy, 213
Palmer, Carson, 233, 236, 238, 239, 240, 241
Parker, Charlie, 160
Parseghian, Ara, 111, 146, 219, 243
Paterno, Joe, 177
Peloquin, Dave, 223–24
Perry, Chris, 3
Philbin, Regis, 137, 241
Phillips, Terry, 60
Piccolo, Brian, 176
Pierre-Antoine, Carlos, 62, 180, 181, 195, 239, 257
Pittsburgh 2002 game: defensive plays, 154–55, 157; and game week, 146–52; offensive plays, 155–56; and Willingham, 157, 158
Plunkett, Jim, 89
Poitier, Sidney, 220
Polamalu, Troy, 233, 241, 255
Polanco, Aaron, 212, 213, 214
Polite, Lousaka, 154
Pollack, David, 218
Porras, Jerry, 140
Powell, Luke, 145
Powers-Neal, Rashon: and Michigan State game, 121, 127; and Navy game, 215, 216; and Navy game week, 210; and Purdue game, 88, 92; and Stanford game, 144, 145; and Willingham, 27

Preston, Audrey, 18, 263
Preston, Buzz: and Boston College game, 194, 198–200; and Florida State game, 182–83; and Gator Bowl, 263; and Michigan game, 4; and Michigan State game, 118, 119, 120, 126–27; and Navy game, 209–10, 212, 213, 215; and Purdue game, 92; and Rutgers game, 227, 228; and Stanford game, 142; and training camp, 38; and Willingham, 18–19, 38
Prister, Tim, 80, 81, 174–75, 205
Proposition 42, 65–66
Proposition 48 students, 8, 65
Pryor, Richard, 116
Purdue 2002 game: defensive plays, 88–91, 93; and game week, 80–81, 84–87; offensive plays, 87–88, 91–93; and Willingham, 80, 84, 91, 92, 93

Quinn, Brady, 275

race and race relations: and Air Force game, 167–68; and black coordinators, 249–50; and Edwards, 202–03; and Hill, 176; and Hollywood, 220; and Hoyte, 152; and media coverage, 64, 247; and Michigan State 2002 game, 114, 115, 116, 117; and Michigan State University, 110; and NFL, 245–51; and Owens, 171–73; and quarterbacks, 250; and Richardson, 201–02; and Simmons, 60; and South Bend, 55, 56, 252; and Stanford, 132–34; and University of Notre Dame, 54–55, 57–58, 99, 100, 242–44; and Watson, 153–54; and Willingham, 20–24, 38, 54, 56–58, 64, 67, 86, 99, 117, 140–41, 145, 161–62, 174, 175, 197, 203, 204, 220–21, 242–44, 245, 249, 251, 254–55, 264–65
Raye, Jimmy, 111
Reed, Neil, 204
Reed, Tom, 113
Reuttiger, Daniel "Rudy," 77–78
Rice, Condoleezza, 132–34, 216–17, 263–65
Rice, Jerry, 36
Rice, Tony, 8, 65, 66
Rice University, 112, 113
Richardson, Mike, 62

Richardson, Nolan, 201–02
Richmond, Kenneth, 56
Rideaux, Darrell, 239
Riley, Mike, 244
Rivers, Philip, 267, 271
Rix, Chris, 179, 180
Robbinson, Eddie, 64–65
Roberts, Eric, 214
Roberts, Ryan, 90, 108, 118, 125, 164, 165
Robinson, Greg, 244
Robinson, Jackie, 244
Rockne, Knute, 6, 8, 17, 46
Rodamer, Ronnie, 148
Rogers, Charles, 114, 122, 123, 125, 254, 255
Rogers, Darryl, 112
Rolfs, Eric, 214
Rose Bowl, 11, 130, 138, 232, 240
Royal, Darrell, 254
Rudy, 16, 63, 77–78
Russ, Jim, 83, 121–22, 213
Rutgers 2002 game: defensive plays, 227; and game week, 218–27; offensive plays, 227, 228–29; and Willingham, 218, 219–20, 228, 229, 230
Rutherford, Rod, 157
Ryan, Nolan, 253
Ryan, Sean, 193

Sample, Joe, 160
Samuel, Tony, 64
Sanders, Deion, 172
Sapp, Gerome: and academic standards, 226; and Air Force game, 170; and Air Force game week, 164; and Boston College game, 191, 193, 198; as captain, 276; and East-West Shrine college all-star game, 274; and Florida State game, 183; and Gator Bowl, 261; and Gator Bowl invitation, 259, 260; graduation of, 270; and Michigan State game, 122–23, 125; and NFL draft, 274; and Pittsburgh game, 154; and Purdue game, 91, 93; and Rutgers game pep rally, 225–26; and USC game, 236; and Watson, 150; and Willingham, 26–27, 226
Sapp, Jason, 118
Sayers, Gale, 176
Schott, Marge, 246

Scott, Tony, 252
Seattle Bowl, and Stanford, 18, 19, 221
Sebes, Nick, 5, 143
Seifert, George, 273
Setta, Nicholas: and Air Force game, 166, 169; and Boston College game, 192, 194; and Florida State game, 176, 179, 180; and Maryland game, 72, 73–74; and Michigan game, 104; and Michigan State game, 121; and Navy game, 213; and Purdue game, 92
Shea, Terry, 134
Simmons, Bob: and drills, 60, 62; and Florida State game, 183; and Gator Bowl, 263; and Maryland game week, 62–63; and Michigan game, 108; and Michigan State game, 128; and Oklahoma State, 60–61; and Stanford, 61–62; and Watson, 84
Simmons, Linda, 61, 263
Simms, Chris, 274
Simpson, O. J., 248
Skaggs, John, 212
Smith, Akili, 250
Smith, Alex, 144
Smith, Bubba, 111
Smith, Chip, 270
Smoker, Jeff, 122, 123, 125
Soukup, Andrew, 86
South Bend, Indiana, and race relations, 55, 56, 252
Sporting News Sportsman of the Year, 253
Springs, Shawn, 171
Spurrier, Steve, 10–11, 12, 135
Stanford 2001 game, 5–6
Stanford 2002 game: defensive plays, 144; and game week, 132, 135–41; and Michigan State game, 119; offensive plays, 142, 143; and Willingham, 132, 135–37, 143–44, 145
Stanford University: and academics, 10, 62, 133; and Georgia Tech 2001 game, 18; and Notre Dame 2001 game, 5–6, 12; and race relations, 132–34; Willingham as coach for, 5, 10–12, 23, 25, 36, 37, 79, 114, 129–30, 134, 137–38, 140–41, 209, 221, 234, 243, 265
Stephenson, Dwight, Jr., 275
Stoltz, Dennis, 112
Stoops, Bob, 246

Stovall, Maurice: and Boston College game, 194; and Florida State game, 181; and Michigan game, 104; and Michigan State game, 121, 124, 126; and Navy game week, 210; and personal style, 257; and Pittsburgh game week, 148; recruitment of, 25; and training camp, 45
St. Pierre, Brian, 193, 195, 198
Student-Athlete of the Year Award, 276
subway alumni, 43, 106, 151, 224
Suggs, Terrell, 218
Sullivan, John, 275

Tagliabue, Paul, 265
Taylor, Bobby, 267
Taylor, John, 36
Teevens, Buddy, 90, 135, 136, 137, 138, 140, 145
Teevens, Kirsten, 140
Texas A&M, 6, 7, 186
Theismann, Joe, 63–64, 143–44
Thomas, Isiah, 56
Thompson, John, 65–66, 204
Thurmond, Strom, 152
Tiller, Joe, 90
Tipton, Dave, 142
Tittle, Y. A., 250
Tolon, Kenneth, 6
Touchdown Jesus, 77
Trading Places, 15–16
training camp: and drills, 35, 36, 40, 41–42, 45, 53–54; and offensive strategy, 35–40, 47, 52, 53; philosophy of, 43; schedule of, 34; and Willingham, 34–36, 42–44, 45, 46, 47, 51–54
Trieweiler, Christina, 83, 84, 150–51, 153–54, 231, 255, 256–57, 261
Trieweiler, Terry, 150
Tuck, Justin, 105, 122, 181, 207, 216
Turner, Ron, 134

Unitas, Johnny, 250
University of Florida, 11
University of Miami, 10
University of Michigan, 98, 158, 185. See also Michigan 2002 game
University of Nebraska, 6–7, 10
University of Notre Dame: and academic concerns, 7–10, 12, 253, 279; and image, 13, 14, 15, 99, 234–35, 251; and race relations, 54–55, 57–58, 99, 100, 242–44; and Willingham, 161, 253, 278–79
University of South Carolina, 9
USC 1977 game, 190–91
USC 1998 game, 260
USC 2002 game: defensive plays, 235–36, 239, 241; and game week, 232–34; intensity of fans, 237–38; offensive plays, 239, 240, 241; and recruiting, 252–53; as threat on schedule, 188, 221; and Willingham, 232, 234, 235, 241

Valvano, Jim, 108
Van Alstyne, Jeremy, 25
Vick, Michael, 250
Vitale, Dick, 102–03
Void, Jerod, 93

Walsh, Bill, 11, 36, 37, 89, 113, 133, 134
Walter Camp All-America team, 218, 255
Walters, Gail, 130
Walters, Trent: and Boston College game, 198; coaching style of, 131; and Laws, 162; and Maryland game, 63, 74; and Michigan game, 107; and Michigan State game, 126, 127; and Troy Walters, 129, 130; and Walton, 218–19, 230
Walters, Trent (son), 131
Walters, Troy, 129–30, 131, 219
Walters, Vanessa, 131
Walton, Lin, 69
Walton, Shane: and academics, 71; and Air Force game, 168; awards of, 218, 219, 276; and Battle, 147; and BET, 221; and Boston College game, 193, 196–97, 207; and Florida State game, 177, 182; and Gator Bowl, 267; graduation of, 270; and leadership, 146, 278; and Maryland game, 63, 66, 68, 74, 197; and Michigan game, 104, 105, 106, 107–08; and Michigan State game, 122–23; and Navy game, 207–08, 212; and NFL draft, 231; and personal style, 257; and Pittsburgh game, 154, 157; and Purdue game, 90, 91, 93; and Rutgers game, 219, 227, 230; and Senior Bowl, 274; soccer background of, 68–71; and Stanford game, 143, 144;

Walton, Shane (*cont.*)
and USC game, 233–34, 236, 238, 239;
and visibility of athletes, 94–95, 96, 207;
and Watson, 255–56; and Willingham,
233, 276
Wannstedt, Dave, 133
Ward, Charlie, 57, 177–78
Washington, Denzel, 220
Washington, Torrance, 180
Watson, Courtney: and academic
standards, 226–27; and Battle, 156–57;
and Boston College game, 191; and
Butkus Award, 82, 231, 255, 258; and
Florida State game, 180; injury of, 261;
and Lott, 152–53; and Michigan game,
105, 107; and Michigan State game,
123; and Navy game, 216; and NFL
draft, 231–32, 258; and Pittsburgh
game, 149–52, 157; and Purdue game
week, 81–84, 87; and Rutgers game
pep rally, 225; and Sapp, 226; and
Stanford 2001 game, 12; and Stanford
game, 144; and Walton, 255–56; and
Willingham, 12–13, 26–27, 84,
256–57, 258
Watters, Ricky, 228, 273
Watts, J. C., 151
Weaver, Tony, 90, 210–11
Weaver, Wayne, 246–47
White, Charles, 237
White, John, 202
White, Kevin: and awards banquet, 277;
and media, 259; and Stanford game,
140, 141; and Willingham, 13, 18,
243–44, 263, 264–65
White, Trevor, 192
Whitfield, Bob, 135
Wilcots, Solomon, 129
Williams, Bobby, 64, 114–17, 125, 127,
128, 242, 245, 251
Williams, Mike, 233, 236, 238, 239
Williams, Tom, 137, 143
Willingham, Cassidy, 23, 124, 140
Willingham, Gail, 20
Willingham, Jerome, 20
Willingham, Joyce, 20
Willingham, Kim, 23, 139–41, 161, 263,
265
Willingham, Lillian, 22–23

Willingham, Nathaniel (father), 22, 23
Willingham, Nathaniel (son), 51, 119, 232
Willingham, Tyrone: and academic
standards, 10, 11, 27, 62, 95, 115–16,
135, 272, 279; awards of, 253, 254, 256;
background of, 20–24, 161; and Bowl
Championship Series, 221–23;
coaching career of, 112–14; coaching
style of, 26–27, 33–34, 51–52, 59, 120,
130, 159–60, 226, 230–33, 243, 257–58,
271, 278–79; college football career of,
110–12, 115, 119, 161–62; as
competitor, 14–15, 184, 234, 235, 279;
and former Notre Dame players, 29–31,
99–100, 277; high school football
career of, 24; and leadership, 28, 82,
276; and loyalty, 112, 114; and media,
78–81, 93, 117, 118, 125–26, 138–39,
174–75, 188, 196, 200–206, 216–17,
222, 237; and music, 160–61, 184, 200,
263–64; Notre Dame's hiring of, 13,
14–15, 16, 18–19; and race/race
relations, 20–24, 38, 54, 56–58, 64, 67,
86, 99, 117, 140–41, 145, 161–62, 174,
175, 197, 203, 204, 220–21, 242–44,
245, 249, 251, 254–55, 264–65; self-
deprecating manner of, 22, 64, 161,
253; as Stanford coach, 5, 10–12, 23, 25,
36, 37, 79, 114, 129–30, 134, 137–38,
140–41, 209, 221, 234, 243, 265; and
training camp, 34–36, 42–44, 45, 46, 47,
51–54; and winning, 11, 26, 27, 66, 81,
117, 136, 174, 177, 185, 219, 258, 277,
279. *See also* specific games
Wilson, Jackie, 160
Wilson, Laura, 140
Wilson, Marcus, 27, 166–67, 191, 193
Winston, Eric, 25
Wonder, Stevie, 200
Wooden, John, 253
Wright, Thomas, 123

Yeager, Tom, 17
York, John, 249
Young, Steve, 124
Yura, Chris, 183, 266–67

Zacharias, Phil, 62
Ziegler, Dusty, 10